# MILLENNIAL BLACK

THE ULTIMATE GUIDE FOR
BLACK WOMEN AT WORK

# MILLENNIAL BLACK

SOPHIE WILLIAMS

ONE PLACE. MANY STORIES

HQ
An imprint of HarperCollins*Publishers* Ltd
1 London Bridge Street
London SE1 9GF

www.harpercollins.co.uk

HarperCollins Publishers
1st Floor, Watermarque Building, Ringsend Road, Dublin 4, Ireland

This edition 2021

1

First published in Great Britain by
HQ, an imprint of HarperCollins*Publishers* Ltd 2020

Typeset in Adobe Garamond Pro by
Palimpsest Book Production Ltd, Falkirk, Stirlingshire

Printed and bound in Great Britain by
CPI Group (UK) Ltd, Croydon CR0 4YY

MIX
Paper from
responsible sources
FSC
www.fsc.org
FSC™ C007454

This book is produced from independently certified FSC™ paper
to ensure responsible forest management.

For more information visit: www.harpercollins.co.uk/green

*For young Black girls everywhere.*
*I hope that by the time you grow up there's no need for this book.*

*Until then, just remember — it's not you. You are magic.*

# Contents

# INTRODUCTION

'If there's a book that you want to read, but it hasn't been written yet, then you must write it.'

TONI MORRISON

**W**elcome! It's so good to have you here, we're going to have such a good time together! But it's important that I'm honest with you from the start – we're also going to have a really hard time together, because understanding the deep-rooted structures that have kept Black women out of top positions and limited their career and earning potential can be pretty heavy. We're going to get into the weeds of how things are and have been for Black women in the workplace, and look at what needs to happen for things to improve. But it's not all doom and gloom, in fact, far from it. Along the way we get to talk about Oprah, make new professional networks based on Lizzo lyrics, and have conversations with really phenomenal Black women who are bossing it in every way. I was going to say bossing it every day, but no one is superhuman, and the 'rise and grind' daily hustle mentality is, well, a lot.

Please hear me loud and clear when I say this book is not just for Black women. It *is* for Black women, but it's *also* for supporters, employers, and anyone who runs a business that they're hoping will continue to be successful and relevant. The book does not say, 'Black women, here are the things about yourself that you have to do, or change, or be, in order to be successful.' Black women no longer expect to work for organisations where they are forced to fold themselves in half, underline one part of their identities and erase another, or contort themselves to fit into workplaces and structures that never had them in mind when they were built.

Within many business sectors there is a lot of talk about diversity (though not enough about inclusion or representation), especially in the wake of the Black Lives Matter movement that galvanised so many in 2020. But all too often, when it comes down to it, the pressure to make any real headway is put back onto the shoulders of marginalised groups, who are expected to pull themselves up by their bootstraps (more on that later) and find their own ways out of problems that they didn't make, and that they're not in positions empowered enough to change. That is not only not fair, it's not possible. As a doubly marginalised group, we don't, for the most part, have the resources to single-handedly fix the system and educate the world whilst doing our day jobs, being a part of our communities, and trying to stay sane.

I wanted to write *Millennial Black* to highlight the workplace issues that disproportionately impact on Black women's careers, and offer methods and solutions to overcome them. In a lot of ways these overlap with the barriers women of all races and backgrounds face, and in other ways they overlap with the roadblocks that come up in the careers of Black people of all genders, but they are never *just* that. They are always only the starting point for Black women. Their struggles are the struggles of all women, compounded by anti-Black racism. Their struggle is also that of the anti-Black racism that Black men face compounded by sexism, which come together to make the unique misogynoir experience (a term originated by queer Black feminist Moya Bailey) – a combination of racist and sexist prejudices faced by Black women on a daily basis in and out of the workplace.

In 2020 many have become more familiar with intersectional feminism[1] – the recognition that the layers and tones of people's overlapping identities impact on their lived experiences, and that one area of marginalisation doesn't cancel out another. Instead, they pile on top of one another, creating a reinforcement of both facets. But we have yet to acknowledge that this is also true of people's experiences of work.

Black women are centred in this conversation and so are their experiences. But this book also includes advice and strategies that would be useful for those from any background facing the frustrations of feeling invisible, being overlooked for promotions, and relentlessly hitting their heads against a concrete ceiling, all whilst being told they should be grateful for even having been allowed in the building.

Pointing out the barriers is not enough, *Millennial Black* is a part of finding solutions. Sometimes the solutions are for us to action as Black women, but most of the time they are for business leaders, senior managers, gatekeepers and allies to action, because this is all of our problem, and we're *all* going to need to take active, and regular, steps in order to be a part of the solution. Even when it feels risky. Especially those of us who haven't suffered generations and centuries of discrimination.

If there's anything that I've learned it's that we can only fix this world together. We can't do it divided – I cannot emphasise that enough. We can't let the desensitivity seep in – the 'If it's your problem, then it's not mine.' 'It's a woman's problem.' 'It's a Black people problem.' 'It's a poor people problem.' I mean, how many of us in this room have colleagues and partners and friends from other races, sexes, religions? . . . Well then, you know – they want to break bread with you, right? They like you? Well then, this is their problem too. So when we're marching and protesting and posting about the Michael Brown Jrs and the Atatiana Jeffersons of the world, tell your friends to pull up . . . We have been denied opportunities since the beginning of time, and still, we prevail. Just imagine what we could do together.

*– Rihanna, acceptance speech for the President's Award at the 2020 NAACP Image Award*

After brief stints as an events planner in Leeds, and an English teacher in Paris, my career has been spent working in advertising agencies in London – a traditionally very white and male industry. I started as a runner, before becoming a project manager, producer, head of production and then taking the position of chief operating officer, all at breakneck speed. At the start of my career I thought the burden was on me to work out how to position myself for success – to be as non-threatening and compliant as possible, to keep my head down, work hard and hope for the best. Now that I've become more senior, I've learned that a lot of responsibility lies firmly in the hands of those who shape the businesses, who define their culture and values, and create the systems that everyone else works within.

I have spent several years having public and private conversations about the experiences of Black women at work, and what needed to change. During that time, I have learned that if racial inequality isn't something people have deliberately sought out to self-educate around, talking about it makes them feel pretty uncomfortable. Particularly white people. Most non-white people talk and think about race daily, it's a part of our everyday experience and our personal identity. It's part of the essential fabric of our lives. But this is a burden unique to racially marginalised people. I can't count the number of times that I've been warned off talking about these 'uncomfortable' topics with 'advice' about the negative impact 'pushing an agenda' would have on my career. Every time someone tried to dissuade me, or scare me into making my voice smaller, it only made me more determined to have more of these conversations – have them louder, and with more people, and to turn those conversations into actions.

I first envisioned *Millennial Black* as a toolkit for working whilst Black and female, and in the under-represented groups, in a business context, of Millennials and Gen Z (anyone born between 1981–2014, ish). Born in 1987, I'm a Millennial and I didn't feel that the shape of my career, or the way I saw things progressing in my industry, was reflected in the more traditional books aimed at female success. I read tips about using my voice and advocating for myself, and knew that the way Black women are perceived when they take those steps is not always, or even usually, in a sympathetic light. I couldn't find the book that I needed which recognised the differences in our experiences that our intersectional identities afford us.

The more I spoke to powerful, inspirational Black women – both in my own life and in interviews for *Millennial Black* – the more I realised that offering a series of 'tips and tricks' for Black women to succeed would repeat the same well-intentioned mistakes that so many people before me had made. I would be reinforcing the idea that Black women, as a group, needed extra help and support because on their own they weren't enough.

We are so much more than enough.

Growing and established businesses need to become the types of environments where a wider variety of people can succeed than ever have done before. More and more clients and consumers are demanding diversity and a range of authentic voices in the teams and companies they work with and buy from, and businesses need to be able to fulfil that need in order to remain relevant. Attracting a diverse range of talent isn't enough, much stronger provision needs to be put in place to grow and retain that talent. That is the key to success.

As they age into the workforce, organisations are employing an increasing number of Millennial and Gen Z team members. Both are generations who repeatedly report that they expect diversity and representation from the companies they work with as a matter of course. 72 per cent of Gen Z[2], when asked about their workplaces, say that they believe 'race equality is the most important issue today'. That's huge, and businesses are going to have to make some wide-reaching, long-term changes in order to meet that expectation.

It's not always easy. Companies have realised that having a team that looks and thinks like a representative cross-section of the population is essential, but what can they do to make it happen? What is a hiring manager supposed to do if the entirety of their recruitment pipeline looks the same? Does it mean that good and diverse talent just isn't out there, or does it mean that companies need to understand how to look in new places and reach out in new ways? What is an HR manager meant to do if the turnover of marginalised staff is much higher than other team members? Does that mean some groups of people are less committed to their professional development, or does it mean that there are cultural and structural roadblocks within their own business that they don't see but which are disproportionately impacting on those team members, effectively forcing them out of the business? *Millennial Black* is a resource for first recognising these issues, and then developing the tools to overcome them.

It's impossible to talk about the struggles Black women face without talking about the struggles endured by *all* women, but to ignore the additional layer race plays is to do a disservice to those hitting not just a glass but a concrete ceiling. A glass ceiling is invisible, most of the time you don't even know it's there until you hit up against it. Being able to see through without the ability to reach out and touch what's on the other side is frustrating, so is hitting your head against it time and time again, but at least it lets the light through. Concrete ceilings are anything but invisible. They are dark, thick, oppressive – and they limit your vision from the very start.

When we, as Black women, ask for more, we do it with the knowledge that our mothers and grandmothers had to fight tooth and nail for every opportunity they got, and succeed as best they could in a world of overt racism. They toiled in workplaces, usually in menial, poorly paid roles where the message 'this is the best you'll ever get' wasn't simply implied through coded language behind closed doors, it was said outright by people with power who knew that nothing could or would be done about it.

I'm happy to live in a time where we don't have to face the same levels of overt discrimination, but that is not to say that the beliefs that once allowed that discrimination to thrive are a thing of the past. These beliefs and behaviours still exist, but in more subtle, slippery, harder to pin down, harder to take to HR ways. They're baked into the expectations that people have of Black women, and those that we have for ourselves. They are enshrined in the recruitment pipeline and the office dress code, the investment process.

I believe that we as a society have come a long way in understanding that the case for race and gender diversity throughout organisations, and especially at senior levels, is not only a moral necessity but an essential consideration for companies who want to remain both profitable and relevant to their consumers. This change is being driven by the next generation of workers and consumers who will become increasingly important as they age into senior positions in the workplace, and take over more and more spending power.

Companies that have made a real commitment to diversity and inclusion have more engaged, productive workers. And they're more profitable. Companies with just 10 per cent greater gender and racial diversity on their boards and in their management made 5.8 per cent higher EBITs (Earnings Before Interest and Taxes) in the UK, and 1.1 per cent higher in the US. And the companies in the top 25 per cent for racial and ethnic diversity are 35 per cent more likely to have financial returns above their industry's national median.[3]

Knowing the benefits of racial and gender diversity at a senior level, it is disheartening to see the lack of Black women in these positions. This gap is not through a lack of ambition: one study found that Black women are 175 per cent more likely to aspire to a powerful position with a prestigious title, and more likely to actually believe that they would be successful in that position.[4] However, despite the ambition and belief, they are not succeeding in reaching these roles in any great numbers. Despite diversity initiatives, women from racially marginalised backgrounds face an incredibly steep drop-off at senior levels. Only one in five C-suite leaders is a woman, and fewer than one in thirty is a 'woman of colour'.[5] So initiatives focusing on simply getting Black women in the door aren't enough. The structures, understanding and desire must be in place to retain, grow and develop these women into senior and leadership positions.

I hope that *Millennial Black* shows businesses the outdated methods and practices which are not only alienating them from a new generation of emerging talent but also limiting their success and profitability. I hope that companies, and those responsible for running them, feel informed and equipped to make the changes necessary to be open and receptive to growing teams from increasingly diverse backgrounds. I hope they understand that diversity isn't enough: inclusion and equity are the essential goals.

In the 1930s the first *Green Book* was published, written by Victor Hugo Green as a guide to help Black motorists in the US travel safely across the country where they were so rarely welcome. *Millennial Black* does the same for Black women trying to find their way through what can be an unwelcoming work landscape in the 2020s, and for companies who want to benefit from what they have to offer and add their value to their business.

When we understand the whole picture we can work together to make it better. We've all already come so far, but there's still a long way to go, and in the words of Oprah Winfrey – the godmother of inspirational Black women – 'I want you to succeed.'

## CHAPTER 1

# WHY MILLENNIAL BLACK?

'There is no such thing as a single-issue struggle, because we do not live single-issue lives.'

**AUDRE LORDE**

I'm aware that both of the words that make up the title of this book will be seen by some as jarring. They're both words that can make people feel a little uncomfortable, for different reasons. Millennials are a group that have so often been the butt of the joke, parodied and analysed in both pop culture and news, to the extent that even identifying as a Millennial is something that some feel is an association they don't want to make. Black can be an uncomfortable word too, loaded because of the stigma that has been associated with it for so long, especially for many who have been brought up to try to avoid using it all together as a descriptor of people. We could avoid talking about these words, and why I've chosen to put them so very front and centre, or we could dive right in. I'm not one for avoiding a tricky conversation, so off we go! First let's start with why Black, and then we'll talk about why Millennial.

## Why Black?

If you're a Black woman, are you Black first, or woman first? All too often in my life, as a Black woman, I've felt the push from others to quantify and order myself in those terms. More Black or more woman? Feminist first or Black activist first? White women and men are not asked to tear themselves in two in this way. They don't have to rip themselves down the middle and then weigh the pieces to see which they were *really* made of more. Because whiteness is seen as a neutral, their race is seen as the baseline by Western society, and so it's negligible, unremarkable in a way that Blackness isn't. It's a blank canvas.

Black women, like all people with multiple intersections to their identities, are not more one thing or the other. We can't choose for the world to treat us as just a woman one day, and just Black the next. We're both, full-time, for all of the good, and all of the bad.

> What I would say for Black women is that I think we should never forget that we have such a unique perspective in life, in the sense that we understand gender discrimination, and we understand racial discrimination. And for sure, racial discrimination is way worse. I think if anyone needs that question answered, ask a Black woman.

> Because only a Black woman can tell you definitively what the two feel like.
>
> — *June Sarpong*

The feminist movement, which was never built with the advancement of Black women in mind, has nonetheless always relied on support from Black women. In return, they have always asked that we sacrifice our Blackness in favour of our womanness, pushing for the advancement of women overall, which has always seen white women as the primary beneficiaries, with Black women left as little more than an afterthought once the battles that we have fought shoulder to shoulder in have been won. The long tail of this is that all too often, in a business context, 'diversity' has meant the advancement of (cis, straight) white women, and movements such as the push for greater representation of women in boardrooms, or the publishing of gender pay gap stats, have failed to take into account the narrowness of the group to benefit from them. This legacy is not lost on Black women today.

> I'm in a space right now where I'm kind of reluctant to call myself a feminist, which is crazy because actually, yes I am a feminist, but a lot of the feminists I see have made a constant effort to erase me and my Black sisters and women of colour in general from the conversation – so to loop myself into something that I see so many potholes in, in order to appease the wider audience, doesn't feel authentic to me. I'm far more of an intersectional feminist, and if anything I'm a Black feminist – because all of our realities are different, and the more we start going under one umbrella and saying, 'we're all for all' without looking at the structure of how power works [the more] we're always going to uphold that same structure unconsciously.
>
> — *Naomi Ackie*

We are Black, and we are women, simultaneously and forever. It is our identity, it is how we see ourselves, and – just as importantly – it's how the world sees and reacts to us.

I know a light-skinned, mixed-race woman might not be the person you'd imagined writing this book, or occupying this space. Honestly, I know. I know that being mixed-race gives me the privilege of proximity to whiteness, and I know that my experiences aren't always going to be representative of all other Black women's experiences. No one can, or should, try to represent a whole group. All too often Black women are treated as a monolith, denied individuality or nuance, denied texture and shade; we must be as one – we must feel all of the same joys, and our bodies must ache and crack in all of the same ways. Because we are one, one voice can represent us all, since we only have one story to tell, and so to understand one of us is to understand us all. That's simply not true, we are as varied and colourful and beautifully individual as any other group, and we need to be celebrated for our individuality, rather than being forced into the same broad-stroked, wide-lens view that has been our lot up until now.

A lot of people talk about oppression Olympics. When you bring up the subject of women's rights as an issue in itself, everyone wants to be seen as a supporter of them. But the moment you mention Black people's rights, that's the moment you're told to hush down. [I'm a woman,] I am also a Black person, and those two things, for me, aren't separate. I come as a whole package. So, I'm looking for those networks that tell me it's OK to be Black, and it's OK to be a Black woman.

[I once] had someone tell me that they don't see colour, and my automatic response, 'Well, then you don't see me.'

– *Lopè Ariyo*

I am Black. I see myself as Black, I identify as Black, and the first thing that the world sees about me is my Blackness. I will admit I had a choice in this, whilst many – most – don't. For years I had relaxed hair, and that, combined with my light skin and eyes, meant that I could move through the world easily. More easily at least. People would think I was 'interesting' or 'exotic' – appealing in some way, rather than treating me with the disdain or dismissal that is so common in Black women's daily interactions.

As I reached my mid-twenties I realised that this wasn't what I wanted. I didn't want an easy ride at the expense of other people. If I had this advantage of proximity to whiteness and white privilege, I wanted to use it, and use my voice to lift the voices of those who are too often overlooked and undervalued in conversations where they have the most skin in the game. So, I made the conscious choice to stop putting any distance between myself and Blackness. I stopped changing the texture of my hair, I stopped staying quiet, or trying to make myself smaller, and I started demanding more.

I want to use my privilege, my access and my voice to tell the stories of individual people, and to treat them as individuals.

I hope that in reading this, Black women find a place where they feel seen, safe and supported. I should be clear that when I say Black women I am referring to anyone who self-identifies as such, I am not here to judge your Blackness or womanness, and neither should anybody else.

The second part of 'Why Black?' is more specifically 'Why Not All Racially Marginalised People?' and my answer to that is – because we are not the same. Yes, all non-white groups in Western countries are marginalised, and all suffer, in one way or another, from white supremacy. And, in fact, quite a lot of the ways that we suffer are the same. But there are some important nuances in the societal expectations of us, and our lived experiences, that are lost when we lump people into large, opaque groups. *Millennial Black* is deliberately focused on the professional working experiences of Black women. It will be the case that many of the themes and issues are more widely applicable, but Blackness and womanness (as defined by those who identify as much) are at the book's very core.

There are (a lot of) instances where research about Black women as a standalone group is lacking. There is a lot of research about women, but often when we dig into the details we can see that the researchers are using the word women to mean only white, cis women. Similarly, there is a lot of research about Black people, but again when we dig into it we can see that it's really Black men who have been the focus of their studies. In this way not much has changed since 1982 when the first edition of the seminal feminist anthology in Black women's studies, *All the Women Are White, All the Blacks Are Men, But Some of Us Are Brave,* co-edited by Akasha Gloria Hull, Patricia Bell-Scott and Barbara Smith, was published. In the instance where academic research about Black women as a specific, singular, stand-alone group is missing I have used research about the 'BAME' female experience overall (using the language that is used in the study, whether that is 'BAME', 'BIPOC', or 'people/women of colour'), and where possible bolstered with testimonials and interviews from Black women about their personal stories and experiences.

The UK is far behind the US in terms of available research that focuses on Black women, with research instead nearly exclusively being focused solely on white cohorts, or all 'BAME' women, which ignores the difference in both history and lived experience between, for example, a Bangladeshi woman, a Chinese woman, and a Black woman. Where I have encountered these shortfalls I have opted to most often use US figures that are about Black women as an individual group, as UK stats that don't offer the same granularity.

## Why Millennial?

Like millions of others, being a Millennial is part of my identity – who I am, and what I have experienced in my life to date. When I first started working on this book, I had a lot of discussions around the title. Was 'Millennial' a negative word? Would people self-identify with it in a positive enough way to want to buy the book, or had it been co-opted by news articles and think pieces about us being lazy and selfish beyond redemption?

In short, had a word that describes a cohort born between 1981–1996 (ish – depending on who you ask) been weaponised in such a way that no one wanted to associate themselves with it?

Personally, I think not. And here's why.

The Millennial part of *Millennial Black* is important. It's important that we recognise that not only do Millennials have different aspirations for their working lives than previous generations, and a different idea of what 'success' might look like – less corner office, more flexible working? Less a job for life, more hybrid skillsets and social purpose? – but that the challenges they (we) face are also very different.

Millennials came into the start of their working lives in what was at that time the worst economic recession there had been seen since the Great Depression. I graduated in 2008 – just as that recession truly bit, stepping out into my working life in an economy no one had any idea what to do with, or how to navigate. Now, in the middle of a global pandemic, Gen Z are experiencing something very similar – stepping out into a world that's unpredictable and unrecognisable.

For those of us who started our working lives around that time, all of our expectations about climbing a professional ladder that resembled our parents' were gone before they even started. And so, we had to adapt. We had to change what we wanted and how we were going to get it. And along the way we found some really great things – remote working, work-life balance, mission-driven enterprises, caring about our mental health. So now the old way of working needs to catch back up with us. Because we changed the game.

I think that Millennials in particular are doing really well at reframing what 'effort' is. It's like, 'Hold on, it's so much more than hopping on a packed tube and sitting at a desk and lamenting your job.' It's so much more than that, it's like, 'What am I leaving behind to go to this job? If I've got kids, how am I making childcare work? How is my work-life balance?' There's just so much to consider now. And when you really break it down, more often than not, you're not being paid fairly, if at all. You're barely making ends meet if you really slice it down. But because, especially being Black and female, I know that my nan or a great-aunt would be like, 'Oh, you should just hold on to that job – just be happy to be there, be happy to be employed. Don't you go making no noise, don't you go making a fuss. You know the rent or mortgage is due at that first of the month, so you put your head down, and you do a good job.' And it's like – no. People of my age are completely ripping up that rule book, because you are constantly reminded of how it could all just change in a blink, and I don't want to be stuck working for someone who doesn't respect me, or who doesn't pay me well. And I know that those older than us have got into the habit of calling Millennials uptight or greedy – and it's like, 'Babe, you're throwing these words around from your house where the mortgage has *been* paid off, because you bought it for what today wouldn't even be a deposit.'

> It doesn't make sense, and I think those who don't want to admit it doesn't make sense just don't want to admit that perhaps they've been looking at it wrong. It's not like it was twenty–thirty years ago, it just isn't now.
>
> — *Candice Brathwaite*

The accusations most commonly levelled at Millennials are that we're flighty, selfish and entitled. We expect the world handed to us but aren't willing to do the work, so we just get bored and churn out of jobs. We have no stick-with-it-ness. This is simply not true; in fact, Millennials are just as likely to stick in a job, and with their employers, as their Gen X counterparts were when they were the same age. According to insights from Pew Research Center, a US-based organisation, 70 per cent of American Millennials interviewed in 2018, and 69 per cent of Gen X interviewed when they were the same age in 2002, said that they had worked for their employer for at least thirteen months, and 30 per cent of both groups had been with them for at least five years.[1] In fact, college-educated Millennials actually stick with their employers for longer than their Gen X counterparts did at the same age.[2] The image of Millennials as flighty seems to be little more than intergenerational projection, which we see every time one generation looks at the one coming up behind them, and worries that they'll be the downfall of us all. But that doesn't mean we'll stick around long-term in businesses that don't serve our best interests, as another study found that 38 per cent of Black Millennials are planning to leave their jobs to start their own business ventures, at some point.[3]

Though the gap in terms of years between Gen X and Millennials isn't huge, the gap in our early working experiences and the way that's impacted our values, working practices and early career opportunities are vast.

The 2008 financial recession had the biggest impact on the youngest workers, both in their personal and professional lives. Due to the disruption in our early careers, 31 per cent of Millennials delayed either getting married or starting a family, and 24 per cent had to move back in with their parents after having already lived alone.[4] Professionally, 49 per cent of Millennials say they have taken a job that they didn't want because they needed to pay the bills, 24 per cent have taken unpaid work to gain experience (in an economic landscape where experience is key) but investing in training and development for young workers became an expense that many employers could no longer afford.[5]

In 1998, 65 per cent of 18–34-year-old full- or part-time workers (the Gen X cohort) reported being very to extremely confident that if they lost their job they could find a new one. By 2009 that confidence had fallen to 29 per cent in those of the same ages.[6]

I believe these difficult early experiences of breaking into the job market changed the way that Millennials think, especially about work, and to overlook or diminish that is to ignore the way that the future of work is developing – and ultimately to be left behind.

So here we are. Millennial *and* Black, together at last. The intersectional experience of being a part of both of those groups can no longer be overlooked or downplayed, as we and Gen Z (the oldest of whom, in 2020, are 24 years old) cement ourselves into our working lives. It's no longer good enough for businesses to overlook or undervalue our racial or generational experiences and identities. It's time for us, and our experiences, and what we expect from workplaces that want to attract and retain our skills, to take centre stage, and for us, as Black Millennials, to make our mark.

# Working Whilst Millennial

## Vanessa Sanyauke

*Vanessa Sanyauke is an award-winning and globally recognised diversity, inclusion and innovation professional. She is also the Founder and CEO of Girls Talk London, a global community for Millennial women.*

**SW:** Vanessa, it would be great to talk to you about Millennials. Through Girls Talk London you come into contact with women of all ages, and I'd love to hear if you think the career expectations and approaches of Millennials are different from previous generations.

**VS:** I think they're completely different. We are more ambitious. We're not trying to wait for thirty years to become a director or have senior roles, we know our skills, we know our worth, and there's no limit. We don't put limitations on ourselves, and I think that's probably why people say, 'Oh, you're lazy, you want things now,' but no, we're ambitious, and we've got so many tools available to us, why should you have to wait until you're 60 to get a role that you can do now? It doesn't make sense to us, and we're calling out that bullshit.

We've seen previous generations suffer with work-related stress, seen the deaths, seen the breakdown of marriages and families, seen the damage that it's done, and we're able to learn lessons from previous generations. So now we're talking more about well-being and mental health and work-life balance, and it's not because we're lazy, I think it's just because we're able to see where things have gone wrong and we want to learn from that.

We're the era of technology.

We're the era of Zooms and Facebook and Twitter and Slack and WhatsApp and all of these tools that make working from anywhere possible, in terms of collaborating and file-sharing and all of that, being able to access files from anywhere – all of that development has just happened when our generation entered the workforce. And that's what makes us different – we are understanding more how we can work anywhere in the world and have more flexibility. I don't necessarily think it's us as a generation, it's just what's developed whilst we've entered the workplace, and I think that when we're older, the next generations are going to have their own developments in terms of technology or things that matter to them, and they'll have their own differences.

**SW:** I think the 'Millennials are lazy' narrative is really interesting, because it just doesn't seem to ring true.

**VS:** It's rubbish. We work hard, so many of us have two or three jobs. Get a group of ten Millennial women and I would say that at least a third have a side hustle. We've always got things going on. If anything, I'd say we're probably the hardest-working, resourceful generation out there, rather than the laziest.

# June Sarpong's Favourite Thing About Being a Black Woman

June Sarpong, OBE, is one of the most recognisable British television presenters and broadcasters and a prominent activist, having co-founded the WIE Network (Women: Inspiration and Enterprise) and the Decide Act Now Summit. In 2019, she was appointed the first-ever Director of Creative Diversity at the BBC.

Oh! My god, so many! I think the Black culture in itself lends itself – even with all of the discrimination and obstacles we have to face – to joy. I think by nature we are fun people! You know, when you go to a Black party, you know you're at a Black party! And actually that sort of informality is part of everything we do. So that is why Barack and Michelle had the most fun parties in the White House – it doesn't matter where somebody gets to, you can still tell that there is that kind of spark, and yeah, I love it.

I think anyone who's fortunate enough to be around that joy, good for you! That's what I say to all of the allies – you want some fun in your life, get some Black friends! So actually, it really is something to celebrate, and something that we mustn't lose, even when we have to face all of the things that we face.

## CHAPTER 2

# TWICE AS HARD FOR HALF AS MUCH

'Tell the truth, to yourself first,
and to the children.'

MAYA ANGELOU

**D**o you remember your parents sitting you down for The Talk? Depending on your race, there are two different things you could be thinking of now. If you're not Black, you're most likely thinking of an uncomfortable chat about sex, that came either too early or too late and made you squirm in your seat.

If you're Black, The Talk probably brings up a different memory for you. You're most likely remembering an equally uncomfortable conversation with your parents about race – or more specifically, about how the world would be different, harder, and more dangerous for you, because of your race. That's The Talk I'm talking about.

> It was something that was constantly discussed [when I was growing up]. For sure. Always. Which meant that you had to do well at school, couldn't be staying out late, couldn't talk back to your parents – you know, the things that your white friends could do weren't allowed in my household.
>
> *– June Sarpong*

The knowledge that we need to be better, work harder, do more is ingrained in us from our childhoods. We are aware that a lot of our lives we will be overlooked in favour of our whiter, male peers. The eyes of the world are on us for every mistake, and every slip-up along the way.

> Black parents do tell their kids that they can't do the things that their white friends do. I think the conversation is universal in as much as the fact that all Black parents have to tell their Black children at some point that they will be seen differently. If you are out shopping with your white friends, and your friends decide that they want to shoplift, you have to leave immediately. Do not hang around there, because you have to know that they are looking at *you* when you go into that store. And I think that's something that's still pretty universal for Black people.
>
> *– Aja Barber*

Every Black person growing up in the West knows about 'twice as hard for half as much'. There are differences of opinion about when the right time to talk to children about it is, or if talking to them about it at all does more harm than good. Some who choose to have the conversation have it young, building it into a narrative of continued conversation over a course of years. Others choose to wait until teenage years to have one frank conversation about stacked odds, systemic oppression and the dangers of simply walking through the world with Black skin. Others still choose to bypass the conversation entirely, not wanting to cause undue worry or pressures in their children's lives.

In the end, I don't think it matters when, or even if, our parents chose to give us this early lesson in unfairness and disparity, because whether via the playground, TV shows or some kind of cultural osmosis, by the time we reach our teens or early adulthood, we're all more than familiar with the message that we have to work twice as hard as our white peers. Not to get the same, but to get half as much.

This talk is given to children of all genders, and so when we look specifically at Black females, it's easy to see how the odds, already stacked against us, get multiplied in the worst ways. As we know, Black women's problems can't be broken down into 'just' Black problems or 'just' women's problems,[1] they are always, and inseparably, the multiplication of them both – everything that holds white women back from having equal representation at the most senior levels of the workplace also holds back Black women. Everything that prevents Black men from stepping into the boardroom is also a barrier to Black women. So, maybe it's more than twice as hard, once we start to consider the role that our intersectional identities have.

Not the cheeriest, I know. But I did say I was going to tell you the truth.

If you're a Black woman, take a second to think. How often do you feel lazy? I don't know about you, but I feel lazy pretty much all of the time. On one level I know this is absurd – my work sees me working my office hours, and then working from my phone, checking emails and Slack messages from bed at both ends of the day, the first and last things I do every day. I have co-founded a non-profit, I speak on panels and at universities, and mentor people. I paused this book and put out a whole second

(first) book in record time, in the middle of a global pandemic. I'm reno-
vating a flat (with my partner, by which I mean we're actually, personally
doing the physical work of knocking down and rebuilding walls – which,
it turns out, is hard), and I'm a very active and invested partner and friend.
And yet. And yet I feel lazy. Recently, my good friend Rory told me that
my ambition was one of the things he admired most about me – 'Really?'
I asked. 'I don't feel that way at all.'

Now you've thought about how often you feel lazy (I bet it's a lot),
think about what you do. At work, at home, as a side hustle, as a friend,
partner or member of your community. So then, why do we feel lazy? I
think it's because we've been socialised to be busy. We've been socialised
to be grinding and hustling and getting that bag, because we know both
that the odds are stacked, and it's on us to make our own dreams come
true through hard work. Which is a lot to take on.

But Black women do take it on – 63 per cent of Black women self-report as being 'very ambitious about their careers' (versus 51 per cent of
white women and 55 per cent of white men), but are under no illusion
that the road ahead is going to be an easy one for them, with 69 per cent
believing that they will have to work harder than their peers if they're
going to be able to advance.[2]

'You need to be twice as good.' That's one thing which a lot of Black
people say they tell their children. I never say that to my daughter.
I don't ever tell her that, because I don't want her to subconsciously
think of other people as more deserving than she is. I just want her
to work her best, and work hard, as any normal person would. If I
was a white woman with a white kid I wouldn't tell her 'work twice
as hard', I'd just say 'work hard, do your best', so that's what I'm
telling my child.

*Lekia Lée*

## Black women's labour participation

Black women are no strangers to working. In America they have, in fact, 'always had the highest levels of labour market participation, regardless of their age, marital status', and whether or not they have children.[3] It seems that this has been true as far back as 1880: according to research into the female labour force, 73.3 per cent of single Black women worked, a rate much higher than their white counterparts, only 23.8 per cent of whom worked. Whilst this participation shrunk after marriage to 35.4 per cent, it still remained much higher than married white women at the time, only 7.3 per cent of whom worked.[4]

Despite this, Black women have not been able to make the same strides in professional standing as white women. I believe this has to do with a large number of factors, including the types of work that were, and remain, open to Black women professionally.

What does it mean that Black women are a large part of the workforce, but notably absent from well-respected, well-paying, high-level roles? Where are these invisible Black women, and what are they doing? The answer is simple: they're breaking their backs working in low-paying, unstable, disrespected roles. And that's where they've always been.

### Occupational segregation

Occupational segregation looks at the make-up of the workforce within different occupations, and is a topic that is usually limited to discussing the gender breakdown of certain occupations. If an occupation has been segregated to a great enough degree, for a long enough period of time, it may even impact on our mental preconceptions of who 'should' be filling certain types of roles.

I try to be gender-neutral and use they/them pronouns for people I haven't met – but cis-normative gendered pronouns are so ingrained in us that even with the best intentions we can find ourselves slipping up.

Do you catch yourself saying 'he' or 'she' when talking or thinking about people doing certain jobs? Maybe when you think of a doctor, you expect to use a male pronoun, but when you think of a nurse, you're more likely to think of someone you'd call 'she'? We all do it with roles that have been historically gendered by occupational segregation. We might have an internalised image of what a secretary will be like versus a business owner. Or a mental image of a primary school teacher, which is likely to be different to, say, a long-distance haulage driver. It's not natural, in as much as there's no natural reason that roles should have been segregated in this manner – and these segregations are becoming, in a lot of fields, more integrated – but it's natural in as much as we've been socialised to do it since before we were us.

Occupations are not only segregated along gender lines, there is also racial occupational segregation, we just talk and think about it a lot less. Being unlikely to work in high-paying management or board-level positions, Black women in the workforce cluster in 'low-status' roles, often in 'service occupations' such as cleaners, food service workers, home healthcare or domestic service.[5] These are some of the lowest-paying occupations, and as such are more likely than most to pay minimum wage (or below), and much less likely to have benefits such as sick pay (37.2 per cent of Black working women in the US do not have access to paid sick days) – which is essential for women with caregiving duties to either children, elderly people or people with disabilities – or progression pathways. These roles are also likely to have irregular hours or unpredictable schedules, making taking on secondary employment, managing caring responsibilities, or having reliable and easy to estimate financial security more difficult to navigate.

White women are the cohort of all working women in the US least likely to work in service occupations, with only 18 per cent of white working women working in these roles. Of working African American women, on the other hand, 27.7 per cent are employed in these roles.

Like-for-like stats aren't available in the UK, but we do know that here too, specifically young Black people are the group most likely to work on zero-hours contracts (insecure working arrangements where no minimum number of hours, and so no minimum amount of payment, is guaranteed), as 37 per cent of Black people aged 16–24 work with these precarious agreements.[6] Whilst data specifically about Black women isn't available at this time, the Race Inequality in the Workforce report, published and launched in Parliament in 2020, found that 'BAME' Millennials are 58 per cent more likely to be unemployed.[7] Those who are working are 47 per cent more likely to be on zero-hours contracts than their white peers and 10 per cent more likely to have a second job.

So, Black women are more likely to have jobs that are insecure, disrespected and poorly paid. To add insult to injury, even in these roles, they are still consistently underpaid for the same work, by comparison to their white colleagues. Poverty-level wages are wages that are low enough that if the person earning them were the sole breadwinner for a family the size of their own they would be left in poverty, even if they worked full time, year-round.[8] In the US, in 2017 around 8.6 per cent of white workers earned poverty-level wages, the lowest percentage on record. Black workers were the only group in 2017 whose percentage of workers on these unlivable wages were not the lowest on record; instead, at 14.3 per cent of Black workers, there are slightly *more* Black workers on poverty-level wages than there were in 1980.

As the Economic Policy Institute is careful to point out 'it is worth noting that in 1986, the average Black worker had a slightly larger family than the average white worker; yet by the mid-1990s, that was no longer true. As of 2017, Black workers had the smallest average family size at 2.7 people – meaning that the significantly higher rates at which Black workers are paid poverty-level wages relative to white or Asian workers is entirely the result of low wages, not larger average families. Indeed, reweighting the 2017 data shows that if Black workers had the same average family size as white workers, their poverty-wage rate would actually rise to 14.8 percent.'[9]

With all of this in mind, it's no surprise that in America 34.1 per cent of Black women are in the lowest earnings quartile, whilst only 12.4 per cent are in the top.[10] Over a quarter of Black women live in poverty, compared to 18.9 per cent of Black men, and 10.8 per cent of white women.[11]

According to UK government statistics from 2019, 'Black households were the most likely of all ethnic groups to have a weekly income of less than £400'.[12] Black women are working hard, and not getting a lot back. As they always have been.

## Other types of work: double duty

Black women are doing back-breaking, unpredictable, insecure work, and not making enough money from it to live above the poverty line, only to go home and pick up a second shift. This second shift, or double duty, refers to the responsibilities Black women often have at home, often as caregivers, and often from a young age, whilst their parents can be away working long hours, for low pay, in order to make ends meet. 80 per cent of Black mothers in America are the main breadwinners in their families,[13] and more than one quarter of families headed by Black women live below the poverty line.[14]

Also in the US (the UK is particularly bad at breaking down research by both race and gender, meaning we need to rely on American research a lot of the time), 77 per cent of Black women with children under 6 years old are in work, compared to 68 per cent of white women.[15] This balance of work duties and the second shift at home is made even more challenging by the fact that, as we've seen, Black women are more likely to work in roles that are badly paid, and unpredictable, meaning that funding childcare might be unattainable for many.

In this way, as well as working twice as hard and getting half as much back in the paid working world, we're also asking – expecting – Black women at all stages of their lives to take on unpaid, invisible additional physical and emotional labour of caring for and nurturing their families, siblings, parents, grandparents and communities.

Outside of the regular workplace, Black women are working twice as hard for very little in return. Destiny Ekaragha, award-winning director, explains in her own words.

It is more than twice as hard. At first, I was working more than twice as hard – of course we have to. The moment we get up we're working twice as hard because the moment we get up our thought process is different to the average white person's in a white space. Because we have to think with that dual consciousness that people talk about. We literally walk in with dual consciousness, and it's tiring, which is why I think you find a lot of Black women ending up in mental health institutions, or with mental health issues, because you are constantly having to dual-process everything in our environments, and the brain is not designed to do that – so that alone is work. That's just living twice as hard. But, because of that, about two years ago, I just decided that I'm not going to do that anymore. I'm not going to work twice as hard. I felt that it was too much, and I just thought, 'I'm going to run myself into the ground if I keep tiptoeing like this. If I keep doing the most.' You know how everyone is like, 'You've got to do the most,' I'm like nah man. I felt like I had enough work that was canon for me to go into a room and the people who are there know that I can do my job, whether you think that I'm right for that job or not – that's up to the person, I'm not right for every job, of course I'm not. But I'm not going to do the extras. I just told myself, when I found out that some of my white male counterparts aren't doing that, then I'm not doing it. If I know that James, Todd, and Chad ain't doing the most – I'm not doing the fucking most. I don't know if I've gained jobs, or lost them from it but for me I'm tired and I think it's exhausting, when you'll find white guys not having to do half the work. And that's when I was like, no. No, I don't want to work twice as hard. I'm not doing twice as hard. I'm going to work fucking hard, I believe in working fucking hard. But not twice as hard, no.

*– Destiny Ekaragha*

## Education will set us free?

People still speak about education as something of a silver bullet for ending occupational segregation, the race pay gap and even racism itself. If Black people – Black women – were better educated there would be nothing holding us back from all of the same opportunities as our white peers. Right?

If only it were true. Although the race and gender pay gap follows us from our very first roles, shockingly, the gap actually *increases* with each educational attainment Black women achieve – with Black women in America who have a bachelor's or higher degrees facing the largest gap between themselves and their white male colleagues (around 35 per cent, an increase from 23 per cent between white men and Black women who haven't completed high school).[16]

In 2015, Michelle Obama gave the graduation address to Tuskegee University's mostly Black graduating class. 'The road ahead is not going to be easy,' she warned them. 'It never is, especially for folks like you and me . . . there will be times . . . when you feel like folks look right past you, or they see just a fraction of who you really are.' She told them that they would not be seen as the hardworking graduates that they were today, who had toiled so hard to achieve their degrees, 'They don't know that part of you. Instead, they will make assumptions about who they think you are based on their limited notion of the world.' She warned them of the 'daily slights' they would have to endure, in what many have referred to as her version of 'the twice as hard' talk. A sobering, but necessary way to send a class of young Black talent into the world.

I think there's a balance. There's a way you can inform your children of how the world is, but empower them with the belief and the tools to change it. So that they're not burdened by it, but they're also realistic about how some people think. So it's a case of telling them 'some people think that way, but we don't think that way in this house'. And I think it's really important to do that because what often happens is – and I've seen it so many times, for a lot of young talent of colour, not just women but young guys – it's a real shock when they enter the world of work. Because also the way [racism and discrimination] is in Britain is so . . . covert. It's so under the radar that you start questioning yourself like, 'Is it me? Is this real?' And I think that there's almost no preparation for that, especially when trying to get those kids into the corporate world where it is very much a dog-eat-dog world, and no one's necessarily got time to be listening to your problems, and your issues. I don't know if we are fully preparing them for the world that they will encounter if we avoid talking to them about these topics, and I think as a result, perhaps we're doing them a disservice, because a lot of them find it very hard – and then you get the kind of emotional issues and problems that come with that. So I do think there's a balance. You know, we can't lie to them, you can't lie to young people, you have to tell them how it is, but you also have to empower them to know that that's unacceptable, and actually their job in part is to help to change things, and to find the people within organisations who also want to change.

– *June Sarpong*

## Once you're in

Another way that we have to work twice as hard is just recognising the mental gymnastics that we need to perform in order to thrive and progress once we're able to break our way into the industries that we want to be a part of, especially if we're the only Black women in the space – which is the case all too often.

You know that whole thing about Black parents telling their kids that you have to work ten times harder? I would say it's fifty times. With non-Black people I've had to prove myself fifty times over and over again in order to get a credit that I know I am deserving of. White people don't have to represent the entire white race, but we do.

– *Aja Barker*

This expectation for Black women to be the face and voice of her entire race and gender is something we will go into in more detail in Chapter 8, but I think everyone is familiar with the mental strain that comes from having to navigate a space as the only person like you, especially when you are expected, by proxy, to be the living embodiment of that entire group. Yes, your successes might shine a positive light on Black women overall, but many Black women feel overwhelmed by the idea that any failure, mistakes or missteps, might well set back the perception, or the progress, of other Black women in the company or even the industry in ways beyond your control. Especially when the odds of success are not stacked in our favour.

Having good mentors, role models and internal sponsors is an incredibly important part of the career progression of all workers – having the expertise and guidance of these people is an incredible way for young people to learn and develop the skills that will allow them to thrive and progress in their careers. It's more than unfortunate, then, that women overall report having less senior-level contact than men, and Black women report more than any other group that they never have any senior-level contact.[17] These senior interactions are not only learning opportunities, they're chances to gain familiarity with stakeholders and decision-makers, and to build human connections, which makes leaders and managers more likely to advocate on behalf of employees for pay raises and promotions, and more likely to have them in mind in their own future leadership pipelines.

In America, the majority of Black professionals (58 per cent) have suffered racial prejudice at work, and were almost four times more likely to have experienced prejudice than white professionals (15 per cent).[18] Despite hard work, Black women remain double outsiders, not fitting into the idealised vision of leadership with either their race or their gender.

In 2019, Glassdoor released its Diversity and Inclusion Study, which found that 31 per cent of employed adults in the UK had either witnessed or been the victim of racism in the workplace.[19] In the same year the Race at Work survey found that 25 per cent of the 32,000 'BAME' workers who provided data had suffered from bullying and harassment within companies with zero-tolerance policies, and that despite these zero-tolerance policies being in place, less than half of businesses carried out reviews into bullying and harassment claims.[20]

It's no surprise then that 20 per cent of Black managers said that they had found racial discrimination to be a barrier to their progression,[21] and that 'BAME' employees are less likely to be rated in the top two performance categories, and less likely to be identified as having 'high potential' by their employers than white people.[22]

I just want to live, and work, in a safe environment, that's all I want.

*– Lopè Ariyo*

## What can be done?

Understanding systemic prejudice and the true unevenness of the playing field doesn't mean we should give up. Throwing our hands in the air has never been an option for marginalised people. Instead, we have always needed to find ways to navigate these spaces. That's exactly what people are trying to do when they prepare young Black people to work twice as hard for half as much – they're not saying that they like it, or that it's the way things should be. They're saying it is the truth that they have found of the world that they're living in, and they want to give their children the best possible chances, and tools, to make the most of the system they find themselves in.

Whilst I see the intention – what parent doesn't want to set up their child for the best possible success? – I think it places an unrealistic and unnecessary burden on the shoulders of Black women. Instead, I think we need to solve this problem by coming at it from the other side, by being clear about what businesses must do in order to tackle structural and systemic prejudice in their workforces, and remove the need for us to prepare our children to work twice as hard for half as much in the first place.

If you're a senior manager, CEO, COO or board member, I'm looking at you. You have the power and the responsibility to make real, long-term structural change in your businesses, and your industries.

And, if the moral case for making this change doesn't move you, then know this – by limiting the opportunities of Black women and marginalised people, businesses limit the contributions that these people can make to the success of those businesses, ultimately causing those businesses to be less successful. By creating clearer, more equitable pathways to success, business leaders improve their own prospects, and those of people from marginalised backgrounds, meaning there is not only a clear moral imperative to improve the system, but also a tangible business case.

### Realise business leaders are responsible for shaping the space

Company cultures don't spring out of nowhere – they are made by the people who drive and shape the business, whether intentionally or not. If you run a business, and you haven't been intentional about the culture that you've created, it is very likely to closely replicate wider society, which in Western countries was founded on the image of whiteness and maleness.

That is something that needs to be addressed if you want to be able to attract, retain, and develop a range of people in your business. And you do want that if you want to stay relevant to consumers, customers and clients.

New businesses and start-ups are thinking about the culture they're fostering from the very start – whether that is prioritising mental health first-aiders, or having a clear and consistent code of standards and shared values that are applied not only internally, but with clients and potential partners. New businesses have the opportunity to be mindful and deliberate in the cultures they create, and can create the environments that we wish we'd found elsewhere.

### Have clear paths to progression

Everyone wants to feel that their career is moving forward. Feeling stagnated or limited is disheartening. Having the sneaking suspicion that you'll never achieve your full potential regardless of how hard you work, how good you are or how many times you go above and beyond is not going to inspire anyone.

People can't be promoted non-stop, and it's to be expected that as people have different aptitudes, some people's paths to progression may naturally be faster than others. The important thing is making sure that the measurements being used to determine promotions are clear and consistent.

People who are, or who feel that they are, being unfairly treated and held back from promotions at work are unlikely to stay in those companies. We can see this in practice – Black women are leaving their employers and going out on their own at surprising rates. According to the 2018 State of Women-Owned Business Report, Black women were second in number only to white men as the largest group of self-employed entrepreneurs.[23] It sounds great, but there's actually a pretty big snag – these women aren't necessarily taking this step because they want to, but because they feel they need to. The report notes factors, including the increased gender and race pay gap, meaning Black women are starting businesses 'out of necessity and the need to survive, rather than a desire to seize a market opportunity'. It seems likely that these women are not actively self-selecting for self-employment, so much as finding the paths to success when working for traditional companies to be blocked to them.

So what? So long as it's happening, and these women are taking steps into business ownership, does it really matter why? Unfortunately yes, it does, because of the impact it has on the types of work women from racially marginalised backgrounds then take on. It's not the glossy story of startup often associated with white male entrepreneurs, quite the opposite. The work that 'BAME' female entrepreneurs do is 'clustered in areas of multiple deprivation' and likely to be low-paid work, and zero-hours sub-contracts, offering these women very little in the way of stability, protection or income.[24]

Black women hitting a concrete ceiling of progression and feeling they have no choice other than to opt out removes members of this already marginalised group, and by default leaves more 'Onlys' (the only person of their race and gender in their team, office, or whole business – see Chapter 8 for a lot more detail) behind them. And so, the cycle continues.

### Creating equality in progression and promotion

It's essential to have a policy for progressions and promotions that all employees know about and can assess freely and easily – mystery and secrecy only make things more difficult in the long run, and people want to have visibility on their careers. Here is a system that I have found works well and is easy to implement.

1) **Define and communicate each level**. For each department in the business (marketing, finance, operations, etc.) make sure there is a clear and public job description, which outlines the level and type of contribution someone in that role should make. For instance, entry-level roles such as an operations assistant, marketing assistant or finance assistant should have skill and role-specific outlines which will be different from department to department, but also have directives which are the same for all people at that level, regardless of department. These directives should be linked to autonomy, responsibility and ways of working, such as 'helps in co-defining tasks with strong support from line manager'. As the roles progress so should the expectations: 'defines tasks with minimal oversight from line manager' to 'owns and carries out tasks without oversight' and then 'provides support for more junior team members in co-defining their tasks.' Everyone at every level knows what is expected of them, and their colleagues.

2) **Make sure everyone knows their level**. Ensure that everyone knows where they sit within the context of the business, or at least their department. They should know the roles which sit more junior to themselves and have performance objectives linked to assisting them. They should know which job roles sit more senior to themselves along with team members they can go to for support. Knowing your level means you know what's above you, and if the job descriptions and outlines are public, you also know what you need to do to move up.

3) **Be consistent**. Do you promote someone when they have successfully shown they can do everything associated with the role they currently have, or when they have shown they can do everything in the next role up? Whichever you pick, make sure it's consistently applied to all promotion decisions, equally.

4) **Lay out a timeline**. It's risky to lay out timelines for promotions to happen in, but it's a good idea to have timelines for when progression will be assessed. More junior roles may be assessed every three months with the possibility to progress then, or if they haven't been successful, reviewed again in another three months. As roles become more senior, the timeline for assessment may become longer, stretching to twelve or eighteen months. So long as people are aware of their timelines and the objectives they are being measured against in that time, the lower the possibility of people feeling undervalued.

### Create an anti-racist workplace – not just a 'not racist' one

It's important to understand the difference between not being racist and being anti-racist. Not being racist is inactive, it's a belief, but it's not a lot more than that. It's not about taking any steps or actions, or making any changes. Being anti-racist is much more than a belief – it's a continual set of actions. Part of being anti-racist is calling out racism and racist structures in every form, every single time they occur. No matter who or where they come from. It can be uncomfortable, but it's the only way to make change, and it should be the baseline of all modern businesses.

One step towards creating an actively anti-racist business is establishing a zero-tolerance policy. And then acting on it. Every time.

Talking a good game and having policies in place doesn't mean anything if people don't stick to them. If the things the company says in internal policies, or public statements, and the way it acts day to day aren't in line, then the body language of the company isn't reflecting the policies. In cases like this, it won't take long for review sites like Glassdoor, which people will check before agreeing to interviews or accepting roles, to pick up on the inconsistencies and make informed choices about whether your company is a good fit for them.

## Don't ask Black women to work for free

> All I can do is laugh. I've cried a lot about stuff like that over the last couple of years, but now I just laugh because I think, what little life I have (hopefully it's long), I can't constantly dedicate it to trying to educate those who don't want to show up for school. It's just not my vibe, you know? It's not my bag anymore.
>
> – *Candice Brathwaite*

The work of making a diverse, inclusive, representative workplace is hard. It's real labour, it's emotionally draining, and it's not something that should fall to marginalised people, either inside or outside of a business, to take on for free.

> 'Why would I do that for free?' When I ask that simple question they're like, 'Oh, I just thought you'd be interested.' I'm not. They think that asking someone like me and saying, 'But shouldn't you want to do this for free?' is fine. Without considering the work and time that will have to go into it. That's a thing people do to Black people, because the conversation around race has always been so devalued, people act like they're almost doing us a favour and it's just nope – you're helping yourself. You're going to make money from this, but you want me to do this for free to allow you to profit?
>
> – *Aja Barber*

Whether it's asking an informal committee to 'solve' a diversity issue within your business or asking a speaker to come in to facilitate a workshop, understand that this is real and difficult work, which should be compensated in the same way as all other work. There is a profitability benefit to having diverse teams, especially at the most senior levels, and so this drive for diversity and inclusion should come from the top.

Having a commitment to diversity at the most senior levels also means that the people who have the tools and resources to make real change are accountable for it. When this is passed off to become the burden of more junior people, not only are you sending the message that it's not seen as important by the business, you are adding to the unpaid labour of a marginalised person, and in most instances – when the proper support and resources are not provided to make real change – setting that person up for failure before they have even begun.

### Set boundaries

If you're a Black woman looking at this and thinking, 'Well, sounds great – but my workplace isn't doing any of that so I guess I just have to keep on keeping on,' then this final point is for you.

It's OK to set boundaries.

It's OK to be firm, and to say no.

Setting boundaries is hard, but essential work. Learning to say no can be scary, but it can also be liberating.

Knowing when to say no to a conversation, additional task or piece of office housework that doesn't serve you can be truly game-changing. Especially when you realise that non-marginalised colleagues aren't asked to invest their time in this way, and so are able to instead invest it into work, projects and training that enables them to progress in their careers, rather than distracting them from it.

I do understand that this is a privileged position. Not everybody works in a safe environment where they're able to say no without fear of long-term repercussions, but it's the baseline that I hope all of us will be able to achieve in the long run, with the support of inclusive workplaces and more diverse leadership teams.

People who don't respect your boundaries or want to compromise on them or take them down all together are people who don't have your best interests at heart. They don't respect your need to take breaks and to only take on your fair share of work. This is something that both Aja Barber and June Sarpong have found in their own working lives.

'People that respond negatively to your boundaries are not people who are your friends,' said Aja. 'I spent my whole life having really bad boundaries, and I think that's the same for a lot of marginalised people. We live in a world where, up until about five years ago, we weren't allowed to talk about race in a way that causes any white guilt, so I think that when we've grown up like that we're bad at setting boundaries because we're so used to having conversations about things that matter to us, but centring white feelings. When Black people started talking about race in a way that didn't centralise white feelings – that's what changed the dynamic of the conversation. And I think for me, being able to do that allows me to have the boundaries that I need to protect myself, and protect my energy.'

June agreed, 'Yes, and that's then for us to have the self-confidence, and the self-value, to make sure we put boundaries in place. And all of those things are really important.'

Twice As Hard

Naomi Ackie

*Naomi Ackie is an award-winning actress and writer from East London. She has starred in* Star Wars: The Rise of Skywalker, Lady Macbeth *and* The End of the F***ing World.

**NA:** I've actually started doing something - and this is an evolution of stuff that my mum would teach and talk to me about growing up - which is handing people back their shit. What I think tends to happen in friendships and relationships, and in business as well, is that when people have their own undealt with baggage, they like to hand it over to other people, so they don't have to take accountability for it. So instead of taking on their stuff and buying into that trope of 'I'm going to take this on and I'm going to help them through their stuff whilst I handle my stuff and juggling all of this stuff,' it's actually creating clear boundaries, addressing that person and going, 'Hey, there's something here that you need to look at. The thing is, I'm not your mother. Or your therapist. Or someone who's getting paid to handle this shit, and so I'm going to hand it back to you, and because you're a grown person, you can either choose to deal with it or not. And until then, if you're not ready to, then don't come to me.' It's really helped in relationships and also in business where I've just gone, 'Oh, I don't have to feel too sad about this for too long, cause what I'm not going to do is take on your baggage and add it on to the stuff I'm already dealing with on a daily, societal basis.' That of course has to come with me knowing what stuff I need to deal with so I don't project that onto others either.

It's insane the amount of jobs I've had where I have to do my own hair, where I've had to bring my own foundation for them to use, it's insane. I can't speak on other industries, but that's something we still have to think about [as actors]. I've had to educate certain designers on the fact that I can't have my natural hair out if we're filming outside, because we don't know if it's going to rain, and if it rains continuity is going to get messed up. If you want, halfway through the day, to change my hairstyle - I've got 4C hair - so if you want to change my hairstyle so in the morning it's like a cropped 4C short hairstyle, and you want to stretch it out within half an hour to do the next shoot where my hair is longer, it's going to take more than half an hour. So, you need to structure your shoot, and it comes down to me to tell you that.

And for me it's like, hang on a minute, you want me to learn my lines, create a character, collaborate with the director and the sound department and hair and make-up and all of that, and you also want me to tell you how to structure the day so that we can get the best performance possible? There are things I am paid to do - I am paid to learn my lines. I am paid to talk to the director at any point that they want. I am paid to spend twelve hours, if not more, on set working with people - and I love it. Absolutely love it. But the things I'm not paid for, I'm not doing.

Specifically with creative industries, there's this ingrained feeling I had that I should feel lucky to be there. Now I'm learning actually it isn't diva of me to say, 'What you're asking of me isn't in my pay bracket, so if you want more of me, pay me more I'll tell you if I can do it, or if I want to do it. Because what I'm paid to do is the thing I'm already doing, and anything more, you're taking liberties, because of the fact that I love my craft and I want everything I make to be the best that I and the people I'm working with are capable of.'

I think my job is about being a people person, working with people and making people feel at ease, it's about creating an environment that feels the most creative and the most collaborative, but the thing about boundaries is that I'm now learning how to switch that off and turn into business mode and say 'No, you're asking too much of me,' when they are asking too much of me. And I think that can be applied to many different areas of your life where you just go, 'Actually I'm seeing some things here where you're trying to pull strings that aren't appropriate, and I'm just letting you know that you can try to do that to someone else over there, but that's not happening with me. And if you have a problem with it, by all means, have a problem.' For instance, there was a situation where they couldn't get a body double with the same skin tone as me, because not one of the crew was a Black woman. No one on the crew had Black skin. And so they were asking me to stay an extra day, outside of the day that I was being filmed, to shoot coverage because they couldn't find a body double. I

said, 'No. That's your problem that, when you brought a Black girl onto this set, you didn't think ahead to when we were going to need a body double. That's your problem, and I'm going home because I'm not staying here another day when I've been working six days per week. No, you figure it out,' and they did, of course they did. And that actually takes the piss more – that I had to push them and say, 'I'm not staying,' for them to go, 'Oh, OK, we really need to sort this.' That's annoying, you know? Then all of the apologies afterwards, and 'let's talk about it' and all of that stuff is like, no, no, no. We don't need to talk about it, I don't need to talk to the producers on the phone and hear your apologies about how you're so sorry and you didn't see this coming and all of that, because you should have, you're a producer. That's your job, so if I do my job and you do yours, we're all good.

**SW:** Absolutely, there's no world where you have to do five jobs, do your own hair, do your own make-up, educate the team, and be your own double because other people didn't want to do all of their one job.

**NA:** I don't have to do that, and that's not what I'm getting paid for. And the privilege of earning the money that you can earn as an actor means that I can make those kinds of boundaries for myself. I have deep empathy for Black women and women of colour who feel like they can't or *actually* just can't. I think I'd never want to come across like it's easy to do those things, and that comes with a certain amount of years, and amount of support from many different people, including my own team, where I feel like I can make a stand for myself, and I feel like they've got my back in that. I guess the challenge is, and what I haven't figured out how to help with, is for those women who are not in that privileged position. How do we as a community help them feel empowered with the choices that they can make? I've spoken to Black dudes who have told me to not take any shit and I've been like listen, you're a Black dude, I'm a

Black woman – you can get away with things that I can't get away with. There are things that you are allowed to do in terms of male privilege that I'm not allowed to do in terms of female lack of privilege! So, I understand, if we all lived in an equal world, we could all do it the same way – but I want to always consider the fact that we aren't all treated the same way in this world. So the way we move and empower ourselves is always gonna be at different levels, but they are all worthy and bring us a step closer to the world that we want to see.

# Natalie Lee's Favourite Thing About Being a Black Woman

Natalie Lee runs a blog called *Style Me Sunday*. She is a big advocate of in encouraging women to feel comfortable in their skin and likes to stick a middle finger up to society's standards and norms. A mother of two girls, she is a fierce supporter of women and a huge lover of beauty and fashion. Natalie talks about many things, from alopecia to ageing to wanting to see more diverse images in the media. She has a podcast, *The Everything Project*, and runs events such as 'The Warrior Woman Project' in association with Dove and Feeling Myself.

" From the curl in my hair to the curve in my spine, from the blood of my ancestors in my veins to the delicious tone of my skin, I have learned that my Blackness isn't something to hide or to shy away from. I love being Black, and my favourite thing is walking around with the confidence and the knowledge that my Blackness has risen despite the struggle and adversity, which makes it even more precious. "

## CHAPTER 3

# THE 'PROBLEM MINORITY'

'I have come to believe over and over again that what is most important to me must be spoken, made verbal and shared, even at the risk of having it bruised or misunderstood.'

**AUDRE LORDE**

How often are you aware of your race? Like, actively, consciously aware? If you're a white person living in the UK or USA, I'd expect the answer is rarely. One of the advantages of not being marginalised is almost never having to think about it. If you read a script or a novel, unless explicitly stated otherwise, characters are presumed to be white, because whiteness is the baseline we are all presumed to start from. Public spaces reflect you, and walking down the road, or going into a room, you can usually guarantee that there will be people who look like you and that you will generally be safe.

This is an idea that Robin DiAngelo explores in her book *White Fragility*, in which she discusses the ways that people can often cling to a 'racial innocence', an idea in which white people see Black people as the 'havers' of race, whilst seeing themselves as the raceless default. Other people have a race – white people are just people.

For me, even though I'm a very light-skinned Black woman who with a quick trip to the hairdressers could probably pass for white if I wanted to (I don't), I can honestly say that not a day goes by that I'm not consciously aware of my Blackness, and the fact that this is a much more pronounced experience for darker-skinned Black people.

It could be the mental maths of being invited to an event and having to quickly calculate the likelihood of being the only Black person there and what my escape plan will be when too many unwelcome hands find their way to my scalp, or curious, socially unaware people ask me where I'm 'like . . . *from* from . . . y'know . . . *really* from?' (Still Birmingham, thank you so much for double-checking.)

I'm aware of my Blackness when I apply for a job or go to an interview – especially earlier in my career when I would have to make the choice to straighten or not straighten my hair. I'm aware this consideration may seem minor or trivial to non-Black people, but it's absolutely not. In reality, it's a choice between presenting yourself in line with a widely held view of professionalism (do an image search of 'women's professional hair' and see what comes up), and being your authentic self, by allowing your hair to simply exist in the texture in which it naturally grows out of your head, without putting it through time-consuming, expensive and damaging heat or chemical processes. Happily, thanks to initiatives like 2019's 'Rip Up the Dress Code' campaign from Project Embrace, an organisation championing afro-textured hair in the workplace in the UK, this may begin to change, but any change in this respect is in geographic time. Glacial time.

I'm never not actively aware of being Black, and that's not necessarily a negative thing – in fact, I have found some real comforts in it and some warm corners to call home.

As I've become older I've discovered that there's a community in this otherness, one that has come to mean a lot to me. There are organised communities that I'm proud to belong to, organisations for bringing people together, striving for change and making a difference in the world, and I am deeply thankful that these exist, but they are not the ones which mean the most to me on a day-to-day basis. The community that I find most affirming and assuring is not an organised one. It isn't vocal or even visible to most people – it's simply other Black women, and the way that we Black women subtly, almost invisibly, interact with one another every day in public places. In streets, supermarkets, offices and train stations, we have built a secret and silent community amongst ourselves, for ourselves.

This is a silent community of micro-interactions, usually invisible to all but the most observant outside eyes. Nine times out of ten when I pass a Black woman in the street, particularly another Black woman with natural hair, there is some small acknowledgement. It's almost never more than a nod or a smile, a simple 'hi' at most. It's a tiny gesture, but to me it's huge. It says, 'I see you. I acknowledge you. I'm rooting for you.'

Sometimes white friends will see these tiny interactions and ask me who the person I just shared a moment with is. The first time someone asked, I was leaving the building I worked in, walking out with a colleague, when she saw me give a little wave and say 'hi' to a woman I saw most days, coming and going from the building. The building was large and housed a lot of offices, so although I saw this other woman pretty much every day, I had no idea which company she worked for, or even her name, but she was someone I looked forward to bumping into as I bustled around the building – even though it was always fleeting. 'Who was that?' she asked? 'Oh', I said, not thinking much of it, 'you know when you're out somewhere and you see someone like you and so you say hi . . . I mean . . . I guess . . . do white women do that?' Her completely confused face quickly let me know that no, in fact, white women do not do that. Because there is no need to. It's something secret, special and just for us.

## The pressure of representing a group

I'm happy to be a part of this secret club and I'd never want to give it up. It makes me feel safer, more supported, and like I'm a part of something really beautiful. It's the good part of my always being aware of being a Black woman. But this constant self-awareness of our race isn't always positive.

It would be naive to imagine that being constantly aware of being 'other', always having in mind that you are part of a marginalised group with a painful history, is a positive experience. Black people have had to work for generations, over hundreds of years, to be accepted as good, positive and equal members of society, and all too often we're shown in the clearest possible ways that we're still not there in many people's eyes. We can't discount the impact that history and ongoing lived experience still have on our day-to-day choices and behaviours.

One of the pressures of knowing that you're part of a marginalised group is the constant pressure to succeed – because we're part of something bigger than ourselves. It's easy to feel that if we mess up, if we fail or if something doesn't go to plan, we've let down more than just ourselves – we've damaged the whole group. And that's a lot to take on.

At work, a lot of Black women, especially those who are Onlys or close to Onlys, say they have persistent anxiety that they are representing, or are seen to be representing, something larger than themselves. They worry that they are viewed subconsciously by their employers as not just themselves, but also as a representative of Black women as a whole. If you do well, then great, maybe the door will open a crack wider for others. And if not, well then maybe that door slams behind you, locking out everyone who would have got in if only you'd been a little better, worked a little harder, and not made a fuss.

Whoever you are, whatever job you do, simply doing that job can be tough enough. Everyone wants to make a good impression, do well and succeed, which is hard to navigate on its own without the fear that any missteps, mishaps or mistakes could make things harder for future Black women to succeed.

No one wants to be the reason the door is shut and padlocked behind them, and that's a lot of responsibility. It's tiring, it's scary, and it's a layer of emotional labour that people in non-marginalised groups don't need to take on.

If you're white, this constant awareness of living within your racialised body and the impact that your actions can have on others like you is unlikely to be your experience.

As DiAngelo points out, 'people of colour' often have their views attributed by others to their race: people presume that our race is the reason that we make certain choices or hold certain beliefs – taking away our 'luxury of impartiality'. This homogenisation based on race is not something commonly applied to white people. As DiAngelo notes, despite the majority of school shooters, rapists and domestic terrorists in the USA being white males, white men as a group have maintained the privilege of being viewed as individuals, rather than being grouped together and associated with the dangerous and negative stereotypes of white males.[1]

> It's baffling . . . straight white men don't see themselves as 'straight white men'. To think that you can be a person and not see your intersections, you simply think that you're just that individual. You're so used to being seen as an individual that you're not used to being part of a group, and that's what we're all experiencing.
>
> *Munroe Bergdorf*

Indeed, I would argue they have largely avoided these stereotypes forming at all, for them to be associated with – since whiteness is often perceived as a *lack* of a race or racial identity, rather than a race of its own, it resists the groupings and stereotyping that other racial groups experience being applied to them.

## The model minority and the problem minority

When striving for success and trying to better our position in the workplace, one of the biggest stereotypes Black women are pushing against has its origins in the idea of model minorities. I feel as though I've been aware of the term 'model minority' my whole life, but as it turns out, I hadn't really understood its meaning or history until now. I had somehow conflated it in my mind with respectability politics, the pressure that people from marginalised groups felt to behave like model citizens to counteract any negative stereotypes against them. Whilst one notion does tie in with the other, the origin of the term, and its distinction between different marginalised groups, surprised me.

First coming into use during the Second World War, the media used the term 'model minority' to report that after the period of being ruthlessly persecuted, Japanese people were rising back up, achieving wealth and position within society due to what they believed to be their innate cultural goodness.

This idea was popularised in 1966 when a sociologist named William Petersen wrote 'Success Story, Japanese-American Style' for the *New York Times Magazine*, which was subsequently picked up by a number of news outlets across America.[2] In his piece, Petersen pointed to the increasing socio-economic success of Asian American people and characterised them as 'model minorities', asserting that their model virtues such as politeness, family values and a hard-working nature led them to success.

The mid-1960s, when this piece came out, was the time of the civil rights movement in America – a time during which Black people in the country were fighting for their basic rights. Whilst in his piece Petersen praises Asian Americans and their values, he used 'negros' as the naturally problematic counterbalancing group by way of comparison. He contrasted Asian Americans and, according to him, their 'naturally' law-abiding and productive group attributes, with the African American 'problem minority' – a group who, he asserted, were inherently more inclined towards criminality and disruptive behaviour, and who were not able to achieve equivalent success due to their innate internal flaws.

This is bad enough as it is – assigning innate behaviours and values to groups of people based on their race – but if you follow the argument through to its logical conclusion, it gets worse; you'll see that it's asserting that racism doesn't exist. Or, if it does, it doesn't have any impact on people's lives or successes – which are purely down to effort and hard work on an individual basis.

At its root, the argument was that if society were truly racist, prejudice would have impacted Black and Asian American people equally. However, since Asian Americans were able to be successful whilst Black Americans continued to struggle in society, the shortcomings that Black Americans face must be within themselves.

Those who want to deny that race or intersectional marginalisation has impacts on people's outcomes still cling to this flawed logic. There are *some* successful people from a whole range of different backgrounds, so race must not be a factor in success at a societal level, they argue. The real factors in success must be at a group or individual level, in the way that marginalised group members behave, instinctively.

And so their logic goes that some racial groups are less good, less hard-working, less polite, and therefore less deserving of success. The only thing holding them back is themselves.

You don't need me to tell you this, but this logic is nonsense. The starting point is flawed, there's a page-one error. When Petersen compares the outcomes of relative successes for the model Asian Americans and problem 'negros' he makes the mistake of lumping all racially marginalised experiences into one. We can only measure differences in outcomes in a meaningful way if the inputs have been the same, or at least comparable.

It's an easy mistake to make if you are a white person and think of yourself and other white people as racially neutral, essentially as people who are raceless, believing instead marginalised groups are the havers of race. In that binary, it's easy to lump all non-white racial groups together and overlook any variation in both the starting points and societal experiences of members of different races. It's also easy, in this case, to lack the understanding of the varying ways society perceives different races, and how those perceptions impact both individual and group outcomes. It basically assumes that the starting point for different groups is the same, which it isn't.

Black people, most pointedly in America, have lived through segregation, the prison-industrial complex, police violence and harassment, housing redlining, hundreds of years of slavery or legal lynching – that's right, *legal* lynching. Despite over 200 anti-lynching laws being put to US Congress since 1918, and many false starts to criminalise it,[3] lynching

– a type of violence which has always historically over-indexed towards victimising Black people – only became a federal crime.*

Asian Americans have suffered huge, real, racial injustices, and I would never want to deny or belittle that history. They have been confined in internment camps, denied citizenship and suffered the appropriation of their cultures, among other prejudices. Their struggle is no less real, at all, than the Black experience – but it is distinct and different.

This model minority stereotype was also *deeply* damaging for Asian people. Though they are assigned as model members of society, this classification still breaks them down into sweeping stereotypes, wipes away their individuality, and puts a huge pressure on them to be successful, at all costs.

The idea of model minorities, and by contrast problem minorities, works well for us as a society, and the beliefs we like to hold – it's in line with our values of living in a colour-blind meritocracy, and so it sticks around.

Its insistence that all achievement and attainment is down to the individual, with no societal impact, has led to stereotypes such as Black people being lazy, unmotivated and uneducated, by way of explaining their lack of access to spaces of success. It's based on the idea that there is a 'right' way to behave – and whilst it may not come naturally to us, if we as Black women were just able to follow those correct behaviours then there would be nothing outside of ourselves to stop us succeeding. It completely overlooks and erases history, infrastructure and societal expectations. There's only us, individually, working hard enough, or not working hard enough. Being kind and polite enough, or not. Succeeding, or not. Either way, it's purely down to us.

## Current impact of the model minority versus the problem minority

The idea that lays the foundation of model and problematic minorities – that some groups achieve more because they are naturally better, harder – working, and more suited to it – is one that we as a society, regardless

---

* Although in 2018 the American Senate passed the anti-lynching legislation Justice for Victims of Lynching Act, the bill was unsuccessful because it wasn't passed by the House before Congress ended in 2019. In February of 2020, a revised version, known as the Emmett Till Antilynching Act passed the House of Representatives,[4] but has been held from passing in the Senate up to the time of writing.

of our individual race, have absorbed over generations. Maybe not in those words, and almost certainly not consciously, but it's there. As a society we treasure the idea that whoever you are, your success is directly related to how hard you have worked and what you deserve. We value against-the-odds stories of people overcoming and pulling themselves up by their bootstraps without acknowledging the role of society's expectations and limitations.

The idea that Black people are naturally a problem group with criminal tendencies has persisted and impacts the way that Black people are treated from the very beginning of their lives, and at times, even before their lives truly begin. Black mothers are five times more likely than white women to die in childbirth, a tragedy of medical racism which impacts the family structures of many Black families before they have had the chance to begin.[5]

In a 2014 study, after interviewing 264 mostly white, female college students, they found a tendency to see Black children ages 10 and older as 'significantly less innocent' than their white counterparts.[6] Whilst white children of the same age benefited from an assumption of childhood innocence, the Black children were seen to be responsible for their (hypothetical) actions, and so mistakes or behaviour that might not be reacted to, or taken as an indictment of a white child, could be more likely to lead to a harder punishment, or a presumptions of guiltiness in young Black children.

Later in life, we can see that this disparity reoccurs in a range of areas, not least within the British Criminal Justice system statistics.[7] In 2016–17 Black people were eight times more likely than white people to be stopped and searched by police. Once in court, in the same year, Black people were four times more likely than white people to face prosecution (for every 1,000 population members, 16 Black and 9 mixed defendants were prosecuted compared to 4 white defendants). I could go on to tell you the same stats about the ways in which, after being prosecuted, Black people are convicted at higher rates, and face longer, tougher sentencing, but I don't need to. You get it.

These pieces of research are saddening but not surprising – they're not new news. In fact, we see this reflected in our own lived experiences when we, as Black women, begin our working lives. In my experience, nine times out of ten when discussing Black women's success at work there is a huge weight of burden placed on us to be the change-makers – both within the organisations and societies we're part of, and within ourselves. We have the expectations that society has built up around both what it is to be Black, and what it is to be a woman, stacked on top of each other, and on top of us – a huge weight to carry. We're told non-stop that if we want to be more successful, Black women should modify their behaviours in this way or that. We should use this tone or avoid using those words so people don't think of us as angry or aggressive, we should wear our hair a certain way and be five minutes early, and keep our heads down and work work work. If we do that, we'll be able to break the stereotype that was established before we were even born, and pave the way for others. But if we slip up, we've proven the stereotypes right, and pushed ourselves, and everyone else, back to the start.

So what do you do when the world tells you that they know who you are before you open your mouth, based on the body you live in – and that who you are is bad? You try to be as good as you can. This is exactly what I believe Black women have been doing for some time.

We are pushing forward in educational attainment – in 2016 the *Independent* reported,[8] citing statistics from the National Center for Education Statistics, that Black women had become the most educated group in the US, earning 68 per cent of associate's degrees and 66 per cent of bachelor's degrees between 2009 and 2010.[9] They went on to say that, 'By both race and gender, a higher percentage of Black women (9.7 per cent) is enrolled in college than any other group, including Asian women (8.7 per cent), white women (7.1 per cent) and white men (6.1 per cent).' Black women are overachieving and outperforming in their academic achievements.

When Black women get into workplaces, this tendency to overachieve in the hopes of being perceived positively continues in a very simple yet meaningful way – volunteering. Specifically, putting themselves forward to take on office housework. Black women self-nominate or accept when they are nominated by others to take on additional, unpaid tasks at work, not directly related to their job roles or development.

Taking on additional tasks might seem like no big deal – they're usually small, they're sometimes quick, and *someone* has to do them, right? It might even seem to be a good way to work your way into the good favour of employers by being helpful and available. However, in reality, the impact that taking on these tasks can have on progression and perception can be bigger than expected. The crux lies in the *types* of additional tasks Black women are being expected to take on, and the impact that has on their time and perception within their workplaces.

## Office housework versus glamour work

Office housework is all of the additional unpaid tasks that businesses have come to rely on to function. In a company without a talent, HR or office-management team it can mean scheduling interviews, preparing and clearing meeting rooms, organising events like seasonal parties, or performing emotional labour to support the team or management. These tasks can be small and simple like making coffee for meetings or note-taking, or large and time-consuming such as helping to find a new office or sitting on internal committees. Though the forms of the tasks can vary between industries and workplaces, the thing that they have in common is that they, and the effort required to complete them, are usually over-looked. Office housework is also referred to as 'non-promotable tasks' – which should give you some idea of just how much businesses value them, and those repeatedly taking them on.

Women, particularly 'women of colour', volunteer or are volunteered to do this work at a disproportionate rate when compared to white men. In Joan C. Williams and Marina Multhaup's 2018 study they found that 'women of colour' were the most likely to report doing more administrative tasks than their colleagues – over 20 per cent more likely than white men.[10] This was also true when it came to *literal* office housework – tasks such as cleaning up the coffee cups and tidying shared space, where 'women of colour' were 18 per cent more likely than white men to report taking on these tasks.

Unlike most tasks in an organisation, office housework isn't usually directly tied to profit-making for the business, and so whilst they can require effort and skill, they are unlikely to be recognised and rewarded (or even taken into consideration) in decisions around pay rises and promotions.

So, what's the opposite of office housework? In their study, Williams and Multhaup coin the term 'glamour work'. In stark contrast to the office housework, glamour work is, well, glamorous. Whilst office housework is unsung and overlooked, glamour work happens in the spotlight. As the term's authors point out, getting assigned, or assigning yourself, the right piece of glamour work can rocket you to success. Glamour work might be building a new team or department, or pitching to a new client – it's big, it's shiny, it has your name on it, and when it goes well, people take notice.

It won't come as a surprise to learn that whilst office housework skews unevenly towards women and 'women of colour', glamour work leans towards white men. Williams and Multhaup found that female engineers 'of colour' were 35 per cent less likely than white men to report having equal access to desirable assignments; white women were 20 per cent less likely. For lawyers, the findings were remarkably similar: 'women of colour' were almost 30 per cent less likely than white men to say they had equal opportunity to high-quality assignments, and white women were 18 per cent less likely.

I understand the desire to offer to help – especially if you're in a junior position, in a new company, or one of a limited number of Black women in a company – I've been there too. Black women have struggled against the image of being aggressive for a long time, and Black people overall, thanks to model-minority stereotyping, have struggled against the stereo-type of being lazy and unmotivated. What better way to show that you're none of those things than to lend a helping hand? It's the least you can do.

I'm also not saying that you should never take on anything outside of your core role. Taking on extracurricular work tasks can be great if it's something you get genuine enjoyment from, if it puts you in social or professional situations with influential people you wouldn't otherwise be with, or if raises your profile or teaches you transferable skills you can apply to this or next role.

The problem is that taking on tasks of this type can have real, negative repercussions for you. As Linda Babcock, Maria Recalde and Lise Vesterlund, authors of a study on women's office housework point out, 'If [women] are disproportionately saddled with work that has little visibility or impact, it will take them much longer to advance in their careers.'[11]

Anecdotally, this experience seems to be something that almost all women can relate to having fallen into at some point in their careers. In February 2013 TV presenter Mika Brzezinski recalled a conversation she once had with Massachusetts senator Elizabeth Warren. Warren had told her that when she had been a Harvard Law School professor, she had found herself, for years, 'holding the mop' for her male colleagues, including taking on undesirable shifts because the men had said no to the hours. Brzezinski summarised by saying, 'There's a fine line between paying your dues and knowing when to say no.'[12]

I've certainly done this myself more times than I can count, especially when I was starting out. In one of the first advertising jobs I had, I was one of only two Black people in the company, and I was picked (lucky me!) to form and lead a culture club – a group of employees that would meet every two weeks to do a temperature check of the agency, gather any problems and (having no actual power ourselves to solve them) take them back to the management to be addressed. I was young, and to me, it seemed like a good idea to begin with – a real chance to make a change and help people at work, and the opportunity for more face time with the heads of the company – what could be better? The result was a million miles away from what I'd hoped. Colleagues who brought their problems to me quickly became annoyed at the lack of change I was able to push through. In my annual review with my bosses, they complained that I was too negative and said they felt like I brought up too many problems – I pointed out that these were not my problems but those of other people, and that I had gathered and presented them at their request. But by then the damage was done. I was a person who complained, and that reputation stuck. The relationship never really recovered and it was one of the big reasons I decided to move on from that job.

You'd think I would have learned my lesson, but no, this has been repeated almost identically several more times in my career. There was the time I was asked to form a diversity and inclusion committee – N.B. Black women are *so often* asked to do this – which essentially just allows businesses to say they have a D and I initiative, whilst actually just putting all of the burden of that work onto the plates of marginalised people, usually without the support to actually enact any changes that are anything more than symbolic or tokenistic.

There was the time that I was asked to mentor a much older and much more senior white man on the importance of basically not being a racist ('I don't think I'm a racist . . . I mean, I don't really like the Chinese, but . . .'). In that situation, *he* was praised for proactively seeking mentorship. I, on the other hand, spent almost all of our time together doing the mental gymnastics of making sure that *I* didn't offend *him*, by reacting in any way to the openly racist things he would say. How could I, I had to work out, say things that he saw as valuable contributions to his 'personal development' without putting my foot in it by accidentally suggesting that he was in fact racist – a dangerous thing to accuse a senior colleague of, even indirectly. Even when they've asked you to teach them to not be racist. Tiring. Risky. And a really inappropriate position for a business to put a junior team member in with no training or support.

In addition to my day-to-day work, there have been countless unpaid hours where I've organised office summer and Christmas parties, bought birthday presents and cards out of my own pocket, despite being in roles where I was most certainly not the best paid, and made cups of tea and coffee for clients and stayed behind to clean up meeting rooms. Only last year, when I was freelancing in a very senior role, I found myself taking drinks orders and balancing a tray of tea and coffee in my hand as I tried to get through the doors to the boardroom to deliver drinks to a meeting that I wasn't a part of – casting myself for some reason as a self-appointed caterer. It felt as though I was still the office runner I had started out as years before. 'Oh you know, once a runner, always a runner,' I joked, but the reality was even though I was the most senior person in the business, aside from the founder, I knew that if I didn't do it, no one would.

There's absolutely something to be said for people of all levels in a company chipping in and doing their part, of course, and this isn't about anyone being too big or important to lend a hand. But it is about the inequity of it all, and now that we've come to see that the split between housework and glamour work is as it is today, it's safe to say something's up.

The reason that this disparity is a problem can be broken down into two parts: time and perception.

## Time

In short, time is limited and valuable, and the time you're spending researching and ordering an inflatable lobster for the office Christmas party (yes, true story, I'm good at parties) is time that you're not investing in something that could progress your career. Or, you know, resting.

Every night you're working late because some non-core task has eaten into your day is an evening you're not spending time refreshing your batteries, making you better at your role tomorrow.

Every hour you spend on a committee that won't be recognised in your salary review, count towards your next promotion or teach you new skills is time that you're not making work that can go in your portfolio or on your CV. It also takes away from your capacity and ability to put yourself forward for or be put forward for glamour projects.

All of this time spent on unrecognised tasks diminishes your ability to reach your full potential. When this expectation falls more heavily on women, particularly women from racially marginalised groups, opting in to create new, positive stereotypes about ourselves damages us in both the long and short term.

## Perception

Although Black women often take on office housework in order to create a good impression, the actual result can be the exact opposite.

Perception is so important at work. At their core, every workplace is a people business, and the decisions that we make are based on how we see one another.

When I'm managing a team, I don't always have full visibility on all of the tasks that each member of my team is doing at any given moment. However, I do usually have a good sense of who is working late most often, coming in early to get their work done or sending non-essential emails in the middle of the night. If I see that someone is needing to extend their hours a lot, my first thought won't be that they are really going above and beyond (unless it's a particular moment, like a pitch, where an agency pulls together for a short period), I'm much more likely to think that they are struggling with their role. Maybe they've been promoted too soon, have poor time-management skills or need extra support.

The chance to lead big projects doesn't always come up very often, so the last thing you'd want to do would be to have discounted yourself in your employer's mind because invisible office housework is taking up your time.

Another important area of perception that comes into play when we put ourselves forward for office housework is around the importance of the work you were doing in the first place. If you're able to drop (or delay) your work in order to plan the party or pop out and buy a gift more often than anyone else, it suggests to people that the baseline of your work is less important and valuable at its core function than that of others.

Because these low-level, low-reward tasks usually, fairly or unfairly, fall to more junior people, when we pick them up we are putting ourselves in those positions. Note-taking in a meeting might seem harmless, but you're much less likely to make a groundbreaking point if your mind is busy keeping track of what everyone else is saying, so they can remember later. Planning a party, offering mentoring or sitting on a committee can be interesting, but what are you *not* doing to make time for it?

One-off actions can quickly form habits in ourselves or assumptions in others. I'm sure we can all think of instances at places we've worked where the phone will ring and it will be ignored by everyone except one person who has to interrupt their work to answer it, despite it not being their job. Or times where a meeting needs to be scheduled, and all eyes turn to the one person who always takes on the task of going through everyone's diaries and finding a time that works for all, and booking a room.

The more we do it, the more we're expected to do it, and the harder it is to say no.

## So, what's the alternative?

You might think that this is the moment where I tell Black women the secret to tactfully, yet firmly, setting their boundaries and say no, whilst avoiding any risk to their jobs. I'm sorry, that's not something I can do. Partially because I'm awful at the tactful side of it (if I say no, I mean no. And I say no often and freely), but mostly because this burden should not be falling onto the shoulders of Black women. They shouldn't have to take the risk of saying no, without knowing or being able to manage any potential fallout, implications or repercussions. Instead, the burden of this lies outside of us, with the people assigning work and building structures.

This really is a problem for managers and business leaders to pave the way in addressing. When we consider the pressures which lead women, and particularly Black women, to take on these roles in the first place – simply saying *'say no'* isn't always a realistic option, or doesn't always feel like one, at least.

There are a few simple steps that leaders mindful of allocating work in a fairer way can follow to try to distribute office housework, and glamour work, more evenly.

### Pay attention

The starting point is simply being aware of the types of task that exist in your business and which groups of people are usually doing them. Are there more white men having the opportunity to pitch high-profile new accounts, and more women doing tea runs and writing up minutes from meetings? If you've not paid attention to the distribution of tasks in your office before, chances are it has fallen into this pattern. Once you see it, you can address it.

### Set an example

People who run businesses are busy, of course – but so is everyone else, just with different types of tasks. For a period, put yourself forward for some tasks – organise a party, buy a birthday card and make sure it gets signed. Having people in senior positions taking on these tasks helps to remove the stigma of them not being valuable ways to spend time, and can help to diversify the range of people who put themselves forward to pick up these tasks.

### Have the right team in place

You can remove the need for anyone, of any background, to pick up these tasks which are necessary to run the business but not in any job descriptions, by hiring for roles dedicated to filling these functions. Office managers, HR teams, PAs or EAs, even on a part-time basis, are really valuable team members. Having these functions filled can take the burden off people to volunteer to pick up these tasks, allowing them to focus their time on fulfilling the roles they were hired for.

### Decide office housework is valuable

The office housework types of tasks we've been discussing are only unpromotable and thankless if we decide they are. Build a culture of recognising and rewarding the people who take these tasks on. Have contributions to the office environment, culture and smooth-running form part of team members' measurable KPIs, linked to promotions and pay rises. In this way, you transform office housework into glamour work and reward people for helping.

If you take this approach, however, do be careful that it isn't all falling on one person or type of person. You may have to intervene if someone isn't pulling their weight in this regard – after all, it's a part of their measurable objectives.

### Delegate – don't wait for volunteers

When a task needs to be done, don't wait for someone to put themselves forward, if we know it's likely to be the same people who end up saying yes (or being put forward) time and time again. Delegate tasks by name, specifically, on rotation, throughout role and position within the company. This also means you taking on some tasks. If you're a company that talks about everyone chipping in – that means you too.

### Empower people to say no

People who move through the world, conscious of the bodies they inhabit, and the negative stereotypes associated with them, have good reason to struggle to say no when asked to take on office housework. They can feel stuck in a lose-lose position – either they take on additional tasks which detract from their professional performance and the time that they can dedicate to their role, or they risk negative consequences. Black women who push back are often seen as being stuck-up, or thinking they're too good for the task. They're accused of not being team players or being difficult and stand-offish much more quickly than a white man is who turns down a task of this nature. Be aware of this. Make sure people know that taking on additional tasks is optional, and valued, and support and listen to Black women when they take the risk of telling you they may not have capacity to take this on.

# Hostile Work Environments

## Vanessa Sanyauke

**SW:** I was reading an interview with you where you were talking about the importance of mentors and having people who look like you in the workplace. I wondered if you could speak a little bit about why it's important to be able to see someone who you can see yourself in.

**VS:** I think it goes to the role modelling, and you can't be what you can't see. And I say that a lot. You can't say to Black women, in particular, 'Definitely, still go for it! Go for senior positions! Go for board-level positions! Start your own businesses!' if you haven't got someone you can identify with and see yourself becoming. How can you expect people to be motivated and actually see that it's possible? And so, I think that it's really important for Black women to have role models – their stories may trigger something. They may have similar upbringings. They may be people who have gone through similar challenges, and understanding how they navigated them can really help. I think being a Black woman in business, or Black woman in corporate life, is completely different [to anyone else's experience]. Not to invalidate a white woman's experience, or to say that we can't learn anything from white women, but I just think that with role modelling and mentoring it's important that you try and align it with similar backgrounds because it's just more impactful.

**SW:** Have you noticed any differences in what women of different backgrounds want or need when they come to Girls Talk London, in terms of looking for mentors or the experiences that they want help with or guidance through?

**VS:** Imposter syndrome is a big one, that's one we get a lot – especially with Black women. I'd say also personal branding – how they can brand themselves internally and externally as well. Those are the two main problem areas.

**SW:** Do you have any thoughts about why imposter syndrome seems to be something that is impacting Black women more?

**VS:** I mean, even in my own career I've felt that. I worked on a contract in-house at a law firm, and I sat on one of their boards, where I was the only Black person there. And you immediately feel out of place, because – it's hard to describe the feeling. It's just so hard. In this particular law firm, the culture was very traditional: white, male and conservative. And I feel a lot of it has to do with leadership – if you've got a CEO or an MD that recognises that you're a minority on a board and makes sure that you feel included, asks your opinion, maybe checks in with you at the beginning of the meeting, or even just says, 'Hi, how are you?' you feel more comfortable. But in this particular place, no one is coming up and even engaging with you or saying hello. Sometimes I have people who don't even behave as if I'm there – as if I'm actually invisible. And I think it's because I'm a Black woman. If I looked like them, I would have been more engaged, and so it's down to leadership.

It's not our fault, it's nothing that I had done wrong, but that kind of feeling when you enter the room . . . even some of the looks that you get. You know, we're all adults here, you can get vibes where you feel people are welcoming or not. You can feel that it's just not welcoming because that culture is coming from the top.

**SW:** I think it's a really, really hard thing to put into words because it is a feeling, and I think that's what makes it so easy for people to dismiss. They think we're being over-sensitive like 'Ooh, they made you feel bad!?' without realising that no, you made a space that I was uncomfortable being in, which meant that I wasn't able to give the value that you've hired me to deliver because you created an unpleasant work environment.

**VS:** I've even heard Oprah Winfrey, the world's richest Black woman, saying about the various boards for businesses she sits on, that she feels like an imposter. She's made to feel like she doesn't belong in the room, and that people are wondering, 'What are you doing here?' – and this is the richest Black woman in the world! If the richest Black woman in the world is saying that, then you can't deny that with all of her money, all of her billions, even to this day, she is made to feel unwelcome when she sits on these massive boards. She's probably the richest person in that room, in terms of

personal wealth, and she still feels, no, she's still made to feel that people are questioning why she's there. So, you just can't ignore that.

**SW:** No, absolutely not. And I think the fact that you said 'she feels like' and then corrected it to 'she's made to feel like . . .' was really interesting – because that really is the crux of it, I think.

**VS:** Yes, she's made to feel that people are questioning, 'What are you doing here?' And it can be things as simple as, when you say something to contribute – I've had it before when I've sat on another board, where I've said something and then a white male says something similar and it's like, 'Oh yeah, great idea'. Or, you know that you've given better ideas than your colleagues but it's like your one's kind of dismissed and theirs are thought of as amazing. I've heard about those kinds of situations time and time again. There's a Black woman in my network, a lady who's very senior, and she sits on a lot of boards in the UK. She said the same thing – that she came out of a meeting one day, where she'd made a suggestion, and five minutes later one of the male white board members said the same thing – and they had ignored the thing that she'd said and only when the white man had said it were they able to understand what she was saying, or to take it on board.

This is where allies come in – good white male allies should be able to see that and say, 'OK, what Vanessa was trying to say is XZY'.

I've heard some women say that they've got some senior men in the room to advocate for them as well, so there are good examples of how people can treat us, as well as bad.

I think we're seeing some of that – I've heard some examples but not on a big enough scale in the UK. It's still a very foreign concept.

# Munroe Bergdorf's Favourite Thing About Being a Black Woman

Munroe Bergdorf is a writer, model, activist and Doctor of Letters, and has become recognised globally for her activism. In August 2020, not only did *British Vogue* name her in the Top 25 Most Influential Women in the Country (alongside Rihanna and the Queen), but *Teen*

*Vogue* featured her on the cover of their coveted September issue. Munroe has most recently been announced as the winner of *Attitude*'s Hero Award 2020, presented by Edward Enninful.

"I would say other Black women. I think that it's instant access to an amazing sisterhood that will support you and lift you up and inspire you, empower you. And you know there are so many different kinds of Black women, so it's like being part of an amazing club, really. You know, the first people, whenever I've come into trouble in the media, the first people who will defend me are Black women. I think it's, again, really important to identify that there are so many different kinds of Black women, but we've all got a common experience which is misogynoir, in whatever form that may take – dependent on our intersections. But we've all experienced that, and I feel like Black women will just stand up for each other in a way that I just don't see in any other group. When we see each other on the street we'll just say 'hi', or compliment each other, and it's really lovely. And I feel like – I don't know if it's because I transitioned like ten years ago, and I've only just experienced it more recently – but I think that the shift of community has definitely been helped by things like #Blackgirlmagic, or internet hashtags helping us to see each other."

## CHAPTER 4

# THE STRONG BLACK WOMAN

'You are not the work you do;
you are the person you are.'
TONI MORRISON

'**I** am a strong Black woman, and I cannot be intimidated.' I think of the moment that Maxine Waters, (Auntie Maxine to a generation of Black women around the world), said that in response to comments made by Bill O'Reilly on Fox News, maybe once a week. What resilience, what strength of character and deeply ingrained self-worth – but at what cost?

The Strong Black Woman is a pervasive stereotype, one that generations of Black women have adopted and held close in both their private and professional lives. But it's a double-edged sword – both empowering and protective, and diminishing and dehumanising. It helped us in the past just as much as it's holding us back now.

I know me saying that the Strong Black Woman has run her course might feel like a personal attack – shots fired – but if you stay with me for just a moment, I think I can make you agree.

Broadly speaking, there are three dominant stereotypes surrounding Black women: the Angry Black Woman, the Overly Sexual Black Woman and the Strong Black Woman. Of the three, the Strong Black Woman is the one that we ourselves hold on to the tightest, claiming it as an identity and using it as an armour to protect us from the world. No one can hurt us, we're brave, we're tough, and we don't take any crap, we're Strong Black Women.

Black women, in countries where we have been treated as less than equal humans, come from a long, and necessary, line of strong women. Whether they travelled to what we now call our homes of their own free will, or not, our mothers, grandmothers and great-grandmothers and those before them faced hardships, living during a time where they had to be on guard, poised, pristine and presenting a good face at all times, whatever the circumstance. Every day, in different ways, their lives were under threat. There were very few places they could work. In America, although women were technically afforded the vote in 1920, many Black women weren't able to exercise that right until 1965 when it was protected by the 19th Amendment. In the UK, while women may have won the vote in 1928, regardless of race, in practice the reality of stigma and political inequality they faced meant it was far from a level playing field. Redlining in the US, and discrimination in lending in the UK dictated, and continues to impact, where they could live.[1] They were hypervisible in every move they made, and people were ready to pounce on any perceived weaknesses they could find.

We all know that if a time machine was invented, we'd only be going forwards, back isn't an option for us. The past wasn't a safe place. What we don't often stop to think about is that this unsafe past is the world where the people who made us *us* lived, and the defence mechanisms and stereotypes that were established then remain with us today.

Pop culture celebrates Strong Black Women – they're the ones in the stories that we like to tell the most. Harriet Tubman, Sojourner Truth, Rosa Parks, Maxine Waters, these strong women stood up and did what needed to be done for themselves, their families and communities to survive.

Let's take a couple of steps back – who is the Strong Black Woman, what does she look like and where does she come from?

## Who is the Strong Black Woman?

Amani Allen is an associate professor at Berkeley; in 2012 she launched research into the Strong Black Women identity, and created a five-part framework for the persona:[2]

- Feeling an obligation to present an image of strength
- Feeling an obligation to suppress emotions
- Resistance to being vulnerable
- A drive to succeed despite limited resources
- Feeling an obligation to help others

Sound familiar? Hiding emotions, trying to be strong, pushing to succeed and helping others – all despite having limited resources and facing daily racialised sexism and gendered racism.

In 2014 Roxanne Donovan and Lindsey West also looked into the Strong Black Woman construct and identified two central, essential traits – strength and caregiving.[3] The Strong Black Woman is not only strong for herself, perhaps she is not *even* strong for herself, instead she is self-sacrificing, putting the needs of others before herself and caring for her family and her community emotionally, spiritually and often financially. But, importantly, she doesn't expect the same in return – she's much too strong to need any help herself.

> 'SBW is perceived as naturally resilient, able to handle with ease all the stress, upset, and trauma life throws at her. Challenges that would break others just make SBW stronger. Her strength is also shown in her independence, self-control, and work ethic . . . She is self-reliant and emotionally contained . . . She does not need emotional or financial support to succeed or to take care of her (and others') responsibilities . . . She works tirelessly and without complaint, always able to do more even if what is asked seems impossible.'

Donovan and West believe that the Strong Black Woman persona is a direct result of slavery – a necessary survival mechanism for a life of unrelenting exploitation, violence, aggression and oppression. This survival mechanism was then passed down, consciously or unconsciously, through generations, where strength and survival went hand in hand.

We like fatty, sugary foods because highly calorific foods used to be hard to find. We have learned through generations of famines and failed harvests that we should eat as much of them as we can now, to prepare ourselves for inevitable long, hard winters with scarce resources. Although the reality of severe food scarcity, for much of the world, is no longer an annual concern, our taste for these foods has stuck with us, beyond its usefulness for survival. In the same way, during conditions of slavery, the traits of the Strong Black Woman were not only an advantage, they were essential for Black women, their families and their communities to survive. Passing these traits down was essential to ensure the best possible outcomes for their children.

We no longer live with legal chattel slavery in the same way, but Black women still do live with inequity and have to navigate day-to-day sexism and racism. So, what's the place of the Strong Black Woman today? Are the traits that once helped us still doing their part or are they holding us back from asking for the support we need?

## Unrealistic expectations

I'd like to go back to some of the findings from Donovan and West from their research into the traits of the Strong Black Woman and take a moment to read it again.

'Challenges that would break others just make SBW stronger.'

'She does not need emotional or financial support to succeed or to take care of her (**and others'**) responsibilities'

'She works tirelessly and without complaint, always able to do more even if what is asked seems impossible.'

The problem with the image of the Strong Black Woman today is that it's become an expectation. An unrealistic one.

The stereotype ties a Black woman's worth to her expertise at over-coming hardships – praising us for our ability to endure more than anyone should have to, expecting us to suffer in silence whilst putting on a strong and brave face. A Strong Black Woman's suffering is glamorised as she is praised for picking up and carrying everyone else's hardships, taking the weight off their shoulders. But she never complains, and never takes the time to process or express her own pain – there's nowhere for her to rest the accumulated weight she's carrying.

I think that the armour of the Strong Black Woman image, which used to protect us, has become too heavy to continue to carry.

Like Shonda Rhimes' Olivia Pope and Annalise Keating, the Strong Black Woman just gets it done. By whatever means necessary, at whatever personal cost. She's busy taking care of her own, and everyone else's, responsibilities with a constant smile on her face, hiding her aching feet and back. Her aching heart.

Pushing forward constantly in this way means that there is not only never a time to rest, but there is also never time to celebrate achievements along the way. This is something that I know I'm often guilty of – working without pausing to take stock of what has already been achieved. Each time I reach a moment that should be cause for celebration, I'm already distracted by thinking about what has to come next, what the next achievement has to be. What I've done is never enough, there is always more to push for, and I'm far from alone in feeling this.

Part of what I was having to challenge myself with last year was being proud of the things that I've done instead of finding holes in them that I can improve on next time because I'm always like, 'It's not enough. It's not enough, it's not exactly the way I thought it would be in my head, so I'm just going to ignore it and pretend that it doesn't count, and just keep pushing forward,' which I do think helps in terms of achievement, but not in terms of enjoying your achievement . . . I spend half of my time trying to create the foundations on which I can then take a break, focus on relationships, take a holiday – because it's just not there yet, the foundations haven't been built solidly enough for me or anyone I know to relax. It just doesn't exist in my head in that way, because there are so many reminders every day when you go into work that this place was not built for you.

– *Naomi Ackie*

Black women continue to need to work hard to gain opportunities that are given more freely to other groups, and to gain respect from their peers and bosses. In an effort to make the best possible impression and shine as brightly as they can, Black women risk overloading themselves, at the cost of their mental well-being. The Strong Black Woman image may well be the armour of choice for Black women, determined to make it in a world full of obstacles, but wearing heavy armour all day every day quickly becomes a heavy load to carry.

I'm tired. To my bones. And I know other Black women are too. To borrow some words from the immense Nayyirah Waheed, '*all the women. in me. are tired.*' How could they not be, under such huge pressure? It's enormously stressful to be not only a Strong Black Woman, but a Strong Black *Millennial* Woman.

## Burnout

As I've mentioned, Millennials have been on the receiving end of a lot of bad press for being said to be lazy, entitled, and spoiled for seemingly wanting prestigious careers that we were passionate about without being prepared to work for them. Or for having big ideas about ourselves but lacking the talent to back them up.

Recent studies and reporting, though, have shown that the old caricatures of the Millennial generation and our Gen Z siblings (who have been referred to Millennials on Steroids[4]) were simply not based in truth.

In reality, Millennials came to adulthood during two generation-defining economic events – the bursting of the dotcom bubble and the 2008 recession, and have reached what should have been our years of professional security amidst a global pandemic which has thrown the working world into chaos, pretty much across the board. This period of confusion, upheaval and fast-turnaround change that businesses are in, in the wake of the Covid-19 pandemic, is going to be the professional landscape that Gen Z are stepping into for the first time.

For the entirety of our working lives, Millennials' jobs have felt unstable, as though they could disappear at any time. I don't know anyone who thinks they have a job for life any more, whether they want one or not.

Job security feels like an impossible dream to a lot of Millennials. The economic crashes made competition for entry-level jobs incredibly intense, with many businesses taking funding away from more junior roles and instead looking for graduates to provide unpaid labour in the form of internships, which were simply not economically possible for many. Many others who had already secured first jobs found that they lost them in last-in-first-out redundancies.

Job security has also been undermined by the continued rise in zero-hours contracts, or the gig economy – making hours and income deeply unpredictable and unreliable for many workers.[5] Women and racially marginalised people in the UK are the most likely to be on zero-hours contracts. A recent report showed that between 2011–2016 there was an increase of 58 per cent in the number of Black workers on zero-hours contracts, whilst the increase for their white counterparts was only 8 per cent.[6] The number of Black women, in particular, rose by 82 per cent in that period, compared to a 37 per cent increase for Black men.

As a generation, we live with the stress of knowing that our jobs could be taken away at any moment, for practically any reason, leaving us without any income, and unable to fulfil the roles of independence, and availability for caregiving in our families and communities, which are so central to the Strong Black Woman persona, who is expected to take care of not just herself, but her family and community.

We're less likely than our grandparents to be selling our physical labour and more likely to be making money from our thoughts, and cognitive outputs. In a lot of ways, this is good – physical work is hard. I was about to say 'physical work is long and hard', but in fact, it's not, and that's the crux of it. Whilst physical work can be, literally, back-breaking, it's self-limiting in the number of hours per day or per week that people can be expected to take it on. The limitation is partially physical constraints (bodies can only take on so much), and partially location-based. If you're mining for coal, or assembling a car, you need to be in the physical locations where that is possible – you can't quickly log in to the coal mine from bed to check in on your canary. Once you're out for the day, you're out, able to create separation both physically and mentally.

The experience of being connected all of the time not only separates us from our grandparents' experiences, it separates us from those of our parents, and even Gen X. Millennials are the first generation to have started their working lives as connected and competent users of digital technology, and Gen Z are the first group to not remember a time before this kind of technology became a part of their day-to-day lives. A recent YPulse survey found that 84 per cent of Millennials are 'always connected' to their work via technology, and continue to check their work email after leaving the office in the evenings.[7] I doubt this will surprise you – we all know that work doesn't end when we leave the office. What may not have occurred to you, though, is that this 'always connected' mentality means that more than any previous generations we are likely to have traded in work-life balance for something close to work-life blending. We're the first generation to do this – we're the guinea pigs. And I don't think it's going all that great.

In 2020, burnout became recognised by the World Health Organization as a medical condition. In its listing in the ICD-11 it's characterised as a 'syndrome conceptualised as resulting from chronic workplace stress that has not been successfully managed'.[8] Doctors are able to give a diagnosis of burnout to patients with the following symptoms:

1) Feelings of energy depletion or exhaustion
2) Increased mental distance from one's job, or feelings of negativism or cynicism related to one's job
3) Reduced professional efficacy, or ability to be effective at their jobs

Millennials are suffering from burnout more than any other generation, with 70 per cent of us reporting feeling at least some burnout, and three in ten reporting that we're very often, or always, burned out at work.[9]

Burnout is more than just being tired, more than being exhausted, even. It's what happens when people are exhausted, all of the time, and feel they have no choice other than to just keep going.

A psychoanalyst who specialises in burnout puts it this way: 'You feel burnout when you've exhausted all your internal resources, yet cannot free yourself of the nervous compulsion to go on regardless.'[10]

Burnout, in a medical sense, can only be applied to feelings and experiences associated with work. So, you can be burned out from over-working, not taking holiday or sick days, and answering emails in bed at both ends of the day, but not from housework, caring for children, or the other myriad of tasks that (some) women hold in their mental to-do lists all day every day.

According to a study by Project: Time Off we, Millennials, are a generation of 'work martyrs' – people who are driven to work non-stop, feeling shame if we take time off for holidays or illness, because we live in fear that if we do our bosses will think we're disposable.[11] These behaviours can be seen in other generations, but to a much lower degree – 43 per cent of Millennials were identified as work martyrs versus just 29 per cent of the overall population studied.[12] What I think is interesting is that we are not trying to hide our martyrdom, quite the opposite – we're the group most likely to *want to be seen* to be work martyrs – in fact, the same study found that 48 per cent of Millennials wanted their boss to see them in that light (compared to 39 per cent of Gen X and 32 per cent of Baby Boomers) and 35 per cent of Millennials also wanted their colleagues to see them in that way (versus only 26 per cent of Gen X and 20 per cent of Boomers).

Despite, or maybe because, our work is so insecure, we're doubling down on it, giving it time and importance in our lives that has not previously been the norm. We're the generation most likely to sacrifice our paid holiday allowances – 24 per cent of Millennials gave up unused holiday days, compared to 19 per cent of Gen X and 17 per cent of Boomers, both generations who grew up and spent the majority of their professional lives in more economically stable times.[13]

27 per cent of Millennials said they felt that taking holiday days would make them seem replaceable and 23 per cent said they would worry about what their boss would think if they took their allotted days off. 30 per cent said they thought not taking their holiday allowance would show their boss how dedicated they were (compared to only 15 per cent of Boomers).[14] We're burning the candle at both ends, and we want you to know it.

There's a problem with all of this extra work, long hours and presenteeism – it doesn't work. Not in the way we want it to. Working long hours is exhausting and an exhausted employee isn't a good employee. In fact, a 2013 study from the *Journal of Occupational and Environmental Medicine* showed that workaholics performed worse than their colleagues, since their exhaustion was likely to lead to illness and mental strain.[15] On top of that, a 2014 study showed that the productive output from a worker doing seventy hours per week was roughly the same as their colleague who did fifty-six hours.[16]

But maybe it's not about actual productivity – maybe it's less important what's being done, and more important to make a good impression to your boss, and secure that pay rise, bonus or promotion? Well, bad news again: work martyrs are actually *less* likely to receive a bonus. People who took under ten days of their holiday allowance per year had a 34.6 per cent chance of getting a raise or bonus within three years, according to Project: Time Off, compared to people who took more than ten days of their allowance, who had a 65.4 per cent chance of receiving a raise or bonus.[17]

Not only is work martyrdom not working for Millennials in their careers, it's not working for them in their lives. Unsurprisingly, Millennials report feeling that their jobs have an oversized presence in their lives, and in their mental health. These jobs with their long hours and stagnant wages are leading them to burnout, and other mental health issues.[18]

## Mental health impacts for work martyrs

A Blue Cross report found that the current outlook for Millennial mental health is troubling.[19] According to the report, Millennials' physical and mental health is declining much more quickly than that of Gen X as they become older, as they suffer more from loneliness and money stress, depression and substance abuse. Blue Cross also found, in the same year, that diagnoses of 'major depression' are rising at a faster rate for Millennials and Gen Z than in any other groups.[20] In fact, since 2013 the number of major depression diagnoses for the group has risen 47 per cent.[21]

So, if Millennials overall are burning themselves out, working hard for jobs that could drop them at any time, and aren't being rewarded for going above and beyond, what's the outlook for the Strong Black Millennial Woman?

We know that Black women are hired at lower rates than men or white women,[22] and that they are more likely to have caregiving responsibilities outside of the workplace, or head single-parent households.[23] When we add this to the Strong Black Woman's characteristics being so focused on being a hard worker, and our understanding from childhood that we'll need to work twice as hard, for half as much, we can easily see how the stresses of everyday life can combine with the pressures of always-on working culture to create the perfect conditions for the Strong Black Woman to silently spiral into ill health.

The Strong Black Woman may be more susceptible to burnout than other groups. Black women may feel that opportunities that come their way are more limited, and so may be more likely to agree to take them on, even if they're already overloaded. It's also possible that Black women take on additional tasks for fear of excessive negative repercussions should they say no – such as being characterised as lazy, divas or not team players.

Because burnout has only recently been recognised as a medical condition, there hasn't been in-depth, intersectional research into how it impacts different ethnic gender groups. However, it is worth noting that it has been observed that women do seem to be more susceptible to burnout due to the types of work we do:

> 'Our results show there are differences between men and women because, from the outset, employees are subject to different working conditions depending on their gender . . . Indeed, female employees often burn out at a faster rate simply because of the nature of their work.
>
> Many women have positions that offer little latitude in decision-making, meaning that their work only provides them with a low level of authority and decision-making power and makes little use of their skills.
>
> This type of position, which men are less likely to hold, causes women to burn out.'[24]

This frustration that comes from being in positions with limited authority and decision-making capacity causes women to burn out. We do know that there are more white women in higher-level jobs than Black women, and so it would stand to reason that Black women would experience more of these frustrations and burnout at a higher rate, though this research has yet to be done.

What there is research around is suicide rates, a common and deeply sad outcome of major depression and other mental health illnesses. In these figures, we can see the extent of the issue for Black women. Whilst overall rates of suicide attempts in the USA fell between 1991–2017 by 7.5 per cent,[25] during the same time period attempts by young Black people rose 73 per cent,[26] and attempts by Black females rose 182 per cent.[27]

## Other areas impacting the Strong Black Woman

You may say that the pressure of always-on environments and work martyrdom isn't only faced by Black women, and you'd be correct.

Millennials, as a group, are overworking, not taking time off, trapped in insecure jobs, and their mental health is suffering as a result. Strong Black Women are known for their exceptional work ethic so it seems fair to reason that if Millennials as a whole are working hard, Strong Millennial Black Women are working even harder.

Women are burning out more quickly than men due to frustrations in their careers, though we know white women have better access to more fulfilling work than their Black peers.

As we know, everything that touches the skin of women, and Millennials, will touch people with intersectional marginalised identities twice as hard – people like Black women.

Black women also face some more unique pressures and stressors at work that their white counterparts may be blind to.

## Emotional labour

> In a way, it's quite interesting that even though we talk about white saviours, there's a similar Black female saviour thing going on. I used to spend so much time educating people on how it feels to be a Black woman, how it feels to be me, and now I'm like, you know, actually, there's Google. There are books. There are TED Talks, there are YouTube video essays – there is a plethora of knowledge, and if you cannot be bothered to go and find out that knowledge yourself, do not come to me and expect me to put it in layman's terms. I'm not doing that anymore. It's boring and it's a waste of my time.
>
> – *Naomi Ackie*

Emotional labour, sometimes called the emotional tax, is different to office housework, but it's just as real, and it's just as tiring, if not more so.

One of the core elements of the Strong Black Woman stereotype is caregiving. She takes care of others, as well as and before herself, despite having limited resources. In the workplace, one of the most common ways that Black women are asked to perform emotional labour is by taking on the burden of explaining, and solving, racism.

I used to think it was great when companies I worked for asked me to join their diversity committees, or to lead a lunchtime or after-work session on inclusion. I've come to learn better.

Instances like this, where the burden to solve a problem – that you haven't caused, but disproportionately suffer from – is placed on your shoulders are exhausting and almost never have a positive outcome. We are asked to dredge through hurt, to resurface pain and pull open old wounds for the benefit of 'teaching' others. Often times not only is the pain of this experience not acknowledged or appreciated, but our experiences are also dismissed by racial gaslighting, with comments like '*Oh, I'm sure that's not what they meant*', or suggestions that we are exaggerating or embellishing – retraumatising us for no positive outcome.

Another form of emotional labour is the feeling of always needing to be 'on guard'. An American report on the subject found that 58 per cent of Asian, Black and Latin employees felt on guard at work – consciously preparing to deal with instances of discrimination and bias, causing 38 per cent of them to consider leaving their jobs.[28] This is a conscious effort, taking away cognitive energy and resources that would otherwise be spent elsewhere.

Being on guard, constantly ready for an attack or discrimination, can be tiring, and so a lot of racially marginalised people opt for an alternative that can seem easier, but also carries a huge psychological strain.

### Code-switching

One common tactic adopted by Black women to minimise their otherness and avoid suffering harassment and discrimination is code-switching. Most Black people are familiar with the idea of code-switching, a term originated by Einar Haugen in the 1950s to reference the ways in which multilingual people transition between languages in different settings. The term has since evolved, and is now commonly used to explain the experience of Black people in the US and UK, changing or 'whitening' elements of their speech, appearance or actions to make themselves more easily accepted, and more palatable, to the white community. For the Strong Black Woman, this might mean taking on more than is feasible, or fair, in order to make a good impression, not just at the start of a role, but throughout her working life. It might mean artificially changing the texture of her hair or the tone or content of her words, in order to blend in more easily. Code-switching is essentially wearing a mask – keeping people from seeing the real you, in an attempt to avoid discrimination.

The feeling, from Black people, of being compelled to 'wear a mask' in order to be accepted by white society, isn't new. In 1896 the poem 'We Wear The Mask' by Black American poet Paul Laurence Dunbar was first professionally published, beautifully outlining this experience – see Appendix on page 355.

Sometimes, code-switching can be fun, and I think we almost all do it to some degree – maybe the way that we speak to our parents is different to the way we speak to our boss, partner or friends. Different people bring out different sides and versions of ourselves, and that can be a good and healthy thing. The problem is when it feels like a necessary survival mechanism to be able to move through white spaces without discrimination, making Black women feel that they're always having to put conscious effort into playing a part, and hiding their true selves from the world.

Whilst it might offer some protection, the trade-off can be our psychological well-being. 'For Black women,' clinical psychologist Dr Anu Sayal-Bennett told the *Guardian*, 'I think it's about showing a proxy-self.'[29] We all know it can be fun to take on a character from time to time, but having to always bend yourself to fit the expectations of others isn't that – it's something much more damaging.

### The impact of stress

It's not surprising to learn research has shown that living with racism is a stressful experience, and that continued experience of stress can have a negative impact on mental health.[30] [31]Stress can also come from workplace harassment, which is more likely to be endured by 'BAME' people than their white colleagues. According to a study by BITC,[32] over a quarter of 'BAME' employees (28 per cent versus 17 per cent of white) reported witnessing or experiencing racial harassment or bullying from their managers, and 32 per cent reported receiving the same treatment from their peers.[33]

Black women, who suffer from both the race and gender pay gaps, are more prone to suffering from financial stress, and are more likely to be harshly disciplined at work, causing employment stress. They are more likely to face microaggressions or plain old aggression both in and out of work. It's not hard to see how stress builds on top of stress, seemingly without a release valve.

The fact that racism causes stress, and stress, in turn, can lead to mental illnesses isn't a shock. It's saddening, not shocking. What *is* surprising is just how much of an unspoken issue Black women's mental health is.

There are countless stories of young Black women taking their mental health into their own hands, in one way or another. Some seek medical help, but feel due to the weight of the stigma that they must keep the information hidden from even those who are the closest to them. Others aren't able to access professional assistance, and so turn the pressure of the pain inwards, resorting to self-harm and even suicide, as we have seen.

Being stressed or overwhelmed, depressed, even, is just not in line with the image of the Strong Black Woman. The Strong Black Woman can't be stressed – or at least she can't show it or do anything about it if she is. She's too busy and too in control. Stress doesn't pay the bills. This is where the damage comes from. When the expectation of taking on the world, with a smile, against all odds, becomes a minimum requirement, the pressure to play a role builds up, and can become unmanageable. It's in this situation that the Strong Black Woman image and reputation becomes a burden, rather than an advantage.

Not being 'allowed' to feel that way, though, doesn't mean it's not many Strong Black Women's lived experience, just an undiscussed one. Dr Burnett-Zeigler, a clinical psychologist writing for the *New York Times* said: 'Black women are more likely to be depressed and when they are, their symptoms are more severe, last longer and are more likely to interfere with their ability to function at work, school and home. Black women are more likely to have feelings of sadness, hopelessness and worthlessness.'[34] And the research agrees with her.

In the UK, according to the Race Disparity Audit, Black women are the most likely to suffer from disorders such as anxiety, depression, panic and OCD. In fact, 29 per cent of the Black women surveyed experienced one of these disorders in the week prior to being surveyed (compared to 21 per cent of white women).[35]

A Cambridge University study found that Black women aged 16–34 were more likely to self-harm than their white peers, and whilst white women were more likely to harm themselves in visible ways such as cutting, Black women were more likely to harm themselves in invisible ways, such as self-poisoning, usually with household cleaning products.[36]

In the UK, Black people, overall, are the group who report the lowest ratings for life satisfaction, happiness and feeling that the things they do in life are worthwhile. They are also the ethnic group with the highest instance of PTSD, with 8.3 per cent screening positive, compared to just 4.2 per cent of white people.[37]

It's hard out there.

Although Black women are more likely to experience these mental illnesses, Black adults overall in the UK are the group least likely to report receiving any kind of treatment, whether medication or therapy.[38][39]

This is where I feel the Strong Black Woman stereotype has outlived its use. Our lives are different now, all of our lives. Black women are dealing with all of the stresses and strains of normal Millennial life, along with the pressures of misogynoir. The pressure to be strong means we're not accessing the support systems that we could be making use of until it's long overdue.

In America, fewer than 50 per cent of Black adults who have mental health issues actually receive treatment – a stat that's not helped by the fact that over 16 per cent of Black women are uninsured, meaning they often can't afford to access services.[40] In the UK Afro-Caribbean people are the group most likely to be diagnosed with severe mental illness, likely because the stigma around accessing treatment means they delay seeking help until their illnesses reach a crisis point.[41]

The effects of stress endured by Black women have physical, as well as psychological, implications. The American Psychological Association points out that African Americans, overall, suffer from increased rates of hypertension and diabetes due to chronic stress as a result of discrimination. 'Perceived discrimination' (feelings of being discriminated against in the workplace, or due to gender or race/ethnicity) can lead to damaging behaviours such as alcohol or substance abuse, poor nutrition and smoking, and can contribute to mental health disorders.[42]

One shocking discovery made in a 2011 study was that stress may cause Black women in the US to be, very literally, old before their time. Looking at women aged 49–55 they found that the repeated impact of long-term exposure to high levels of stress on Black women, impacted them at a chromosomal level. The pressure of dealing with this stress meant that Black women went through an accelerated ageing process, so that by middle age 'Black women are 7.5 years biologically "older" than white women' of the same chronological age.[43]

We have taken on these burdens at what we now know to be the expense of our mental and physical health. I am grateful to the Strong Black Woman, she got us to where we needed to be, but I think now the time has come to lay her to rest. She's already worked hard enough for us all.

## Letting go of the Strong Black Woman

> When a white person calls me a Strong Black Woman I get really bothered – I'm like, 'Don't call me that.' You know? People think, 'Oh, Aja is so strong,' and it's like, no . . . things can be too much. And because I do feel a lot, I have to set boundaries.
>
> *Aja Barber*

I really, truly think the Strong Black Woman has given all she can at this point, and it's time to thank her for her service, and let her retire. She was exactly what we needed when we were viscerally fighting for our very survival on a daily basis. We probably wouldn't be here without her. I know we still face challenges but they're different now, and the way we approach them needs to be different too.

When we say no to being Strong Black Women, and allow ourselves a little weakness, we don't let down the generations that came before us. They had to be that way to survive, and for us to survive. They sacrificed everything, and the world never saw them for it.

Thanks to the sacrifices of Black women in previous generations, we can choose better for ourselves. But to do that, we must drop the things that no longer serve us. They didn't work themselves to the bone so we could do the same – they did it so we wouldn't have to, and I think protecting ourselves is the greatest tribute to their sacrifice we can make. As the researchers looking at the trope said themselves, 'this thing called strength, this thing we applaud so much in African American women, could also be a disease.'[44]

I believe that our strength now lies in our communities – the ones that we build for ourselves with the widest possible range of people. Those communities are valuable because they allow us to be vulnerable. Sometimes we're being strong for them and lifting them up, and other times they're doing that for us. The weight of the world is a lot to carry all of the time, but we get by with a little help from our friends.

As I explored earlier, work martyrdom doesn't work. It doesn't lead to more promotions, pay raises or bonuses, and doesn't increase job security. Taking on emotional labour doesn't make you more valuable, it just allows the people who should be tackling inequity to delegate it to someone else. Code-switching doesn't make people think you're just like them – and losing yourself playing a part is more trouble than it's worth.

Don't be ashamed of mental health issues. We don't have to be perfect, high-functioning superwomen every day. We've come a long way, and the world owes us more than that now.

For a long time I thought I was only worth what I could produce for other people. I didn't go on holiday for years and years, worked when I was sick, and worked all weekend, every weekend. I worked on bank holidays, on Christmas Day, and prided myself on answering every email that came in within a matter of minutes, regardless of the time, or how important it was – and still I was always in constant fear of making a mistake or being fired. I was never not stressed, and I was utterly miserable.

This was also at a time where I wasn't really sure who I was, or what I wanted, and I was placing a lot of my value and self-worth into the hands of other people – if I was valuable to them, I was worth something, regardless of how that made me feel. Research has shown that women who most highly align themselves with the Strong Black Woman image are those with lower self-esteem, and this is precisely what I was doing.[45]

As time has gone on, I've learned to delegate, I've learned that things can wait until tomorrow, and I've learned to cut myself some slack. I've built up a support network of people who love me, and whose love for me has nothing to do with what capitalist output I can make for them, or how I can help them. I've learned that spending time with them, and with myself, doesn't make me bad at my job, it makes me better at it. When you're exhausted, you can't help anyone – you can't give from an empty cup.

Fill up your cup. Rest. Work when it's necessary but don't pull out heroics every day when no one is looking and no one cares. Allow yourself vulnerability. Ask for help – no one who is good for you will think any less of you, it just gives them a new way to love you, and people love helping people they love. Set clear boundaries.

I don't know exactly what kind of self-care will work for you but being a Strong Black Woman, every hour of every day, isn't working for any of us anymore. So, let's try something new.

# The pressure of being
# a Strong Black Woman

## Lekia Lée

*Lekia Lée is a former broadcast journalist who has worked both in Nigeria and the UK. In 2010, inspired by her then 5-year-old daughter, she founded Project Embrace to end hair discrimination, increase afro hair representation and encourage her daughter and girls like her to embrace their afro-textured hair.*

In the UK, as a Black person, because of how Blackness has been politicised, we can't be seen to be failing in any way whatsoever. We have to always be performing, and even when we perform it's not good enough. So, we always have to make sure to do everything right, correct, because people look at us suspiciously all of the time. It's like sometimes, going into a shop I feel like I need to buy something so they don't think, 'Oh this Black woman, she's just come in to look around, she doesn't even have money.' I've experienced it many times, and many Black people have had it, where a security guard is following you around and I'm thinking, 'Do I look like a thief?'

If we go to the airport, we have to dress up well so people don't look at us suspiciously, because we don't have the space to be anything other than perfect. We're always under scrutiny, and we have internalised that, so we are also policing ourselves as well.

I think a lot of the mental health problems on the spectrum come from being under so much pressure to perform. And because we're human we can't always be perfect, and that does affect our mental health and mental well-being. Take me for example, I thought, 'By this age, I've got to do this, I've got to tick this box and that box,' which is a lot of pressure.

So, it's that. There's no room to fail, there's no room to not always look your best or be your best. And then there's also a very narrow idea of what a Black woman should be, and how a Black woman should present herself, and so anything outside of that very narrow definition is frowned upon.

I think a lot of the time we also blame ourselves – I know I do, because every time we go to talk about our experiences of race we are thrown with, 'Oh, you're playing the race card', and you can't even talk about your own pain because then you'll be gaslighted. And that I think compounds the difficulty, it makes it difficult to even acknowledge it. And then even within the mental health system, there aren't people who understand you, you know? We're expected to be strong – and many of us are strong, but everybody's got some . . . there are days when you can be strong and days when you won't be strong.

Sometimes I still hold on to that idea of the Strong Black Woman to keep me going – I really do. But I'm almost trying to understand, or to know, that it's OK not to be strong all of the time. It's OK to cry. Also, I want to show my daughter that I don't hide my 'failures' and I'm trying not to look at certain things as 'failures'. So when I'm confused and worried about something I'll tell her – not everything, to be honest with you, at 14 there are certain things I don't want her to internalise. I mean, I can't protect her from everything but I want her to understand that it's OK to not do everything 'right'.

I really try to talk to her, explaining, 'It's not you, you don't have to be great at everything every time.' I think I also have to show her the sides of me that didn't work, and the things I tried that didn't work so that she knows that it's OK. I used to tie my self-worth a lot to succeeding and it's only within the last year that I started learning that, you know, even if things don't work, or they don't work the way I want them to, I'm still worthy of a holiday. I'm still worthy of buying myself clothes. I'm still worthy of taking a day and just relaxing and not doing anything. But it's something I still have to keep telling and reminding myself as it's not part of my subconscious thinking at the moment. I still have to consciously tell myself, 'Lekia, don't beat yourself up.'

# Liv Little's Favourite Thing About Being a Black Woman

Liv Little is an award-winning journalist, cultural consultant, creative director, author and curator. She's also the founder of gal-dem, a media company committed to spotlighting the creative talents of women and non-binary people of colour. Liv's career spans audio, journalism and TV and film. Liv has been voted a Future Leader, LGBTQI+ broadcaster of the year, a rising star at WOW and included in the inaugural BBC's *100 Women* series.

"Oh, I mean, I wouldn't want to be anything else. I love all of it. I love the community. I love the support. I love the solidarity. I love the heart and soul and the connections, and the people that I have around me. I wouldn't want to be surrounded by anyone else.

I'm in love with a Black woman as well. I think Black women really do show up for each other, you know. I think we really do turn out for each other, we support each other and I think that solidarity, in a world that tells you that you're not valid or worthy or important, is just so special.

No one's ever asked me this question before so I'm like – it's all amazing! We're amazing! It's great, look at all of it – the dynamism – there's just so much. We don't see ourselves reflected and we're not waiting for anyone to do it, we're doing it for ourselves, we're creating our own networks and our way of supporting each other.

Being a Black woman is a powerful thing."

## CHAPTER 5

# THE ANGRY BLACK WOMAN

'You have to act as if it were possible to radically transform the world. And you have to do it all the time.'

ANGELA DAVIS

L et me start by saying I'm a fan of anger. I know that might sound strange but let me elaborate.

The anger I'm talking about isn't the shouting, screaming, throwing hands kind. The anger I'm referring to is the type that lights a fire of righteous rage in the belly, the type that galvanises, unifies and forces change. I think anger like that can change the world.

Anger tells us when something isn't right, and it motivates us to fight for our rights and demand more. Anger should be an agitator for change – we know that angry politicians and revolutionaries, given the right channels, can use their anger to change the world, hopefully for the better.

Throughout history, disenfranchised people have found ways to turn their anger into actions with huge, global impact. When Rosa Parks refused to give up her seat, she may or may not have been tired, but she was most certainly angry.[1] Harriet Tubman didn't risk her life going back to rescue her fellow enslaved people time and time again because she felt chill about the whole thing. These women, and many more like them, galvanised their anger into action, and we owe them a huge debt of gratitude for it.

In 1981, Audre Lorde gave an incredibly powerful keynote presentation, 'The Uses of Anger: Women Responding to Racism', at the National Women's Studies Association Conference.[2]

'My anger is a response to racist attitudes and to the actions and presumptions that arise out of those attitudes.
My response to racism is anger. That anger has eaten clefts into my living only when it remained unspoken, useless to anyone.
Black women are expected to use our anger only in the service of other people's salvation or learning. But that time is over.'

A lot of what we take for granted today we owe to the righteous, motivating, productive anger of Black women in previous generations. So why are we so afraid of anger now? When did it become a dirty word? I think to understand that we need to look at the Angry Black Woman stereotype – where it started, and how it's used to limit Black women's voices today.

It's not controversial to say that in the workplace, not everybody is given the same rights to anger. The same words or actions can be taken in very different ways, depending on who they come from, as many of the people I interviewed had experienced first-hand.

> I'm very passionate about my work – the arts are one of the few things I'm passionate about – and I think that sometimes, the moment you're passionate about something (as a Black woman), and you believe what you're saying to be true, or you want your ideas to be heard, you're suddenly classified as angry.
>
> – *Destiny Ekaragha*

> What happened to me is that I did stand up for myself in a kitchen I was working in when a sous-chef was treating me unfairly, and I was immediately seen as the aggressor. It was very depressing because there were people who were around me who could see the things that were happening – it wasn't like he did it in private, he did it outwardly, and he didn't do it to other people. And . . . well I have my suspicions why he did it specifically to me. But again, I can't necessarily say that because if I shout either sexism or racism then, you know, I look like I'm trying to play the victim. I *am* a victim but it looks like I'm trying to *play* the victim just so I can have . . . I don't even know, I guess from their perspective it looks like I'm trying to have benefits, but I can't really understand what benefits they think I would be getting by calling out racism or sexism.
>
> – *Lopè Ariyo*

Forms of expression taken as passion and conviction from a white male leader are read as anger and a lack of control from a Black woman – even if they're saying the same thing, in the same way, to the same people. Displays that are taken as a humanising sign of commitment and investment from a white man are subject to tone policing in Black women and seen as a signifier that she is unable to speak, or think, clearly and calmly on the same subject – and so her voice, thoughts and opinions are less important because of the implication that they must be clouded by irrational emotions.

I saw first-hand recently how different women are allowed to speak about, experience, and express anger in very different ways.

I went to see a panel on diversity in creative industries. All of the panellists were white, blonde women, except for one Black woman.

When it was the Black woman's turn to speak, she spoke calmly and with great consideration about being angry. She said that the anger that she had felt had been a catalyst for her in setting up a business and a non-profit, and was starting to talk about the ways that it motivated her in the work that she was doing. As she was speaking, giving examples of the great work that she was doing and how her anger had played a part in making that work possible, a small murmur of disquiet rippled through the (again, mostly white) audience. Soon enough, one woman decided that she would be the audience's self-appointed spokesperson. She stood up and *shouted* at the woman on the panel. She shouted (very angrily, might I add) that anger had no place in our lives or our work, and that for the speaker to suggest it did was deeply inappropriate.

The Black woman on the panel said something to the effect that there would be a Q&A later where they would all be glad to hear from the audience, but for now, she was in the middle of speaking, and because she was the one who had been invited to be a part of this event, it was she who had the microphone, so she wanted to be able to finish saying what she had been invited to speak about. This response only served to make the angry woman in the audience even angrier – angry enough that not only did she continue shouting, she escalated the scenario by climbing onto her seat so that we could all see and hear her better. 'Oooh,' she taunted, 'she has the microphone. She's special. She's so special that we all have to listen to her talk about being angry like it's a good thing, when we all know it's toxic. I'm sorry,' (she wasn't sorry) 'but there's just no space for anger in a healthy workplace and we shouldn't have to listen to this.' Honestly, I'd love to say I've never seen a less self-aware person, but, you know, I've met some wild people.

I was really shocked by this woman's response – but I was also shocked by the response of the rest of the crowd (including her friends whom she had come with and was sitting next to), and the other panel members.

There was no one who said either 'Sit down and stop it' or '. . . You seem pretty angry for someone who's so offended by the very idea of anger . . .' Instead, everyone sat and watched this white woman shout down the only Black speaker, for daring to suggest that there have been times where she's been able to harness the power of her anger for good.

I'm not the first person to talk about the stereotype of the Angry Black Woman. In fact, when it comes to misogynoir, the Angry Black Woman is one of the most pervasive, damaging and dangerous stereotypes.

## Who is the Angry Black Woman?

I think the interesting thing about being a Black woman is that we straddle both white supremacy and the patriarchy at the same time. Because we're raised as women, this idea of being out of control, or standing outside of your station, or thinking too highly of yourself, is taboo in female culture and then it's also taboo in Black culture. And so when faced with those phrases of 'you're so aggressive', 'you're so angry', 'you're speaking out of turn, know your place' and all of that stuff, it's very easy to internalise it and think, 'Oh gosh, how do I fix this situation so I don't sound angry? So I don't sound like I'm full of myself and all of that?' Actually, where I'm at now, I'm like, 'OK, keep it coming. I'm comfortable with being and sounding angry, 'cause sometimes I am, and usually for good reason.

*– Naomi Ackie*

Of all of the stereotypes about Black women, despite being one of the most pervasive, the Angry Black Woman is one of the most difficult to research.[3] There have been so few academic studies looking into the formation and continuation of the stereotype itself, and the dangerous outcomes that can come as a result of being tarred with its brush. This lack of research is seen by some as a suggestion that researchers and academics haven't invested in looking into this particular area because they believe it to be true, and therefore not worth investigating.[4] [5]

So, let's quickly jump into the history of the Angry Black Woman to see where she's come from, and then let's look at where she's going.

Many trace the birth of the Angry Black Woman, also known as the Sapphire, back to the American minstrel show *Amos 'n' Andy*, a radio and subsequently TV show that ran in America from 1928–1960.

In the nineteenth and twentieth centuries minstrel shows were a popular form of entertainment, first on stage, then radio and then television. These shows, which were often the first and most enduring contact with a 'Black person' that audiences at the time had, featured white actors performing as caricatures of Black people. White performers would paint their faces with greasepaint and burned cork, creating grotesque depictions of Black people, their lifestyles and mannerisms, and depicting black women as loudmouthed 'Negro wenches'.

The *Amos 'n' Andy* audio minstrel show, written and performed by white men playing Black characters, featured a character named Sapphire Stevens, a Black woman, married to a 'get rich quick' con man, whom she constantly publicly berated and humiliated for his shortcomings. Sapphire Stevens was an overly and irrationally angry, out of control Black woman and her name has come to be synonymous with the Angry Black Woman stereotype that has endured since.

The era of minstrel shows as mainstream entertainment wasn't short-lived, and neither was it solely confined to America. In fact, in the UK the BBC broadcast *The Black and White Minstrel Show* for twenty years as Saturday night entertainment from 1958–1978 into homes across the nation.[6]

In the early days of the stereotype, just like Sapphire Stevens' character, the ABW reserved her anger for Black men – berating and belittling them publicly, inappropriately, and with little cause. As time has gone on the stereotype has expanded, and now we can see the Angry Black Woman trope being used in a much broader context.

It's not at all hard to think of examples of the Angry Black Woman in pop culture – TV shows and films are full of finger-snapping 'sistas' with a hand on her hip, and a chip on her shoulder. These characters take out their unjustified and uncontrolled anger on the innocent people all around them. Maybe she's shouting at an undeserving passer-by on public transport or taking out her oversized hoop earrings to physically fight another Angry Black Woman over some trivial slight – the media uses the Angry Black Woman as part comic relief, part boogeyman.

These depictions are not limited to fictional characters – the stereotype has passed beyond entertainment culture, and into the way that we perceive Black women in their day-to-day lives. Michelle Obama has spoken several times about being characterised as an Angry Black Woman when she was America's first lady.[7] Maxine Waters and Oprah Winfrey have had the caricature used against them, and of course, so has Serena Williams.

In 2018 when Serena Williams controversially lost the US Open to Naomi Osaka there was a deluge of coverage in the press characterising her as angry, aggressive and out of control. Not least of these was the cartoon by Mark Knight run in Melbourne's *Herald Sun* which depicted an oversized Williams, with the exaggeratedly wide nose and enlarged lips that are a staple of racist caricatures, jumping up and down on a broken racket, with a baby's dummy lying by its side. She is shown as destructive, petulant and childlike in her inability to control her anger. Osaka, on the other hand, is in the background, her blonde hair prominent, her skin unrealistically white, looking up calmly at the umpire as he asks her 'Can't you just let her win?' (You can look it up, but you've probably already seen it, and it's gross.) The quickness to characterise Williams in this way was not shocking given the Angry Black Woman stereotype – but it was deeply saddening.

## The mosquito effect

And so, with the idea of being angry – yeah I'm angry, of course I'm angry. Of course I'm angry, but that's OK. Why does angry have to be a bad thing? When was it labelled this thing we should be afraid of? Anger is a notification system in our body that something's out of balance. And things are out of balance. The day I stop being angry is the day I can look around and see that everyone else is being treated equally. And if people aren't angry then there's something wrong with them. That's my opinion. If you're not angry – if you look at the world now and you're not disturbed, I don't know what world you're living in. So actually, if anything, that's a validation of my humanity – yes, I'm angry. Because I care. Because I live in this world and because it's a tiring, beautiful, complicated thing to be a racialised woman in this world. It's not all bad, and it's not all good, but it's definitely a unique experience.

*Naomi Ackie*

There will, of course, be instances where Black women are characterised as angry because that's precisely what they are. We have every right and every reason to be angry – as well as anger being a basic human emotion, afforded to all other groups, Black women are trying to survive in an unequal world that was simply not built for our success.

I think what may seem confusing to some people, who do not suffer from micro- and macro-aggressions on a daily basis, is why sometimes actions or comments that can seem small to them can result in 'overreactions' from Black women.

I've definitely become exasperated at things that might not seem, as isolated incidents from the outside, to be a big deal. I've been irritated when someone puts their hands in my hair for the fifth time after being asked not to, even after I've spent the time explaining the reasons that it's not appropriate (it's my body, which you don't have the right to touch, it's othering, it's objectifying, you don't do it to white women. Also, I've asked you not to, so just stop). I've been annoyed when people have asked me to cast an advert 'diversely' only to respond to that the shortlist of potential participants looked 'like a Benetton ad', and that when they said diversity they were thinking 'more like, a range of accents, or a child with a missing tooth' (both real examples, sadly). I've been frustrated by going to meetings and joining committees about diversity in companies I've worked for only to find that once again 'diversity' means women, and only white women, and possibly working parents, but beyond that there's nothing else on the agenda.

It's important to be clear – when I say I've lost my patience or been annoyed, I don't mean I've exploded. I haven't shouted or raised my hands. Of course not. I haven't kissed my teeth (I don't know how – I just can't get the knack) or put my hand on my hips and snapped my fingers. I may well have rolled my eyes, I'm good at rolling my eyes.

What I have done is told people clearly, calmly, and in my big-girl voice, what's not acceptable, and what they need to stop or change in what they're doing. And people don't always like that – not at all.

The response when I'm pushing back on is usually gaslighting, indignation, defensiveness, some kind of comment about me not being able to take a joke, or a combination of the four. To them, it's no big deal, just a one-off trivial moment. Something small that I shouldn't give a second thought to – they want to tell me that if it were them, *they* wouldn't be making a fuss.

Recently I was walking to work through the park as there was a groundskeeper going by on a sit-on lawnmower cutting the grass. An older man was coming towards me, walking his dog. When he saw me he pointed to the mower and as he drew level with me he stuck his hands in my hair to ruffle it, 'careful of that' and said, nodding to the mower, 'it will have that lot right off in a second.'

'What you just did to me,' I told him, 'was a racially motivated action and comments.' I could have phrased it better, I'm sure – but I wasn't planning on being touched by a stranger on the way to work and having to take the time to explain to them with some kind of pithy one-liner why they were wrong, I was just trying to commute.

He was quick to correct me, 'No, what I said was a fun and funny comment.'

'You touched my body, and you made a comment about my hair, which is a racial characteristic.'

'It. Was. Funny,' he insisted as he walked away. 'Maybe you just don't understand jokes.'

People who don't suffer from this regularly often fail to see how, like a game of microaggression Buckaroo, things pile up one on top of another, until one final comment or touch pushes it over the edge and means that something has to give.

The place I've seen this laid out the best is in an online video by Fusion Comedy called 'How microaggressions are like mosquito bites'.[8] It compares microaggressions to mosquito bites – making the point that some people get bitten much more often than others, and a lot of bites can drive you to distraction. We all get bitten from time to time, and one or two bites spread out over a long time is just a small inconvenience. When you're getting bites on top of bites, all day every day, another bite becomes a much bigger deal. When your already irritated skin has the blood sucked out of it once again, you might react to it with frustration, or even anger, which can seem out of proportion. After all, it's the first time that particular mosquito has bitten you – what's the big deal?

I think this is a good example to use to explain to people why things can build up, and responses may seem overblown when other people may not bat an eyelid at them. Sometimes we're angry because we've been dealing with things that other people don't have to even consider, all day every day.

This was a conversation I found myself having last year with the CEO (at the time) of a very large, annual design festival and awards. They had been dealing with an issue involving several of their speakers dropping out of their speaking engagements at the event at short notice because it had come to light that whilst some speakers were being paid for their time, others weren't.[9]

A few days after this all publicly unfolded in the industry press, I was at an event which concluded with a Q&A, where the CEO was on the panel, so I took the opportunity to ask him about the incident, which seemed to disproportionately impact Black women. I was shocked by his answer. He told me that Black women's fight for equality, 'like feminism, is obviously a movement based in a lot of anger' which he now understood, having spent time talking to people (from what I could tell, most if not all of whom were white), which made their 'overreaction' in dropping out of their speaking slots make more sense to him. This was within the first month of me becoming self-employed, and I had rather hoped that this person would be a good contact, someone I'd be able to collaborate with professionally. From this moment I knew that wouldn't be the case. In front of a room of people, I tried to explain to him that that wasn't a helpful way to characterise a whole movement and group of people. I said there was a lot of baggage behind characterising both feminism, and particularly Black women as 'based in a lot of anger', and that if he was going to continue to speak in public and answer in the news cycle, it would be worthwhile fine-tuning that particular message. 'Well', he responded, 'they certainly seemed angry to me.' Again, I tried to explain that they were most likely angry with him, because he had done something wrong. But that didn't mean that they were, as people, inherently angry, or that that was a fair way to characterise the baseline of a whole movement. He wasn't interested in talking any longer.

He didn't stick around to chat after the panel.

Not too long later, he stepped down as CEO (though he was made chairman), and the organisation publicly rethought their payment policies.

Talking to him was the first time it truly sunk in for me that when we, as individual Black women, are justifiably angry about inequalities such as literally being short-changed, it is characterised as an overreaction, and expanded in people's minds as a representation of our group's temperament as a whole, at all times.

Injustice is maddening, and it's natural and correct to feel angry about it. But it's not the only source for potential anger, of course. Black women feel and have the rights to the same ranges of emotions as everyone else. However, there is one particular cause for potential anger and frustration that may be somewhat unique to Black women's experience of adulthood, and that is feelings of helplessness and powerlessness.

## Relationship to the Strong Black Woman: feelings of powerlessness

We expect that by the time we reach adulthood people will have a level of autonomy and empowerment in their own lives. This expectation is especially true for Black women, who are expected to be strong, and to uplift themselves, their families and their communities.

The Strong Black Woman is the sister of the Angry Black Woman. The SBW might be 'sassy' or 'fierce', but it's understood that everything she does is for the betterment of her family and community, rather than for her own personal gain. She sacrifices her own well-being for the greater good, breaking her back by carrying the world on her shoulders.

It's easy to see why so many Black women have and continue to align themselves to the SBW image as a source of strength and protection, whilst doing everything in their power, from self-tone-policing to limiting the range of emotions they display in public places, to put as much distance as possible between themselves and being labelled as Angry Black Women.

By celebrating the Strong Black Woman we have built an expectation of Black female empowerment, celebrating and idealising trailblazing Black women leading from within, whilst uplifting and protecting those close to them. The problem with this (aside from the pressure that this causes) is that we simply haven't allowed Black women, on the whole, to access the tools, power or social standing needed to be able to achieve this elevation of her community. They are fighting a losing battle, one which would leave anyone feeling maddened.

Black women are still underrepresented in politics and positions of power in their communities and workplaces, leaving them feeling helpless and powerless to be able to effect the change that is expected of them.[10]

One place where Black women are extremely *over*represented is in low-paying unstable work, and because of both the race and gender pay gaps they face even when they do ascend to the most senior positions they are unlikely to be fairly compensated for their work, keeping them from achieving the financial liquidity of other groups, allowing them to make real lasting change in the spheres most important to them.

According to the National Committee on Pay Equity, in the US, Black women's median earnings were equal to only 64 per cent of white men's.[11] Despite this, more than 80 per cent of Black women are key breadwinners for their families.[12] Families in the US headed by Black women have a median income of just $18,244 per year (compared to those headed by single white males, where the median income was over double that, at $39,240 annually).

These gaps in both income and life situations mean that many Black women simply don't have access to the financial resources necessary to make the kind of long-lasting change that they feel is expected of them.

Of course, financial means aren't everything – people can also use their voices and change the world. But when Black women who raise issues are so quickly written off as overreacting or even making things up, we take away all forms of their access to the power needed to make change.

This frustration of the imbalance between what's expected and what's achievable for Black women would drive anyone to despair, and dare I say, very justified anger.

But what about the other side of it? What about when we're classified as Angry Black Women without even being angry?

## You don't even have to be angry (to be an Angry Black Woman)

A Black woman doesn't even need to be angry to be an Angry Black Woman. I know, I know.

In the same way that hysterical used to be a word used to silence (white) women who spoke in any way other than a monotonous, passionless drone, angry is the word that is still being used to do the same to Black women.

Black women cannot raise their voice in white spaces, we cannot. I've learned to be very diplomatic and clear, like 'This is what I want. This is what I'm saying. This is what I'm going to do,' but it literally has to be in that flat tone, and even then – even then – I'm met with a bit of friction. Even then.

What can also happen is, if you convey your thoughts in a passionate manner, and it happens to upset a white woman – now you're a bully. Because she starts crying and now you're bullying. So now it's like not only are you an Angry Black Woman, you're a bully as well, so you're always sort of walking on eggshells.

But I do have to say, I am at a stage now, a place now, where I'm not afraid to say my opinions. I can't be. Especially as a director – my job is making decisions, but I am very aware of who I'm talking to, and which space is the safest.

– *Destiny Ekaragha*

This eagerness to see anger in Black women, even when it's not present, begins in childhood. An African American Policy Forum report examined data collected from schools in New York and Boston, and found that Black girls were six times more likely to be suspended from school than their white counterparts (and more so than Black boys who were three times more likely to be suspended than white boys).[13] The report found that 'Black girls may be subject to harsher disciplinary interventions because they are perceived to be unruly, loud, and unmanageable . . . [T]eachers sometimes exercised disciplinary measures against Black girls to encourage them to adopt more "acceptable" qualities of femininity, such as being quieter and more passive.'

You can be called angry, if you're a Black woman, for pretty much any behaviour or action that is anything less than subservient. By being loud, passionate, confident, or a thousand other adjectives that are celebrated and encouraged in other groups, Black women are not conforming to society's expectations of either Blackness or womanness – both of which require subservience and obedience to more dominant groups.

When a Black woman steps outside of those expectations in the workplace by being outspoken, even in the most deferential ways, and even once they have reached senior positions, others are quick to label her as angry, and to delegitimise her words and thoughts.

## The consequences of being labelled an Angry Black Woman

So. Angry or not, justified or not, the chances are that if you're a Black woman out in the world someone has classified you as an Angry Black Woman at work. (Don't forget, bossy, intimidating, unapproachable, sassy, etc. are all ways of calling Black women angry whilst avoiding the specific word).

Sure, it's annoying to have your emotions monitored and policed, but what is the actual harm that come from being tarred with the Angry Black woman brush in your professional life?

### Limiting Black women's legitimate expression

Just as tone policing dismisses arguments on the basis of how they are expressed, without engaging with the content of what's been said, one of the powers of the Angry Black Woman stereotype (and we're talking bad powers like a sea witch stealing your voice, literally, not good powers like a fairy godmother making you a couture dress) is its ability to silence Black women, by limiting the range of emotions that we can express if we want to be taken seriously.

For some people, being angry (or passionate, spirited, or deeply invested, as people can generously call it when the person in question is a white man) can be a positive thing. In fact, studies have shown that men who express anger in the workplace are more likely to be granted higher status and more powerful roles.[14]

For others, not even *being* angry, but simply being *perceived* to be angry, can be a huge professional disadvantage. Angry women are labelled as banshees – they're hysterical, their wombs are roaming all around their bodies, they must be on their periods.

Whilst characterising white women in that way is obviously unacceptable, it's also temporary. When people make snide comments about the 'time of the month' in response to a white woman expressing anger or discontent, they're acknowledging that this state is temporary, unusual and will pass soon enough.

This isn't true for Black women. The Angry Black Woman stereotype doesn't leave space for that nuance, or the possibility of multiple states existing in one person. Because the stereotype is built from one-dimensional fictional characters, people to whom it is applied are treated in the same one-dimensional manner. Once a Black woman is branded as angry, it's not seen as being linked to a passing moment or a justified reaction to a situation. No, it's the be-all and end-all of who she is. Even if she wasn't actually angry to begin with.

The fact that the Angry Black Woman label endures beyond any singular instance of perceived anger makes it a really useful (read: awful) tool to delegitimise anything that comes out of Black women's mouths – in the moment of perceived anger or at any time afterwards.

In this way, the Angry Black Woman stereotype bites twice. It discounts our expressions once the label has been applied but before that even takes place, the threat or fear of being perceived in that way causes Black women to self-edit their tone, words, and even facial expressions. Which is a tiring burden to take on.

This feeling of constantly being on guard, monitoring, changing and limiting our expressions is a form of social control, used against Black women to limit our range of emotions, and only serves to further limit Black women's personhood to one-dimensional public personas. It forces us to be the embodiment of 'when they go low, we go high' – always picture-perfect in our eloquence, articulation, tone and facial expression. This task of self-containment and internal policing is a burden, forcing us to limit our true selves and quash our authentic range of emotions, but to do anything else – to express passions, discontent or indeed anger, would lead to us immediately being dismissed as wild-eyed, untamed and dangerous.

I love Michelle Obama, but I also realise that her experience is *her* experience and trying to apply it to all Black women is dangerous. We understand her existence as a figure for Black women to look towards and look up to is great. But I think when you say 'when you go low, we go high' and you try to (and not that she's tried to do this), but when you try to blanket that for all Black women, what that means is you're disallowing them the ability to be angry when things go wrong. You're disallowing them the ability to analyse when things go wrong. You're disallowing Black women anger, and you don't care if our anger is righteous or not. I don't think there is one way to be angry, whether it's unrighteous or righteous anger, it's still valid.

What she's talking about is her experience, and what worked for her – but I just think that that level of pressure for Black women is unfair.

Why are you angry? People rarely look towards that. And so this, this idea that we have to be above the fray at all times, it creates a great deal of pressure that you can't maintain, and nobody else has to do that.

When a white woman is angry, her anger is understandable and people look for the root. They investigate why she's angry and how they can make sure she isn't angry again, they look for ways that they can create an environment that allows her to be happy all the time, or whatever. But when Black women are angry it's just, 'urgh, she's so angry' and there is no investigation of where that comes from, and what the source might be. And more often than not, when you investigate the roots of a Black woman's anger you will find an injustice.

I think the next stage of our evolution as a society is understanding the individuality of Black women – to look at who we are and what we've done, rather than applying antiquated racist tropes to every Black woman you meet because you haven't met enough. I think that many people's limited experience and exposure to Black people means that their personal references are too narrow, which means they apply ideas and behaviours to some-body who that might not work for. Again, this monolithic idea of Black womanhood is denying individuals their individual humanity.

*– Daniellé Scott-Haughton*

### The presumption of wrongness

When we see the stereotypical angry Black woman depicted in film and TV, nine times out of ten, she is in the wrong. Her feelings of anger or upset are real only in as much as she is really feeling them, but more often than not the things that she's irate about either don't make sense or aren't founded in truth. She's overreacting to a trivial slight, and has blown things well out of proportion, creating a whirlwind around herself that sucks everyone else into her mess. In these situations, when anger is being so readily applied without cause, the only rational response is to simply ignore her, and the things she's complaining about.

In this way, Black women's anger is used as a weapon against them, discrediting their voices by claiming overreactions, and discrediting their experiences by naming them unimportant.

This is incredibly damaging because it means that every time a Black woman raises a real problem, *she* herself risks being seen as the problem. Whether she raises it in a calm and collected manner, or with legitimate anger, the stereotype of the angry Black woman means that it's unlikely to be treated with the legitimacy it deserves – effectively silencing Black women when they try to speak up, or speak out. It's the ultimate gaslighting – taking our real and valid issues and manipulating them until we are framed as the problem in ourselves, meaning that nothing we say is treated with the credibility it deserves.

## Coded words for angry

I remember the most recent time a boss referred to me as angry. It was totally unexpected because it came during a meeting where I was actually getting a promotion – moving from being the head of production to the chief operating officer of the business I worked for at the time. My boss was giving me feedback and reading out a list of things that would become my new job description. He was reading it out loud from a document on his screen which we could both see, and there it was, buried in the middle of a long paragraph, 'angry demeanour', halfway down a page that, in order to accept my new role, I needed to sign.

'Hang on a second,' I said, 'go back up a little bit. Did you just say "angry" in a document that you want me to sign?'

I couldn't believe it. This was a man who, more than once, had shouted at me at the top of his lungs, like I was a misbehaving child, for asking questions that he didn't want to answer. A man who had reduced me and many other staff members to tears on several other occasions. And he thought I was going to sign a document which said that my demeanour was 'angry'. No way. 'You actually think I'm going to sign that?' I asked, shocked and upset that this was a situation I was facing as part of a promotion conversation, but scared of showing it for fear of furthering the label of 'angry'. 'Oh, I mean, erm, I guess not necessarily.' He floundered, suddenly aware that he had made a faux pas, but still not understanding why. When the meeting ended, I asked him to send me the document, unedited, for me to read through – hoping it would serve as a record of the wording that I could keep as I made up my mind what to do next. He sent it through, but first he removed the wording. In a way, great – no need to feel pressured to sign a document with that characterisation of myself – but on the other hand, with no proof, I had no real chance to escalate.

After that experience, in the hope that I could use it as a teaching moment (and that he wouldn't make the same mistake with anyone else), I gathered a whole host of resources to explain to him why that was a loaded term to use when describing a Black woman, especially with no examples or evidence to give to back up the claim.

It was scary to do, no one likes to be called out on their bias, even when it's unconscious (especially when it's unconscious?), and our relationship wasn't in great shape at that point. But it felt like the necessary thing to do, especially as I was pushing the business to hire more diversely, and to be a safe and inclusive space for those new hires. I didn't want to bring a wider group of people into the business only to inadvertently find themselves in a toxic environment with a boss who wasn't aware of the implications of the language he was using. I spent a fraught evening online gathering up news articles and studies about characterising Black women in this way – the history, the impacts, the deaths – then organised a meeting and took him through it all. I put it into an email and sent it over, to give him the chance to read and take it in without me watching him.

It was a lot of work on my side, both emotional and administrative – finding the articles, highlighting the most relevant passages for him, preparing what I was going to say to make sure I came across as helpful and approachable, rather than as though I was going to take him to a tribunal (which I couldn't since I didn't have the original, unedited, document).

He said he was sorry, that he wasn't aware of the stereotype, and would be mindful in the future.

Sidebar: I want to take a moment to say that not being consciously aware of a stereotype, but still perpetuating it, doesn't mean you're one of the good guys. Ignorance is no defence. It means that without you questioning it, or interrogating it, these stereotypes have slipped in and are impacting the way you see and treat people. 'Not meaning to' or 'not knowing' doesn't reduce the impact of damage that you're having on the people around you.

I felt glad I had advocated for myself and for other Black women he'd be interacting with in the future. But my positive feelings were short-lived. The next time he was angry with me, instead of 'angry' he reached for the word 'aggressive', and when I challenged him on it he replied, 'I didn't actually call you angry, I said aggressive, so you can't say anything.'

It was clear that whilst he'd learned to be careful of his exact wording, neither the sentiment nor his bias had changed – he had just had to find more coded ways to express it. I don't know if he really thought that just switching the word angry to another word (so close that it would be the first synonym in any thesaurus) was actually a solution or if he was being antagonistic, thoughtless, or all of the above. My efforts, and risks, to try to educate him hadn't sunk in in the way I'd hoped. Rather than understanding the deeper social implications, he's heard nothing more than: 'don't say "angry" or you'll get taken to court.'

I'm not alone in this experience – far from it. I asked Black women for synonyms of angry that had been used about them in the workplace, here are some of the answers I received:

- Aggressive
- Bossy
- Bullish
- Intimidating
- Hysterical
- Overreacting
- Sassy
- Feisty
- Fiery
- Spicy
- Unapproachable
- Difficult
- Abrasive

These words all do the same job as 'angry' – they diminish our thoughts and words, and control our expressions. Whilst the words may vary, their impact and damage remain consistent.

It's not the specific word that causes the harm, it's what is betrayed about your value in the accuser's eyes, their conscious or unconscious bias, and their perception of your very humanity and right to express emotion that does the damage.

It's not like it's the most comfortable thing in the world to speak to strangers [about this]. If I'm in a pitch meeting – I don't know these people, and I'm essentially having to ask them, can you see me as a human being? Sometimes it's a reminder that there are some people who don't see you as a human being. And that can wreak havoc on your mental health . . . I double-check everything because I'm over the walking on eggshells thing. I don't want to live my life like that. My work is most of my life – I don't want to spend most of my life second-guessing and worrying. I don't want that.

– *Destiny Ekaragha*

Feeling the need to always be on guard, and the expectation of facing discrimination in our home and working lives, means living in a constant state of fight or flight mode – which is an adrenaline response. We, as human beings, are only meant to have adrenaline bursts for short periods, so that we can take ourselves out of immediate danger, but being exposed to these states for extended periods has been found to have long-term health impacts. Researchers believe that living in this state of uncertainty, with the consistent feeling of being endangered or unfairly treated, may be responsible for health disparities between Black and white women in America, including Black women's higher propensity for cardiometabolic risk,[15] stress, hypertension and type 2 diabetes.[16]

## What next? Debunking the Angry Black Woman persona in the workplace

This work of debunking and rebuilding how Black women are perceived in the workplace cannot lie on the shoulders of Black women alone, it needs to be work that is taken on by those in leadership and managerial positions – because I believe that the crux of the issue lies the perception of Black women, rather than in reality.

Like other stereotypes, the Angry Black Woman only exists if people believe in her. Stereotypes survive and endure best in spaces and communities where there are limited opportunities for real-life interactions with the stereotyped group, which would allow the myth to be debunked. People who have strongly held beliefs about people at a group level, whether based on race, gender, sexuality, nationality or anything else, tend to have had limited interactions with people from that group. This lack of direct interaction allows them to form a homogeneous group in their minds, rather than being individuals with their own personalities, strengths and weaknesses, and lived experiences.

Again, one of the simplest ways to avoid this dehumanising view forming of team members is to avoid creating an environment of Onlys. Almost every back woman I had the pleasure of interviewing had experience of being an Only in a large number of the places where they had worked, and in those working environments, their experiences were much worse than when they were in representative groups.

They felt, and were, hypervisible, meaning that they had to go through the emotionally draining process of constantly self-tone-policing and code-switching to avoid being misunderstood or taken the wrong way.

When there are more than a token number of Black female employees in a space, the pressure is relieved and spread a little more evenly. There is less of a feeling of responsibility to represent a whole group, and less of an expectation from the wider company that you will have to. In greater numbers, there is more chance of being recognised as an individual and being afforded humanity, and the expressions of emotion that come along with that.

## Understand that not all voices are heard the same way

Women have been told to lean in. Be assertive. Ask for what you want. Know your worth. We are powerful women who are in control of our own lives, careers and destinies. However, not all voices are heard the same. While a non-Black woman might be celebrated for leaning in, it can be seen as being overbearing and demanding in a Black woman, whom society expects deference and subservience from.

This knowledge should be applied in two ways. Firstly, it should lead to an understanding that the fear of being seen as aggressive and over-bearing may hold Black women back from asking for what they deserve, stunting their progression. Make sure that promotion and pay rise processes are transparent and manager-driven to encourage the progression of groups who may not feel comfortable advocating for their own best interests for fear of a backlash.

Secondly, managers and those in positions of being instrumental in the progression of other team members should receive training about the Angry Black Woman stereotype and its consequences as part of diversity and equality training. Make sure they are aware of the fear marginalised groups can feel around advocating for themselves and empower them to act on behalf and in the best interests of the teams they manage. Also, make sure they are trained around giving quantifiable and constructive feedback to their team members, and frame goals and targets in the SMART (Specific, Measurable, Attainable, Realistic, Time-based) framework. Feedback such as working on having a 'bad vibe'/'negative energy'/being 'unapproachable' are too loose and unspecific to give people the necessary basis to make any real change.

## Assess if real change is necessary

Before giving feedback to a Black woman about her demeanour, assess if it's necessary and true. I'm by no means saying that there has never been a Black woman who has been unprofessionally angry or short-tempered, but take a moment to assess whether or not you, or someone who is feeding back to you about an employee, would have the same feedback about any other team member who was acting or presenting themselves in the same way. When we meet someone new, race is the first thing we notice about them, followed by gender.[17] Before you shake someone's hand, or learn their name, you've taken on this information, and will have started to form an expectation of them which can shape your attitude towards them for the rest of your relationship – especially if you don't get to know them well on a personal level. If you're in an HR or managerial position, bear this in mind as a potential unconscious bias before deciding where fault lies and asking for change.

## Don't put the burden of change onto the disadvantaged group

Sometimes, too often, we want to empower people by 'allowing' them to solve their own problems. We want to see them coming up with tactics and approaches that will lift themselves up and out of difficult situations – the masters of their own successes, against the odds.

Teach a man to fish and you'll feed him for a lifetime, as they say. But, if the man you're trying to teach to fish is in a sinking boat, or the only rivers he can access have become filled with toxic waste that has seeped in and killed all of the fish, your well-intentioned lesson is destined for failure. You will either walk away from your foray into teaching feeling frustrated – you gave him everything he needs but he just won't learn, or you walk away satisfied that you've given him a strong foundation and as soon as he gets the knack he'll be set for life. Even though all you've really done is take up his time and leave him hungrier than when he started.

I'll admit, men, fish, it's all a bit abstract – so let me give you a real example of an idea that seems like it's empowering, but actually puts the very group it's trying to help at a real disadvantage.

A few years ago I was working in a senior role, holding down the fort until an MD (who had already been hired but was serving out a long notice period) could join the business. I was there to spot problems and look for efficiencies, as well as keeping the day-to-day running of the business ticking over.

I was getting a handover from my predecessor and we were going over the pay rise and promotions process. 'I give women pay rises when they ask for them', she told me proudly, 'women don't ask enough and I want to reward them for asking. It's really important to me, as a feminist.' I couldn't understand what she was telling me – did she mean that any time a female member of staff asked for a pay rise she was given one? Surely not. After some deeper investigation, it became clear this wasn't what she meant, what she meant was she *only* gave pay rises to women if they asked. No asking, no pay rise. And if they asked for an amount that was less than had been budgeted then they only got what they had asked for. Because, feminism?

I was really floored in two key ways by just how broken this logic was.

Firstly they, like most businesses, plotted budgets months in advance. At the start of every financial year they looked at who they had, who they needed to recruit for, and who they needed to give pay rises to – these numbers, and the other projected overhead costs of running the business were plotted against projected income and used to form the basis of our working budget. Though these weren't an exact science (and they were reviewed at the start of each quarter), they already knew what they anticipated increasing salaries by, and for whom. In short, they knew who was due for a raise, and roughly what amount, whether they asked or not.

The second break with logic was that this 'don't ask, don't get' mentality wasn't applied to the men in the business. Male employees weren't made to ask for what they deserved, or guess the cash value, it was simply awarded if it was due as part of their annual review process.

When companies try to empower marginalised people, not by creating fair and equal systems and structures, but by 'giving them the tools to help themselves' they put an unnecessary burden of responsibility onto their shoulders. In instances like this, not only would Black women have to deal with reduced access to earning power, but they would also be forced to take on the mental labour of making a case for a pay rise or promotion that would simply be given to her if she were a man. In those meetings I saw women come in with presentations, spreadsheets and pre-prepared speeches to prove their worth, whilst the men didn't have to use that time and energy in preparation.

## Are you giving people a reason to be angry?

If someone is pushing back a lot or expressing continued discontent, it might be because they have a reason to be unhappy. If you have a small number of Black women in your business or you are successful at recruiting a diverse group of people, but can't seem to retain them for as long as non-marginalised groups, you may have a systemic problem that you're yet to recognise or address. People's actions speak loudly – if people are happy in a business they will stay longer than if they're not (depending, in part, on their feelings of being able to find alternative gainful employment), and leaving a job speaks pretty loudly. If you have a stream of people who are unable to progress, or even remain, in your business, there's a strong possibility that there's an issue that doesn't impact on you, and so you have overlooked it. The team that made Apple Health didn't include a period tracker in its first rollout, because the team was largely male and hadn't appreciated the importance of this element of health tracking for people who menstruate. Early automatic taps, hand driers and facial recognition tools didn't work for Black people as their skin couldn't be seen by the AI – because the homogeneity of the teams creating them meant that those skin tones were overlooked.

Overlooking or not being attuned to a problem that you don't experience first-hand is natural – we can't always be aware of every element and nuance that will impact every group. It doesn't necessarily denote maliciousness or a lack of caring or consideration. The same can't be said for refusing to listen when these issues are raised to you. Dismissing feedback about inequality in businesses as unreasonable and unjustified behaviour isn't good enough. Sometimes people are angry because you've done something wrong, and in those instances, your role is to listen and to find solutions to enable you to retain talented employees who are simply advocating for what they deserve.

# Being Perceived as an Angry Black Woman

Nana Bempah

*Nana Bempah is an executive producer working in film and advertising, and founder of Pocc – a creative community, support network and organisation seeking to accelerate equality for ethnically diverse people in the creative industries. In addition to rapidly becoming the leading community to connect Black, brown and ethnically diverse creatives for help, support, opportunities and collaboration within the industry, Pocc brings about transformation through campaigns using non-traditional ideas, behaviours and activism.*

I started my career a while back, and looking back I remember a discomfort. This understanding maybe harks back to school days – there's a thing where you find yourself operating in an environment where you appear to have two options – to assimilate or speak your mind. To survive, you are in a contact state of flux between the two. So I would always go into spaces, try to understand what was going on and what was happening, and then find out how best I could thrive and survive within that environment and achieve my goals, and I think that that's probably something that has stuck with me since the very beginning. For sure, we know it's not the way it should have to be, but when you are not the default identity – white and male and middle class – you have to find ways of adapting in environments that weren't built for you. Like when people are going down the pub and talking about their family holiday homes in Spain or France and making universal assumptions that are based on their own lives and you're going, 'OK . . . well that's not my life, but this is where the networking gets done so where do I sit in this moment? Or how can I still relate in this moment so that I can still achieve what I need to?' Looking back, there were definitely

times I seriously questioned what I was doing there.

I was in my late twenties when I first became Head of TV and Film at an advertising agency, it was a big position, so my experiences were impacted not only by my race and gender, but also by my age. Sitting at this intersection, I noticed it most in terms of the respect that I would get for the things that I said, and the ways that people would treat me. There were so many instances, at multiple workplaces, where people would call me aggressive, and rude, and I actually had an annual review once where that was the feedback. They said they'd gone round the agency and they'd got feedback from people, 360-degree feedback, and what they reported back to me was, 'You're really good at your job and you get things done, you know what you're doing. But you come across as rude and aggressive, and you walk around like you own the place.' And that is mad feedback to receive. I don't think anyone who knows me would describe me in that way. I asked friends and family about it afterwards and they couldn't believe that would have been said about me, you know, from knowing me. There's definitely a thing that if I had been in a different body, that of a white male, then that behaviour would have been seen as assertive and confident. It's all to do with the position I have been assigned in their minds as a Black female which dictates and sets the limitations on how they think I should act. Like, how dare I speak and carry myself with the same confidence as a white man?!

It's really wild, I've definitely had people – men as well as women – who would say 'You know, you're really intimidating'. When people feel intimidated, that's not *my* issue. It's not my issue that you are intimidated by me. That's *your* issue. I'm just a person, being. And for whatever reason, you've constructed something within your mind which finds me intimidating. Is it because I'm a Black woman who is confident in my ability? Is it because as a Black woman you expect me to shrink myself down so you can shine more? Or is equality intimidating for you? I don't know. I experienced these things in individual and isolated situations through the years and somehow developed a mechanism of not fully taking them into myself as I knew this would weigh me down in the pursuit of my goals. And this is something that has happened throughout my career, and probably my life. I really didn't have the capacity to take all of these instances metaphorically home with me every day and spend time ruminating on them as it would have been massively challenging for me to walk into those environments day after day and succeed in what I wanted to do, and I've always been very goal-focused.

However, as with every woman or person, every Black woman is different, so if people need to walk out of these situations, or the equation of why they are there doesn't add up, then that's what you have to do. You have to protect your mental health. I have always tried to focus on why I'm within an organisation, and on making sure that I succeeded in whatever my personal goals are when I'm within that environment. I had to find a way to make it work so I could survive within those environments, and reach the senior positions I knew I deserved.

It's hard, though, it's very very hard. We all know that we shouldn't need to choose between leaving an environment or finding coping mechanisms to deal with that environment – it's bullshit – but let's be real, a lot of the time this is the reality many Black women in the creative workspace, if not all industries, are navigating. Yeah, we could try another route where we fight the system from within, but what happens to your goals then?! While you're preoccupied doing that, Becky has got the promotion and is celebrating with a trip to Mykonos. Or even worse, you have been removed from the agency because you're seen as the troublemaker – which has definitely happened to me on occasions where I've spoken my mind. It's not easy. You have to do what you have to do to survive – I can't stress that enough. And perhaps that's why I feel so passionate and dedicated about what I do with Pocc – I had certain personal goals back then, I achieved them and feel now is the right time for me to challenge and change the system, while I have more mental capacity to do so and literally nothing to lose.

I think my parents did well – instilling within me confidence and the massively important lesson that people don't get to define you. Had I not had that, then it would be more difficult to challenge the stereotypical images and perceptions that people have built of what a Black woman should be. And what I am is an individual – I'm none of those things that people have picked up from stereotypical representations. So, they see me and they've already decided that I'm aggressive and I'm going to be snapping my fingers, and I've got an attitude or whatever – and all of these things they're feeling intimidated by, but I didn't give them that. I'm just a person, an individual having a conversation with you, while you're telling me you think I'm intimidating because of external conditioning that I've had nothing to do with.

And you know, we have to remember that everyone's story is individual, and, like I said before, there are certain things I felt I could deal with in a certain way – whereas other people may feel that they just need to get out of those environments, and justifiably too – it's survival. People need to, everybody needs to do what is best for them. All I can do is tell my story and things from my perspective, including how I felt and how I was able to manage and hope that will help other people to assess where they are at, not that they have to take the same route that I took, but just that all of the routes are valid. Ultimately they just have to do what's best for them until these systems of oppression are shattered.

# Vanessa Sanyauke's Favourite Thing About Being a Black Woman

66 Ooh let's see! I'm not sure how to say it, but I think my favourite thing about being a Black woman is our resilience, and how strong we are. We are incredibly strong individuals, and incredibly resilient in terms of what we go through and how we're perceived in society, how we're perceived in the workplace, how we're perceived even in our own communities – when you look at sometimes how Black men talk about us. I'm amazed by how we're able to juggle so many different things, and that we have overcome so many barriers. I think that's what I enjoy, and what makes me really proud to be a Black woman. Our resilience. 99

CHAPTER 6

# THE OVERLY SEXUALISED BLACK WOMAN — DEHUMANISED AND OBJECTIFIED

'And the speaking will get easier and easier. And you will find you have fallen in love with your own vision, which you may never have realized you had. And you will lose some friends and lovers, and realize you don't miss them. And new ones will find you and cherish you. And you will still flirt and paint your nails, dress up and party, because, as I think Emma Goldman said, "If I can't dance, I don't want to be part of your revolution." And at last you'll know with surpassing certainty that only one thing is more frightening than speaking your truth. And that is not speaking.'

**AUDRE LORDE**

Taking away Black women's humanity and reducing our bodies to objects that can be owned and used by others, either for sex or work, is nothing new. In fact, it's a decidedly old story.

It could be argued that sexual assault and violence against Black women was one of the sparks that lead to the ignition of the civil rights movement in America. In most tellings of her story, Rosa Parks doesn't really exist in the world until the act of civil disobedience in which she refused to give up her seat on a Montgomery bus in 1955. In that moment, she materialises in our collective consciousness, more as a symbol than a woman in her own right. In reality, when Rosa Parks stayed exactly where she was sitting, she was 42 years old, and the radical act of sitting down wasn't her first subversive action – she had already been working as an anti-rape activist. From the 1940s, Parks worked for the National Association for the Advancement of Colored People (NAACP) investigating violence and lynchings against Black men, and rapes and sexual assaults suffered by Black women. When working with rape survivors Parks was responsible for documenting and cataloguing the epidemic of sexual violence suffered by Black women at the hands of white men, and campaigning so that those women would have the opportunity to appear in court to seek justice for their experiences, something that was often not afforded to them.

Diminishing Black women's autonomy and turning them into sexual objects for the gratification of others started with colonialism and slavery, and we can see the legacy of those actions still impacting society to this day. Enslaved Black women didn't own their own bodies, instead, Black women's bodies were literal property to be bought, sold, and used as desired by their white owners.

Though this is an uncomfortable history, it's important to understand, as the history of objectification of Black women and their sexuality goes a long way in explaining why they are the group today who suffer the highest rates of workplace sexual assault, abuse and harassment.[1]

## Owning Black women's sexuality

Historically, there have been two popular perceptions of Black women in regard to their sexuality – the Mammy and the Jezebel. The stereotypical Mammy's sole purpose and joy in life is to feed the family of her owners and take care of their children. To think of Mammy, think Aunt Jemima, before the 2020 rebrand – she's big, she's round, and she's entirely non-sexual. The Mammy is a construct of a racist society and a tool of pro-slavery propaganda, normalising Black house slaves, showing them as round, happy, jolly 'members of the family', more than satisfied with their role as someone's possession.

The Mammy's cultural counterpoint in this is the Jezebel – a hyper-sexualised, animalistic creature driven by her uncontrollable lusts and untamed sexual appetites. The Jezebel has no real worth or value outside of her body, she's a one-dimensional sexual temptress who lives only to serve the sexual pleasures and desires of others.[2]

Whilst the Mammy caricature, once popular in advertisements for a wide range of products, died away somewhat after the civil rights movement, the stereotype of the Jezebel has proven more enduring.

During the time of chattel slavery, Black women were property, and as property they had a value that depended on their potential outputs for their owners – their potential return on investment. In order to be sold, Black women were stripped naked and made to stand on auction blocks, to be assessed by potential buyers. A Black woman who would produce numerous and healthy children was the most desirable, as these children would either become new, cost-free workers, or could be sold for a profit, and in either instance would increase the wealth of their owners.

Rather than having the usual parental lines of responsibility and care we recognise today, children born to enslaved women remained the property of the slave owner, sometimes even after their parents were emancipated. In 1829 in the legal case of Hamilton versus Cragg a previously enslaved Black woman was granted her freedom, and tried to take her child with her.[3] The court found that she had no rights to the child because 'she was Black chattel whose body "issues" and physical and sexual being belonged to her white owner'.[4]

Since Black enslaved women were valued for their ability to reproduce, and children were just further potential money-making hands, making sure that Black female slaves did, in fact, reproduce, by whatever means necessary, was seen as simply good business. Historians estimate that 58 per cent of enslaved women aged 15–30 were sexually assaulted by white men.[5] This culture of rape was only exacerbated after importing people from Africa was banned in 1808, meaning that rape and forced pregnancy became 'necessary' for the economic continuation of plantations, and was justified by pointing to the insatiable sexual appetites of Black female slaves.[6]

As subhuman property there was no consent as we understand it today – Black women's bodies were owned and could be made use of by whatever means and for whatever purpose her owner desired. And yet there were Black women who resisted. There are countless cases of enslaved Black women who resisted or attempted to avoid the sexual advances of white men, only to have their husbands or children sold or killed as retaliation.

As Andrea Williams wrote, 'Perhaps she remembers her great-great-grandmother who wanted to protest but only rolled her eyes and willed herself not to scream when the white man mounted her from behind.'[7]

In the UK, 'marital rape' didn't become a crime until 1991. Up until that point, it was believed that the marriage contract itself was consent and so the idea of a husband raping his wife was a contradiction in terms. Literally impossible. Knowing that this was the case up until so recently, it won't come as a surprise to hear that the Black women we've been speaking about, at the time of slavery, weren't protected under the law. In fact, more often than not they were blamed for their attacks. Their owners would claim that the Black woman's uncontrollable desires had seduced and overpowered him – not only was he not to blame, but there was also nothing to be blamed for, he was only giving her precisely what she wanted, and he was, in fact, the victim in this attack. She was literally asking for it. During the 1800s, in order to avoid any ambiguity over who was and was not protected by law in America, the language used in the laws around rape was made to be race-specific. A rapist was defined as a man who would 'unlawfully and carnally know any white woman against her will or consent'.[8] This language made Black women simultaneously unrapeable, and always available for sex.

And so, Black women's sexuality was taken away from their ownership, and the crimes committed against their bodies were used as proof of their subhuman characteristics and lustful natures.

Of course, at this time, Black people were not 'people' under the law. Under the US constitution at the time, enslaved Black people were classified as three-fifths of a person. But we shouldn't think this was a purely

American issue. In the UK colonisers returned from trips to 'exotic', 'new' lands, and brought home with them Black women who were kept, naked or nearly naked, in cages and displayed to the public to view for a fee. For an increased payment, wealthy audience members were allowed to touch, poke and inspect the bodies of the Black women before them. This was the fate of Sarah (Saartjie) Baartman, a woman brought to London from South Africa in the 1800s, who was 'exhibited' in circuses, museums and bars as part of a freak show wearing minimal, flesh-coloured clothing or just a few feathers.[9] According to accounts from the time Baartman was displayed to an audience who saw her as essentially an animal, on a 'stage two feet high, along which she was led by her keeper and exhibited like a wild beast, being obliged to walk, stand or sit as he ordered'.[10] After her time in London, Sarah (Saartjie) Baartman moved to Paris, most likely having been sold, where she was under the custody of 'a showman of wild animals' who made her a part of his travelling circus act. She was examined, studied and used as 'proof' by people in the medical profession of the innate inferiority of Black people, and the superiority of the white race.[11] After her death, her dehumanisation continued – her genitals and brain were pickled and preserved and her skeleton was kept on display in the Musée de l'Homme for around 150 years after her death, at which point it was moved into storage behind the scenes at the museum. Although when Nelson Mandela became president of South Africa in 1994 he requested the repatriation of her remains, it wasn't until 2002 that Sarah (Saartjie) Baartman's remains were finally returned to South Africa – 192 years after she left.

If you're shocked, that's good. That's no way to treat any person. But that's exactly the crux here – she and other Black women were simply not seen as people.

Legal chattel slavery is over, but some of the legacies of the lies told about the sexual appetites and availability of Black women have lingered to this day. Researchers looking at unconscious bias and implicit associations about Black and white women's bodies held by people in 2018 found that 'Black women are implicitly associated with both animals and objects to a greater degree than white women.'[12]

The findings of this implicit association study back up a 1997 study of fashion magazines and adverts which found that Black women are disproportionately shown as being animal-like predators, and are shown more often than white women wearing animal print. In fact, 70 per cent of all adverts that featured animal print also featured a Black woman.[13]

And so the dehumanising, objectifying and animalising of Black women's bodies continues today.

## Current implications

All of this matters because it's the context in which perceptions of Black female sexuality were formed, and the legacy that we as a society have inherited. We are living with the consequences of that sexualisation, and we're still suffering because of it. The rate of sexual assault against Black women in America is three and a half times the rate suffered by any other race, though a tendency for Black women to underreport assaults may mean that it's even higher than that.[14] A lack of reporting is sad, but not surprising when we understand that when a Black woman does report a sexual attack, it has been found that she is likely to be seen as being more promiscuous than their white peers, and more likely to be held personally responsible for her attack.[15] She is less likely to have the attack defined by others as rape, and less likely to have the people she confides in believe that the attack merits police involvement.

As Tarana Burke, a Black women who is one of the founders of the #MeToo movement said: 'It's painful to see people preference the pain of other people over ours and not give any credence to the trauma, the layers of trauma that happen in our community, particularly around sexual violence.'[16]

Whilst Black women may no longer be legally unrapeable, we do still seem to be perceived as such. Not only are people less likely to believe and more willing to blame Black sexual assault survivors after the fact, but it has also been shown that people feel less compelled to intervene when they believe a Black woman is *at risk* of sexual assault than if the potential victim is a white woman.[17]

A history of being stereotyped as lustful, animalistic temptresses has left us underprotected and overly preyed upon.

Women's intersectional identities, as always, play a big part in their experiences. It's important to note that LGBTQIAP+ women can be at a heightened risk of rape and sexual assault. In fact, a recent survey found that 54 per cent of lesbian, bisexual and trans 'BAME' women had experienced unwanted sexual contact or touching compared to 31 per cent of white lesbian, bi and trans women. 45 per cent 'BAME LGTBQIAP+' women reported being sexually assaulted whilst at work, which is a rate twice that of their white counterparts. They also reported serious sexual assault or rape three times more than white women (27 per cent versus 9 per cent).[18]

> I think that feminism has prioritised white women for so long that white women have gained a personhood in the eyes of the patriarchy that Black people and other minorities [like trans or gay women] just haven't. So, white female bodies are protected to a much greater degree than any other body. I think we also need to take into consideration how white women will rally for other white women in a way that they just won't for Black women, it's almost like white women protect that change of identification of personhood, which will reduce the amount of harassment that they experience.
>
> I don't think that racism or sexism is always necessarily active in abusing people. I think that that abuse comes by proxy of not recognising someone's personhood or humanity. And if you're not going to recognise someone's personhood or humanity then you're more likely to abuse them, by proxy. I'm sure.
>
> *– Munroe Bergdorf*

## Devalued sexual capital

Of course, there are some roles, such as escorts, porn performers and sex workers in the adult entertainment industries, where sex, or sexual contact, is a part of the job.

In looking at these roles, we can clearly see the imbalance that exists as a result of the legacy of the objectification of Black female bodies, and the idea that Black women are not only available for, but desirous of, sex at all times. We see this imbalance clearly in the unequal sexual capital between performers of different races in sex work, where Black female performers are paid just three-quarters, or even half, of what white female performers tend to make, according to a National Public Radio (NPR) interview with Mireille Miller-Young, a professor of feminist studies at University of California, Santa Barbara. As Miller-Young commented, this is notable on two accounts. Firstly, this pay disparity 'reflects the ways in which Black bodies have historically been devalued in our labor market since, you know, slavery to the present.' But there is a secondary point to be drawn, in that, as she went on to say, 'it speaks to the ways in which there's this simultaneous problem that was like a deep desire to have those bodies present and to consume those bodies as commodities, but a deep disgust for Black people, our humanity and our bodies, at the same time that allows that devaluing to function.'[19]

By underpaying Black female performers, we see and continue the legacy of devaluing Black sexuality in our society, and treating it as something that should be freely available to those who want to access it, without having to treat it with the same care, respect and reward that we apply to white bodies and sexuality. After all, the logic seems to go, why would we pay a premium to access something that has been taken so freely for so long?

## Sexual harassment in the workplace

Sexual harassment at work is extremely common – shockingly so. A study by TUC and the Everyday Sexism Project found that 52 per cent of women overall, and almost two-thirds (63 per cent) of women aged 18–24 said that it was something that they had personally experienced.[20]

The good news is, if we look at long-term trends overall, reports of workplace sexual harassment and assaults do seem to be decreasing. Between 1996 and 2016, according to a study by the American organisation the Equal Employment Opportunity Commission (EEOC), the probability of white women reporting sexual harassment dropped by more than 70 per cent.[21] However, the story isn't quite the same for Black women – whilst the rate did also fall, it was by the much smaller amount of just 38 per cent. Not only this, but Black women are disproportionately impacted by sexual harassment at work, relative to their percentage of the workforce – which is to say that although Black women make up only 11 per cent of the workforce, they account for 14 per cent of the sexual harassment charges brought to the EEOC.[22] Between 2012–2016 there wasn't a single industry in America where Black women didn't file sexual harassment reports that were disproportionately high compared to their percentage participation in the workforce.[23]

In 1996 African American women were twice as likely as white women to report sexual harassment, by 2016 that number had grown to become were four times more likely.[24] These odds are not moving in a good direction.

Although the numbers are already much too high, it's likely that they're hiding a much worse truth. It's thought that concerns around job security and the possibility of difficulties in finding new employment mean that women from racially marginalised groups are less likely to report sexual harassment when they experience it, meaning that the figures that we have may well be artificially lowered by gaps in reporting.[25]

These concerns about potential backlash are not lost on Tarana Burke, 'The stakes are higher in a lot of instances for us than they are for a lot of other women, that creates a dynamic where you have women of colour who have to think a little bit differently about what it means for them to come forward in cases of sexual harassment.'[26]

Black women may be cautious, or even fearful of reporting sexual harassment or abuse over concerns of it being perceived as a personal, moral failing on their behalf, or due to concerns over losing their jobs and having difficulties in finding new employment.

Heartbreakingly, these concerns can be well-founded – in some industries, Black women are the most likely to suffer negative consequences from their employers if they report sexual harassment at work, with 34 per cent reporting at least one negative action taken in response to them making a report (versus 26 per cent of Latinas and 17 per cent of white women).[27] This leaves many Black women feeling safer by not making any formal reports of their experiences, and instead resorting to 'solving' this problem by themselves – using tactics such as changing shift patterns or reducing their working hours (and therefore their pay) to avoid their abuser, which causes a shortfall in the available statistics.

Researchers think that this over-representation of Black women among sexual assault victims is no coincidence. In an interview with *The Independent* newspaper in the UK, Dan Cassino, one of the researchers behind the EEOC report said, 'Over the past twenty years, we've made great strides in reducing sexual harassment in the workplace, but those benefits have all gone to white women, and mostly to young white women . . . It seems as though men have gotten more careful about who they're harassing and have been targeting women of colour, who may be less likely to report the harassment.'[28]

Could it be, then, that this abhorrent behaviour is part of a calculated risk on the part of the abusers? Have sexual predators learned that Black women are so poorly treated when they report being the victim of workplace sexual assault, from not being believed to suffering repercussions, that it bolsters their bravery in taking these actions? Are they also using their power and status, and Black women's history of the stereotype of oversexualisation, to hone in on Black women as the continued victims of their attacks?

Having looked at the EEOC data from 1997–2016, Yasemin Besen-Cassino of New Jersey's Montclair State University thinks so: 'Sexual harassment in the workplace is an expression of power – a way for men to assert their dominance,' she reported. 'The shift from sexual harassment of white women to African-American women indicates that harassers are conscious of power relationships, and choose to target more vulnerable women in their workplaces.'[29]

Research from the University of Toronto, looking into the intersection of sexual and racial harassment in workplaces, takes it one step further, asserting that sexual harassment is a tool which is used to maintain the status quo in traditionally white and male spaces. 'A major tool for maintaining this inequality is on-the-job harassment: Women and minorities often face hostile receptions in traditionally male- and white-dominated domains, which discourage them from entering and remaining in those domains.'[30]

On the day that I'm writing this, Harvey Weinstein has been found guilty of rape. He's probably the best-known current example we have of a man using his power in the workplace to attack and intimidate women for his own sexual purposes, which prompted me to relook at how the racially marginalised women who he abused were treated. Though there were a huge number of women who made accusations of rape and sexual misconduct against Weinstein, there were only a very small number that he publicly responded to deny by name, including Salma Hayek and Lupita

Nyong'o – both of whom are racially-marginalised women. Though they weren't completely alone in having public statements of denial issued about their claims (there were three other women his representatives also issued statements around), the way in which he responded to them *was* unique. In his denials about the white victims he chose to respond to, he said nothing more than that he and his accusers had 'a different account of events',[31] however, he sought to undermine Nyong'o and Hayek's personal credibility in response to their claims, saying that Nyong'o had 'sent a personal invitation to Mr Weinstein to see her in her Broadway show *Eclipsed*', and claiming that Hayek was angry that it was his vision for the film *Frida* (the film they were working on together when he sexually harassed her), rather than hers, that had made the film a success.

This is something that Hayek has been vocal about, particularly in a Women In Motion panel interview with *Variety*: 'He only responded to two women,' she said, 'two women of colour. It was a strategy by the lawyers because we are the easiest to get discredited . . . it is a well-known fact that if you are a woman of colour, people believe in you less. And believe what you say, less. So he went back, attacking the two women of colour in hopes of discrediting [them] . . . It's a proven fact that women of colour are less listened to . . . You know what, the good news is that there's so many, because if there hadn't been so many, probably people would have thought that we made that up.'[32]

Michelle Taylor, known online as Feminista Jones, agrees that the difference in treatment that the white and non-white women received in Weinstein's statements was not a coincidence, but a 'message to Black women that they can't be harassed, they can't be assaulted'.[33]

## Moving forwards

I know that everything about this can seem heartbreaking and over-whelming, but there are some things that we can collectively do to make things better for ourselves, and for those who come after us. The impetus for ending sexual assault and harassment should never fall onto the shoulders of the victims, but we can work together to change how we perceive and respond to these incidents, and business leaders can work on creating workplaces that are truly safe environments.

## Don't blame yourself

Rape, sexual harassment or sexual assault is never the victims' fault. Not ever.

It doesn't matter what you wore, who you smiled at or what you said. Nothing that you have done, or could do, would make a sexual assault, or harassment, your fault. It's really important that you take the time to recognise, understand and believe that, because it's a fact – but it can be a hard one to accept.

Although it's absolutely not their fault, victims can suffer from feelings of guilt that can be hard to overcome. It's important to have people who will listen, believe and support you through difficult times. Whether that's a personal or professional support network, or both, using your community can help you to avoid feelings of shame and isolation.

As Yvonne Traynor, a member of the organisation Rape Crisis said: 'The reasons women do not report it are that women tend to take responsibility for themselves and feel that maybe there was something that they did for it to happen, and they feel ashamed and do not want anyone to know about what happened. It is really hard for women to come forward and talk about it.'[34]

This shame protects harassers, and the businesses where they are allowed to thrive. The idea that women are to blame strips us of our power – and so where we can, in instances where it feels safe, we need to use our voices and speak about our experiences and hold harassers to account.

## Don't downplay your experiences

I don't know about you, but I have a real tendency to downplay or minimise the things I'm experiencing. If something is upsetting me, I'm fast to point out that other people have it much worse, and I'm just making a fuss. If I'm hurt or sick, I'll delay going to the doctor for weeks, or even months, because I don't want to waste their time when they could be helping other, sicker people.

This is a habit I need to unlearn, and I really need you to unlearn it along with me.

If something has happened, or is happening to you, which you know to be wrong, but you find yourself making excuses, or even gaslighting yourself, on behalf of the offenders, saying and thinking things like:

'It wasn't that bad.'

'Worse things have happened to other people.'

'They didn't mean it.'

'It was just a joke.'

'I don't want to make a fuss.'

'It's not as though they did [insert terrible thing] to me.'

Then I'd really like you to rethink how you're framing things.

As outlined in the UK Equality Act 2010, sexual harassment is any unwanted contact of a sexual nature, with the purpose *or* effect of violating dignity or creating an intimidating, hostile, degrading, humiliating or offensive environment. This includes (but isn't limited to) sexual jokes or comments, catcalling, wolf-whistling, making comments about another person's body, flashing, unwanted sexual advances, showing or sharing pornographic material, touching, groping and rape. The common factors are the effects that the conduct has on the victim, and that it is unwanted, regardless of the perpetrator's intentions. Sexual harassment in the workplace is unlawful. And you shouldn't have to deal with it.

You are important, and your safety and well-being is the minimum that you should expect whilst at work. Anyone who oversteps a boundary needs to be dealt with appropriately, and by the appropriate person – in part because of what they might do to other people, but also because of what they've already done to you. Because you matter just as much as anyone else you might want to protect.

## Stand in solidarity

There is a lot of evidence[35] that for many women, types of behaviour which are most certainly sexual harassment have become so normalised and commonplace that they feel that they should 'put up with them',[36] rather than raising or reporting the behaviours as an issue. One of the things that can contribute to this feeling of normalisation is how colleagues and others who witness sexual harassment taking place respond to it. If people stand by, without intervening or supporting the victim, the unspoken message is that there's nothing wrong.

As Dr Rachel Fenton, a researcher into bystander intervention, explained to Parliament, 'the environment in which [the harassment] happens is really important, in terms of what other people's reactions are . . . If you are met by a sea of silence and nobody shows any kind of solidarity, it reinforces that reporting is not the right thing to do.'[37]

Visibility is not enough, we need structural change, we need institutional change, we need allies – this involves everybody.

I think the key really is just making people aware that this is your issue as well, and if a group of people are actively oppressed in society and you're not, that means that ultimately they're being oppressed for your benefit because you're being prioritised over them. I think that a good way of illustrating this is the experience of people with disabilities. People that are able-bodied are prioritised over people with disabilities. We can get everywhere in this country without having to take into consideration 'Are we going to be able to move?', and if you relate that to society, whiteness, throughout the ages, has always been prioritised over Blackness. Cisgender people have always been prioritised over trans people. Heterosexual people have always been prioritised over gay people. So when you make people aware of this, that you have a privilege just being who you are, racism is your issue as well – if you don't want to be prioritised at the detriment to somebody else. If your moral coding says that that is wrong, then this is your issue too. So I think once you make people more aware of that then they're more inclined to see it actually happening and to open their eyes and actually do something about countering it.

– *Munroe Bergdorf*

Allyship is not a passive state, it's an active pursuit that can feel risky in the moment. You can't just decide you're an ally – you have to do the work of allyship and use your voice and actions to protect marginalised people whenever needed.

Allies give us power and resilience when ours is running low, and allies don't let the people they support stand alone. When someone is under attack they can be like a deer in headlights, paralysed by the moment – and this is when speaking up on someone else's behalf can really help.

I'm not saying speaking up, or speaking out, is easy – it's not, particularly for marginalised people. And depending on where you work, I'm also not saying it's risk-free. What I am saying, though, is that two voices are stronger than one, and so are three, four or five.

Using your voice in solidarity with sexual harassment victims is especially important and effective if you're a man. 'Women are seen [by their employers] as a bit of a problem. They are complainers, they are holding grievances and are bringing the organisation into disrepute,' explained Yvonne Traynor, giving evidence to the Women and Equalities Committee about reasons so much sexual harassment at work goes unreported, explaining 'there is a huge myth in this country and around the world that women lie about what is happening.'[38]

The lack of belief in women's words when they speak about harassment and sexual violence they face is a huge issue – both in holding abusers accountable and in a woman's likelihood in coming forward to report incidents, especially for Black women who have historically been blamed for sexual attacks taking place against them.

Speaking out in the moment if you witness harassment is an option, but it can be scary, especially since workplace sexual abuse is likely to be perpetrated by someone in a powerful position relative to their victim.[39] Intervening at the moment that something is going on is not the only way to stand in solidarity – if for some reason it is impossible in the moment, it can also be valuable after the fact to make sure the victim knows that someone believes them, will listen to them process the experience, will work with them to find out what their options are, and will go with them if they want to report to their business, a regulatory board or the police.

If someone decides to speak out, knowing they have people who believe and support them can make a huge difference.

## A note on NDAs

NDAs (non-disclosure agreements) are a normal part of most contracts that you sign at the beginning of a new job. They protect the business you work for from having private or sensitive information about themselves or their clients leaked. So far, so good.

The problem with NDAs arise when businesses settle sexual harassment claims, and then pressure victims into signing new NDAs specifically related to their abuse or settlements, something that happens all too often. In these instances, new non-disclosure agreements are effectively used as gagging orders – preventing victims from talking about their experiences, sometimes going so far as stopping them from being able to go to the police, whilst protecting the business, and allowing the business in turn to protect the abusers they employ without risk of damage to their public reputations.

In February 2020 the Advisory, Conciliation and Arbitration Service (ACAS) released guidance to employers and employees about the use of NDAs in reporting workplace sexual harassment. The guidance is clear that NDAs cannot be used to stop someone from reporting discrimination or sexual harassment at work or to the police, whistleblowing, or disclosing a future act of discrimination or harassment, and that 'NDAs should not be used to hide a problem or brush it under the carpet.'[40]

This is important to be aware of, because there is a long precedent of these agreements being abused to intimidate and silence victims, rather than giving them the support and closure they deserve.

A piece of written evidence from a victim given to the House of Commons Women and Equalities Committee outlined her all too common experience: 'I was told that I must sign a settlement agreement for no money, or I would be "badmouthed", not given a reference, and my new employer would be called and told about the harassment claim.'[41]

If you make a claim of sexual harassment or assault at work and are told that you have to sign an NDA, you have the right to refuse. You have the right to take a reasonable period of time to speak to a solicitor (in many instances the business must cover the cost of a solicitor for you, up to a point – though this is not usually publicised by businesses and so it's worth taking some time to look into) and to consider your options, and you have the right to refuse in cases where you don't think signing will be beneficial to you and bring you closure or peace of mind.

## Employer responsibility

It is important to remember that all of the weight should not fall on victims' shoulders, and that employers have a huge responsibility, and part to play in safeguarding their staff – whether contracted employees, freelancers, volunteers or interns. That protection should extend to shielding employees not just from internal issues, but from harassment or abuse from third parties, such as clients.

At the moment, the law in the UK requires employers to protect their employees' personal data, and prevent money laundering by requiring them to follow strict rules and requirements. The same level of vigour is not required for businesses to protect their employees from workplace sexual abuse.[42]

A survey of employers by the Equality and Human Rights Commission found that one in six employers had done nothing to make sure that people who made sexual harassment claims weren't further victimised.[43] Of those who said that they had taken action, many were only able to point to their business's written sexual assault policy, rather than outline any concrete steps that had been taken, or to offer any examples of it having been applied in practice.

Researchers have also argued that since it's been confirmed that socially low-status 'women of colour' are at a higher risk of being harassed compared to low-status white women and high-status women of any race,[44] 'sexual harassment should be defined differently for ethnic minority women, meaning that "sexual harassment should be defined as a form of both gender discrimination and race discrimination because they are historically and experientially tied to one another."'[45]

It can be incredibly difficult for Black women to 'distinguish and disentangle sexual harassment from racial harassment,'[46] to the extent that it has been found that 'women did not report race and gender harassment as separate incidents,'[47] instead regarding them as intersectionally inter-linked.

So, what can businesses do? First of all, people in senior positions in business must simply agree that sexual misconduct at work is unacceptable and needs to be taken seriously in every instance. They need to commit to investigating all reported instances thoroughly, and fairly.

When allegations are overlooked or swept under the carpet, or when abusers are protected at the expense of their victims, businesses create a culture where misconduct of this type is normalised, and the same people are enabled to become repeat offenders.

Businesses need to understand the power imbalances at play in workplace sexual abuse. Sexual harassment is usually perpetrated by someone more senior than their victim, and in businesses where there are large differences in power between people in different roles or positions, hierarchies can make it difficult to negotiate in coming forwards.[48] This is particularly true for Black women who are overrepresented in junior roles and desperately underrepresented at the highest levels. Through misguided loyalty, or self-preservation instincts, it's not unusual for businesses to draw inwards, protecting powerful, senior people with a track record of making the company money, at the expense of more junior team members, who can be seen as more disposable.[49] In cases like this, sexual abuse can become something of an open secret in an organisation, helping it to become normalised and further discouraging future victims from coming forwards.

One way to avoid this is by having an independent service available to employees, which can hear and handle their complaints. If there is an independent person, a union body, or even a phone line that isn't run by or employed by the organisation, people who have been victimised may feel more at ease coming forwards. This solution bypasses any concerns about personal or professional relationships between the abuser and internal resources such as HR, and offers victims a safe route to speak to someone and understand their options without risk to their reputations, or being seen (unfairly) as a troublemaker.

Workplaces must have a clear, zero-tolerance sexual harassment policy. But that needs to be the start, not the end of the conversation. It's not good enough for the policy to exist – everyone, at every level, must be aware of it, and it must be enforced. It must act as a deterrent to potential abusers, and a shield for victims, should abuse occur.

Like anything else, a sexual harassment policy is only as good as the people enforcing it. This means that it's essential to provide training about it at all levels. It's important to make sure that people know not only what constitutes sexual harassment but what the consequences are, and what to do if they are victimised, or are aware of someone else being. Managers and leaders should receive additional training about appropriate interactions with their more junior team members, and how to help a team member who reports an incident to them. It's important to emphasise that they should never penalise or take negative actions against someone making a claim but should instead inform them clearly and accurately about the options available to them, in an easy-to-understand way, and support them in their choices of next steps.

There is a good chance that people won't feel comfortable confiding in their managers. To safeguard against this, businesses should make sure that information about how to make a complaint is available, in accessible language, to all employees, without them having to give their names or other identifying information to access it.

In the UK, the House of Commons Women and Equalities Committee, made up of a group of MPs including Jess Phillips, said 'It is time for the government to put sexual harassment at the top of the agenda.'[50] The report recommended a change to the way that NDAs were used in sexual harassment cases, which has since come to pass. I hope that with increased awareness, and governmental pressure, we can take strides in addressing workplace sexual harassment and working towards eradicating it.

I hope that the history of the oversexualisation and availability of Black women's bodies, without their consent, does not also have to be the future. We can all, at whatever level we are in a business, be a part of making that change – from putting into place robust systems and structures, if we are in a place to do or, or simply listening to, believing and standing in solidarity with victims, holding abusers and the businesses that protect them accountable.

Getting a Seat at the White Table

Candice Brathwaite

*Candice Brathwaite is a* Sunday Times *bestselling author, TV presenter and contributing editor at* Grazia *magazine*

Sometimes, I think it's important to recognise that sometimes the harshest enemies do look like us – and that can be a bitter pill to swallow. I don't think that conversation gets shared so publicly because BAME people are correctly insular, because we're trying to protect ourselves, so it's not every conversation that comes to the forefront. And so, for any women reading this who are like, 'This is all cool, but I don't even have support from women that look like me', your angels will come. But you also have to leave space to understand that there is – and not just in work but in a BAME woman's life – there is so much trauma before you show up on the scene, that it's never about you. It's never about you. And you don't have to play nice with people. Like my friend always say, 'All skin folk ain't kin folk' – just because the other woman in the office is Black, it doesn't mean you have to put up with her being snarky or belittling you, because you want to show a united front. In the workplace especially, put your oxygen mask on first, sweetheart. And let her deal with her issues. But I know there were many times when I would really try to ignore what (now that I'm a grown-up I know) was bullying by other Black women, or just out-and-out bitchiness. But I just wanted to be likeable, like, 'Oh, you know, we're both Black, we're in this together.' Sometimes you're not.

That's hard because being in the working world as a woman of colour is lonely. It's lonely. And it's not something we want to say because it doesn't feel inspiring for young Black women trying to get the job of their dreams, but it is going to be lonely. The higher up I go on my career climb, the quieter it becomes. For sure.

I think when I was getting started with Make Motherhood Diverse I was like, 'Come, Black mums, let's all join hands and skip into the sunset' and the resounding response was, 'No, fuck that – we do not want to even think about infiltrating a space that has solely been controlled by white faces. We are not interested. You are a fool for this. You are a *fool* for this.' I felt like Black mums online were sitting at this really crowded table, where there were only three buckets of stale KFC, and white women were at this opulent, decadent place where it was all quinoa and avocado, and there was *too much* food at the table. And not only was there too much food, but there was also so much space between each chair. And so then, I feel like at one point I was the only Black mum who stood up and was like, 'Wow, you see how they're eating? That's a bit mad. Don't you want to eat at that table?' 'Oh god, no. God no.' In the early days, people were pulling on my skirt hems, 'Sit down, sit down, don't even look at their table. Make do with what we have here'. And, metaphorically, I dragged myself from that table, slapped myself down at the white table, and was like, 'Sis, let's eat.'

Now, that's not to say that the

reception at the white table was always welcoming, I think on the surface it was all giggles and 'Yes, sure. Would you like to give her this small plate of avocado to keep her quiet and happy?' and then, as it went on and it seemed like I was never going to take my chair back to the KFC table, the mask began to slip, and so many more white women just became supremely annoyed by my existence, and they let that show. But I'm eating hella good now. There's too much food for me. And now more women of colour have got up from the KFC table, and they're like, 'Actually, can I sit here?' 'Yeah, you can, babe, you can. So come, take this chair.' You know?

So, that was a really proud moment. But in the beginning it was a really lonely fight, and no one wanted to back me on that. And I think that's how it's going to be for a lot of women reading this book. You may find that in the early days especially no one wants to have your back in the staff room, or in that meeting, even the people you'd most expect, and you're gonna have to really pull on whatever it is inside of you that's telling you to press on – because there is no other option.

Sometimes it feels like there's a choice between walking the plank and getting back on this burning boat. Life has taught me that there is always a dinghy in the sea. You're going to flap your arms a bit and be a bit cold, but a safety net will appear. So, I don't have a choice now, I just have to go.

# Daniellé Scott-Haughton's Favourite Thing About Being a Black Woman

"Oh, it's the friendships. That's my favourite thing – it's the friendships. And the reflections of myself in other people, and the way that we hold each other with words, and encourage each other and – oh God, yeah. My sisterhoods are my favourite thing about being a Black woman. And those are intergenerational, they exist between women in my own age group, but also older women who are able to give me insight into how things have developed and how some things have stayed the same. It's the sisterhoods that are my favourite thing about being a Black woman."

## CHAPTER 7

# THE CONCRETE CEILING

'If I didn't define myself for myself, I would be crunched into other people's fantasies for me and eaten alive.'
AUDRE LORDE

**B**lack women are still not, in any great number, reaching the topmost positions in businesses.

We're all familiar with the trope of the glass ceiling – women reaching a certain point in their careers and being unable to get any further. They can see the top, they can see the light shining down, it seems almost within touching distance, but every time they try to get there – *bop* – they hit their heads on some invisible barrier holding them back from ever quite achieving it.

The glass ceiling is incredibly frustrating – you can see what's possible and where you want to go, and you don't hit your head against it until you've climbed to *nearly* the top of the ladder. It's so close you can almost touch it. Almost.

The glass ceiling is much more applicable to white women than it is to Black women. To have got up to that tantalisingly close level, and to feel that it's in your power to reach the next level, you need to be able to see yourself there, at least in your mind's eye. The upper echelons of business achievement need to look like a space that you could be a part of, and for many Black women, even visualising themselves in that space is more than we're able to conjure up.

The dual barriers of sexism and racism come together as misogynoir, and misogynoir changes the ceiling above Black women's heads from glass to concrete.

The glass ceiling lets the light in, but the concrete ceiling that hangs above the heads of Black women doesn't do that. With the concrete ceiling above you, there's no light, only shade. You can't see the sky, and you certainly don't feel that with just one more almighty stretch you could reach out and touch it – with a layer of concrete between you and it, you can't even know for sure that there's a sky out there, at all.

White women who enter the workforce now, in most industries, are likely to start their working lives seeing women who look like them in senior positions and may be able to take from that some hope that they too, with enough hard work and tenacity, can reach that level. Black women are still very unlikely to see role-model examples of women who reflect themselves, early or even later in their careers. They're not reaching for the stars to emulate these women, as the role models don't exist in the first instance to offer an aspirational target to aim for.

In fact, despite 43 per cent of Black women versus 30 per cent of white women believing that they can succeed in a position of power, according to a Business in the Community report first published in 2015, the overall number of Black British people (of any gender) in top management positions decreased by almost half (42 per cent) between 2007–2012.[1] The authors of the study suggested that a number of UK sectors 'appear to be closed off to BAME people when it comes to leadership opportunities', since 74 per cent of 'BAME' people who had made it to leadership positions were clustered within just three sectors: banking and finance; distribution, hotels and restaurants; and public administration, education and health.

What this means in practice is that all too often Black women watch those around them, often those who were more junior to them, who they have spent their own time and energy training, being promoted above themselves, and get the message loud and clear – others can work towards the sunlight but their place is in the gloom.

If you are not a Black woman, ask the Black women in your lives if this has happened in their careers. In my experience, nine times out of ten if you ask a Black woman about this she'll be able to tell you in the blink of an eye about at least one job where she's worked away – she's become the person who holds the knowledge, oils the cogs, trains the new starters, knows where the bodies are buried and the papers are filed. She has done all of this, as well as her actual job, only to come in one day and find that, yet again, one of those people she trained up, showed the ropes to, and helped along the way has been promoted. Above her. Sending her the clear message that her years of work, experience and the very knowledge-sharing that has allowed those team members to flourish, mean nothing when they're within her Black, female body.

> I would train up people at the radio station [where I was the only Black woman] and they would get promoted over me, and I'd be like, 'What? What's going on? Is it because of . . .' I don't know, because they don't tell you.
>
> – Lekia Lée

Whilst there have been pushes for greater gender diversity in senior roles, up until the Black Lives Matter movement of 2020, race has largely been left out of the discussion, meaning that Black women have not reaped the benefits of this diversification push to anything like the extent of their white counterparts.[2]

So, what is it that's holding Black women back from breaking through that ceiling and reaching the top roles in their professional lives? What happens to Black women who, frustrated with the blockers in place in traditional employment, choose to go it alone and set up their own businesses? Is this self-structured model the recipe for success for Black women held back in other spheres, or do they face more of the same barriers when seeking investment and growth opportunities?

> In the UK we're very much socialised to stay in our box. That's the class system, and people of colour tend to by default be on the lower end of the class system, just because people always assume you're working class when you're of colour, even if you're not, and so the thing with it is that it also limits your vision of what's possible.
>
> *– June Sarpong*

## See it to be it

Representation matters.[3] I mean, it *really* matters. Seeing yourself in others offers examples for us to model ourselves after – whether it's a mentor, a boss, a manager, or even a fictional character with a strong resemblance to us in one way or another. Seeing life's possibilities being attained by someone with whom we can feel an affinity makes things seem just a little bit closer, and more possible for us, too.

Seeing someone like us achieving things that we might not have even thought possible before allows us to visualise ourselves in that position. It allows us to imagine, for a moment, ourselves in a life that we might never have dared to dream of before – and that's important. Really important. But that's not all. Even more than that, it allows us to open up our minds, and to dream even bigger. It allows us to *build* on that image. If *that's* possible, who knows what else might also be? Suddenly we're invited to imagine a whole world of possibilities for ourselves that might simply never have crossed our minds before – and that's magic.

I know what it did for my life – it was when I saw Steve McQueen win a BAFTA for *Hunger*. I thought Steve McQueen was white. I really did, I didn't know. I saw *Hunger* everywhere because I was at the BFI at the time – I think I had made *Tight Jeans* already and so I was at the festival, and Steve McQueen was on everybody's tongues. I saw a poster for *Hunger* with Michael Fassbender on it – it never occurred to me that it could be a Black man who made the film. I just presumed it was a white dude. And so I remember watching the BAFTAs at my friend Tamana's house, and they said, 'The winner is Steve McQueen', and this big Black dude stands up, and I said, 'Oh my days, get out of the way, man, what are you doing?' because I thought he'd stood up and got in the way of the white people that were walking. So I thought, 'Oh my God, he's still standing, what is he doing?' And then he walked, and he carried on walking. 'Wait . . . wait!' I was literally shouting, 'Steve McQueen is Black!!' and my friend Tamana replied, '. . . you didn't know?' and I screamed, 'Fuck no, I didn't know! What are you talking about?'

I'll never forget when he stood up, and you know, it's BAFTA, so there weren't many other Black people there. So this random Black dude stands up and I thought, 'What's uncle doing? What's going on?' I couldn't believe it. And then, then he said something that changed my life – he stood up there and he said, 'Mum, you were right. We do have to work twice as hard,' and then he sort of bopped off. Like, it wasn't no grateful speech, the dude picked up that award with an air of, 'Yeah, yes, of course, I would have this award,' and I couldn't believe it. And at that moment I felt like, 'A Black man made a film about the Irish hunger strikes, and he's up there winning a BAFTA for it. Nobody can tell me what I can and cannot make. Ever.' I was 25. I was 25, and since that moment, it hasn't changed. You can't tell me nothing. You can't say nothing. When I get scripts people still say that because I'm a Black woman I should only make such and such things, like, no. No one is putting me in a box. I won't allow myself to be put in a box. I will make the things that talk to me. Steve McQueen is my mentor – he just doesn't know it yet! Every interview he did for *12 Years a Slave*, I watched every single one of them. I thought, this guy is so honest, and so himself, it gave me the confidence to be like – I'm just never not going to be myself.

– *Destiny Ekaragha*

The power of representation doesn't only work in one direction; our dreams can absolutely be made bigger by the people who we're able to see ourselves in, but in our careers, we are not only impacted by who we see ourselves in, but also by who can see themselves in us.

People, on the whole, are drawn to those who remind them, to some extent, of themselves.[4] It's natural – familiarity makes us feel safer, whether it's similarities in race, educational level, social standing, or values, we have a natural shorthand with people who remind us of us. We're inclined to take small similarities and overstate them in our minds[5] – increasing our perceived areas of similarity beyond the areas that we have evidence for, literally projecting an image of ourselves onto the other person.

I would argue that our tendency to take singular or small similarities and extrapolate them into larger sets of similarities goes both ways. This means that we not only have the ability to take small similarities and grow them into affinities and positive relationships based on very little, I believe we also do the same with obvious differences – mentally building them up to the point that seeing our areas of similarity with some people can feel insurmountable, without being blinded by our differences, however small they might be.

People in management positions are more likely than not to be both white and male,[6] and may find it difficult to relate to, or see themselves in Black women – people who are obviously, externally different to them in the key qualities of both race and gender.

Researchers refer to Black women's status as the 'double outsider' – kept out of the consideration space, and away from opportunities as a result of the distancing caused by both their race and gender.[7]

The double impact of not having access to positive role models of other successful Black women early in their careers, paired with a lack of affinity with their managers, can be particularly damaging for Black women. A key part of a manager's role is to invest in and advocate for their team members – putting them forward for new opportunities, assigning them challenging but not impossible projects, and making cases for their promotions and progression when appropriate. When this support is lacking, the chances of individual success are deeply reduced. As Baroness McGregor-Smith CBE notes in 'Race in the Workplace: the McGregor-Smith Review': 'All BME groups are more likely to be overqualified than white ethnic groups but white employees are more likely to be promoted than all other groups'.[8] I would suggest that managerial support, buy-in and investment in people who leaders see themselves in versus those who they don't, plays a substantial role in this difference, limiting the possibilities for Black women without them even being aware.

## Employer expectations

As well as not having the same level of investment from their managers, Black women can also suffer from a lack of a managerial vision for their future progression prospects.

When people who are in non-marginalised groups first think of diversity, their view of it can be relatively narrow – often stopping at recruitment and failing to take into consideration retention, development or progression. Instead of seeing the value that a diverse, inclusive and representative workforce can offer to their business, they can get tripped up by tokenism – believing that one 'diverse hire' is enough (please do understand that individual things or people cannot be 'diverse'), and by making that hire, they have 'done their part', and couldn't reasonably be asked for any more. This means that they can fall into the trap of being satisfied with, or even congratulating themselves for, getting a small number of people through the door into relatively junior positions, and not considering their futures beyond that.

I can't count the times that I've been told by employers that they've 'given me everything I've ever wanted' – without them ever having thought to actually ask me what it was I actually wanted, or having had the imagination to consider that my ambitions might be bigger than theirs, or what they had the means to offer to me. In their eyes they had 'given me' a job with a good salary, and so I should be thankful for that – rather than looking for the same progression opportunities of my white, or male, peers.

N.B. On the whole, people who are employing you aren't 'giving you' anything – they went through a process of interviewing and finding someone who they thought would add value to their business, usually within a predetermined budget. They found you, and they decided that the financial cost of your salary was lower than, or at the very least equal to, the value that you would add to them. That is to say, you are an investment to them, and smart businesses don't make investments without forecasting a return on those investments. Businesses, by design, get more out of you, financially, than you do out of them, which is fine – it's the deal we all make when we work for a business. We give them our time and expertise and they give us a salary (and hopefully the chance to learn, acquire new skills and build a network), but we should never feel guilty about 'taking' a salary or asking for what we deserve – businesses aren't people and you don't owe them anything.

Whether it's in conversations about salary, progression or responsibility, it's something I've heard countless times from many different people. Though at first it seems innocent enough, 'We've given you everything you've ever wanted' is actually an incredibly dangerous phrase. It means, 'Why are you asking for more?' It means, 'I think you're being greedy.' It means, 'You should be grateful for what you have' and 'I'm never going to take the time to actually ask what your dreams and aspirations are.' As soon as I hear that phrase, I know my time in a business is limited. An employer who says it is really saying they don't see anything more for you – they're reinforcing the ceiling over your head, and you'll have to move hell to break through it.

UK-based race equality think tank, the Runnymede Trust, commissioned a report with the best name I've ever heard: '"Snowy Peaks": Ethnic Diversity at the Top'. Included in the report's findings is that 20 per cent of Black managers surveyed believed that racial discrimination had been a barrier to their succession.[9] The report cited research conducted by the Diversity Practice stating that 70 per cent of Black women surveyed said that they had experienced workplace discrimination based on their race, and 65 per cent said they had experienced the same based on their gender.[10]

The prevalence of bias in businesses is also highlighted later in the report, when people of different racial backgrounds are asked to respond to statements about the companies they work for:[11]

- 'In my organisation recruitment at senior levels is based solely on merit' was believed to be true by just 32 per cent racially marginalised respondents, compared to 55 per cent of white respondents
- 'Prejudice and bias exist in my organisation and impact on day-to-day decision making' was agreed to by 45 per cent of racially marginalised respondents versus just 26 per cent of white respondents
- Only 40 per cent of racially marginalised respondents believed that if they asked for career support from their employer they 'who held this view' would receive it, compared to 61 per cent of white respondents having this view

This is backed up by other research that has shown that 'BAME' people have lower access to opportunities for workplace development,[12] especially in businesses where progression structures are informal. In those instances, despite Black women being 175 per cent more likely (22 per cent of Black women versus 8 per cent of white women) than white women 'to aspire to a powerful position with a prestigious title',[13] their lack of mentors and sponsors at senior levels means that they don't have the same access to advice, support or guidance in how to position themselves for these roles – or even to know when they are being recruited for.

Research has shown that the biggest barriers to professional success that African American people face are race-based stereotypes, more frequent questioning of their credibility and authority, and a lack of institutional support.[14] In fact, 43 per cent of Black women in their survey identified the lack of an 'influential sponsor or mentor' as a large barrier to their progression.

These opaque practices ensure that people without the opportunity to build up social or sponsorship relationships remain in the dark as others progress around and ahead of them, adding more layers to the darkness above them, making it harder and harder to both progress and even to see the opportunities for progression.

It's also not unusual to hear from Black women that they have worked hard, and achieved all they set out to, only to find that without their knowledge, the goalposts had been moved.

> Sometimes it has felt like the bar keeps being pushed . . . I've had a few experiences where I've felt like I've reached and even excelled the bar, and then the rules get changed. And I'm like, 'Ah, OK I see you now. OK.' We're knowingly working in a system that historically doesn't want us to reach a high level because of the threat that that could mean. Because of underlying fears, and underlying prejudice (or very overt prejudice), or anything in between. That's changing now but only because collectively we keep pushing back.
> – *Naomi Ackie*

## Double trouble: the race and gender pay gaps

I cannot express just how much I want people to get comfortable talking about money. I really believe that the fact that talking about money is so taboo is a total scam, designed to keep people in the dark about their own economic worth, and reduce their ability to properly advocate for themselves.

Information is power, and businesses that have properly constructed pay bands or renumeration models, and have put in the time and work to ensure they're minimising unconscious bias and the pay discrimination that can result from it, shouldn't be resistant to employees having discussions amongst themselves around their salaries.

Not talking about money only benefits businesses who don't want you to spot if you're being short-changed. In both the UK[15] and USA,[16] employees' right to discuss their salaries with their colleagues is legally protected. Which means that even if an employer says that payments and salaries are confidential, there's nothing they can do to stop you from disclosing. In fact, businesses that do try to ban these conversations, or insert clauses into contracts prohibiting these kinds of discussions, can be reported to regulatory boards.

The fact that these conversations are not banned doesn't mean, though, that you can demand the information. HR departments and talent teams will never, and should never, disclose a colleague's salary to you, and you shouldn't ask. This should be a conversation with your colleagues whom you have good personal relationships with in moments that feel natural and equitable – you should never force or pressure anyone who isn't comfortable, as well as your friends in other companies and industries. It will give you a good idea of where you sit, if you're in line or overdue for a pay rise, and if you might need to look at making a move to another company to make the most of your earning power. Talking about salaries is, however, prohibited if it's used as a form of bullying or intimidation. Don't do that. Talk to people who you have good relationships with, and be just as open and vulnerable as you're hoping others will be.

N.B. There are a number of things that can impact on salaries, such as working reduced hours, previous related experience in a different company, and level within a company, that you need to bear in mind when comparing your compensation, and when possible you should try to understand the full package. Many good employers will have public pay bands, and will advertise jobs with the salary listed – they lose nothing from this and employees, and potential employees, can gain a lot.

One of the reasons that speaking about money is so important, particularly for people from marginalised groups, is that starting from their very first roles, Black women are simply paid less for the work that they do. And I don't only mean that they're paid less than men, they're also paid less than white women, quite a lot less, in fact. The much-discussed gender pay gap impacts women, as a group, and their earning potential. The much less-discussed race pay gap impacts the earning potential of non-white people. And they both come together in that magical way that so many things – usually negative things – do for people with identities of inter-sectional marginalisation, to bite Black women twice. Meaning that even if they reach the top levels of their careers, they're still hampered by that legacy of deficit.

In 2017, in the UK, the Equality Act made it compulsory for businesses with 250 or more staff members to report their gender pay gaps, on penalty of a fine, public naming (and shaming), and an investigation by the Equality and Human Rights Commission if they fail to file their data in advance of the annual deadline (though this requirement was paused in 2020 during the Covid-19 pandemic for reasons I can't really understand, since it seems to me that in a time of recession and financial uncertainty for so many, having the data is just as important, if not more important, than ever). Soon the same requirement is hoped to come into place with regards to any racial pay gaps, but until then leveraging our networks for informal conversations is one of the most valuable tools we have.

Research has shown that if the gender and race pay gaps continue to close at the rate that they are currently, white women will achieve pay parity by 2059, whilst Black women will have to wait (work) until 2130 for the same.[17] In 2017 (the most recent data available) in the UK Black African women in full-time work faced a 19.6 per cent pay gap with white British men.[18] In the same period it's widely reported that American women were paid on average $0.80 for every dollar[19] white males were paid, a number that shrinks to $0.61[20] on the dollar for Black American women. That gap of $0.39 on every dollar adds up. A lot. In a single year it adds up to an average loss of $23,653[21] – which makes a typical lifetime loss of $946,120 over the course of a forty-year career, according to the National Women's Law Center.[22] These pay gap numbers mean that a Black woman in America would have to work until the age of 86 to accumulate the same earnings as a white man who retired at 60 to close the pay gap that she suffers due to nothing more than her race and gender.*[23]

Some argue that the basis of the gap is educational attainment. They assert that, on average, marginalised groups and women are less educated than their male counterparts, and so are in worse-paying jobs, because they are able to bring less value to the businesses they work for. This is proven to be untrue since, as we already know, the pay gap actually widens the more educated a Black women is, and is at its largest for Black women with bachelor's and advanced degrees.[24] People who make this assertion

---

* We need to give a shoutout to Chinese women for their monumental glow up. Not only have Chinese women in Britain closed the pay gap with white British men, they've actually overtaken them by 5.6 per cent. Interestingly, though, whilst this has been happening the pay gap between Chinese men and women has widened, with Chinese women going from 4.6 per cent below Chinese men in the UK, to a gap of 11 per cent over the past decade.

are usually the same people who say that the pay gap is a choice – because men and women, and people of different ethnicities, choose to do different jobs, which command different salaries. (To those people I'd say check out occupational segregation on page 29.)

There are others who argue that talking about money is a recipe for disaster. Chances are one of you will find out that you're earning less than the other, and awkwardness and hurt feelings will undoubtedly follow, ruining any relationship. Of course, there is a chance that people might not like what they find out, but that's kind of the point, and finding out you're being underpaid is, I think, better than knowing, and knowledge is power.

Finally, people have also argued that pay gaps don't actually matter. You found a job that you wanted, they told you the salary, and you were happy enough to accept it, so why should what someone else is earning have any bearing on how you feel, at all?

To those people, I say this: sorry, but you don't know what you're talking about.

The wage gap is about so much more than the number on your payslip. In fact, the wage gap is about pretty much everything. It's about the freedom that being able to build up financial security gives to you, which is everything from being able to save up to leave a situation or relationship where you're not safe, to being able to walk away from a role where you're not being respected or treated well.

Being underpaid is exhausting, it adds yet another layer of stress to already stressful, marginalised lives. Knowing that you have cash in the bank, rather than getting down to net zero or going into debt at the end of each month, is a huge burden to take off your mind. Even something as small and simple as a weekly food shop hits different when you're able to walk around a supermarket without needing to do the mental calculation of what's in your basket versus your bank account and what you need to be able to support your family.

Being underpaid means that what might be a small inconvenience to someone who has been properly paid, like a broken-down car, can spin you into months of debt. Someone who has been paid enough to have savings in the bank can fix a problem like that without giving it much of a second thought, but when you're living on a knife-edge a car breakdown might mean having to borrow money or go into debt to repair it. It might mean losing your transportation to work, and so losing your ability to earn. If you're a driver on a zero-hours contract it might mean losing your job, and the only means you have of providing for your family.

Having enough income that you can save some away each month means the possibility of building wealth, which can be put into resources for your community, your family, or yourself (you deserve nice things!). It means being able to afford tuition, or childcare, or put a deposit down on a home to own. It means being able to make investments and earn interest. Once you have money, getting more is suddenly much easier – but when you're suffering from the pay gap, twice, even starting out on that journey can seem an insurmountable challenge.

Money makes money, and being able to make investments like homeownership, or buying stock, can, over time, grow and become generational wealth, which Black people have traditionally lacked. Generational wealth is, in my opinion, the greatest unspoken privilege there is.

The double pay gap places a concrete ceiling not only above the heads of Black women, but over the heads of their children, depriving them of capital in the moment to the dollar value of the shortfall, as well as taking away the advantages and security that the accumulation and interest of those funds would have provided with a much longer-term view.

It's not that Black women aren't interested in these kinds of money moves, by any means, but there has to be some initial capital to get the ball rolling – and if our wages are being garnished, invisibly, before we even start, these opportunities are held out of reach of many Black women.

The wage gap is also about personal value. Paying someone less because of their race and gender is a very clear message – you value them less. The work you're asking them to do is no different, and neither is their output. All that is different is the value that you've put on their time and efforts, and I don't think any of us should be comfortable with that.

## Lack of access to funding and investment

Many Black women grow tired of constantly smashing their heads into the concrete ceiling of workplaces with problems and biases that they didn't create and aren't equipped to resolve. So they make the choice to leave traditional PAYE positions to start their own businesses or go freelance.

This is especially true of Millennial women currently, and Gen Z seems set to follow our lead. We no longer feel constrained by the same expectations, or images of success as previous generations, and are breaking out on our own to forge our own paths, on our own terms.

The idea of starting something of your own is tempting, tantalising, even. I know, that's how I felt when I left my PAYE role after I didn't think there was anything left I could do to progress. I had spent the best part of a year working on an acquisition strategy for the agency I was at – managing the paperwork, forecasting, finances, even beating the ambitious profit targets and leading on setting up a new international wing of the business. Finally, success: the deal was going through, our small agency was going to be acquired by a huge, multinational one – all of the hard work had paid off. We hired a space in a swanky bar and brought all of the team together to tell them the news. Myself and one of the agency's founders headed over a couple of hours early to hash out details and get things set up. Together in the taxi on the way there it was just him and me. I had been clear – this was work I was doing to make the acquisition happen because, for various reasons, it was right for the business at that moment, but I was very dubious about wanting to work for the new company myself. The type of work they made didn't excite me, and I knew that going from a small org to a giant one would mean a downgrade in title, responsibilities and learning opportunities for me. It wasn't until that taxi journey that I realised how right I was. He spent the journey to the announcement to the team telling me how I should make sure I stuck it out for at least two years to give it a good go and what a good opportunity this was going to be for me and my career (when anyone tells you something is going to be a 'great opportunity' for you, or talks about what 'great exposure' something is going to be – which is something they usually say when they're not paying you properly, or at all – it's the moment to start keeping a closer eye on them – they're always *always* up to something).

Thank goodness I trusted my intuition and made the choice to leave – I found out later that if I had stayed they would have given me a title that I had moved away from almost ten years before. I had worked hard to pull myself up the corporate ladder and staying in a place that didn't value me would have been a big snake to slip back down.

When I quit my boss said he was shocked, but to be honest he would have done the same in my position. Which led me to wonder why he'd be shocked – why was what he imagined for me so different from what he'd want for himself?

For me, setting up my own limited company felt like the best, maybe the only, way for me to take charge of my own destiny. I wouldn't have to work in someone else's structures or bend to their changing whims. I wouldn't have to push through initiatives that I didn't believe in or have to manage people who I never would have hired. My successes, or failures, would be down to me, and me alone.

I think for a lot of Black women, this opportunity to define and create their own value, outside of more traditional working structures, feels essential. It feels important and invigorating to have something that is truly ours, for better or worse. This might offer some more insight into why Black women are second only to white men as the largest group of self-employed entrepreneurs.[25] Black women are resilient, it's a word that came up in every single interview I did – when the odds are stacked against us, we will find a way. And so, setting up and running something that you have control over is incredibly valuable.

## Are Back women always better off setting up their own businesses?

In short, if you're a Black woman, and you're talking in terms of cash, the answer is likely to be no. I'm sorry. I wish it were different!

The majority of businesses set up by women are rooted in a need to survive and carve out their own part of the world, and are most often in low-paid industries and made up of unprotected zero-hours contracts.[26] But, of course, this isn't universal. There are also plenty of Black women who are launching businesses with ideas that can change the world, if they're able to reach enterprise level.

But the path to funding, especially for solo Black female founders, is far from easy. Black women, even once on their entrepreneurial journeys, continue to be bitten by the legacy of the impact that having been financially short-changed in their early careers leaves behind. When they move to set up their own businesses and begin exploring the funding options available to them, they often find that many of the finance options which are often essential in the setup of successful companies aren't available to them. In fact, according to the US Federal Reserve, over 50 per cent of Black-owned businesses had been turned down for funding, which is twice the rate of businesses with white founders (there was no data broken down by both race and gender).[27] They also pointed out that even when Black-owned businesses are approved for funding, they are still the group least likely to achieve their full funding needs, instead receiving smaller percentages and needing to try to seek out investment from multiple sources.

Black women, having suffered from the impact of the combined race and gender pay gaps, and without usually having the advantage of large amounts of generational wealth, often have lower personal wealth and savings than many other groups – which makes the process of securing a business loan both much more difficult and less likely. Instead, many Black women who start their own businesses are put in the position of needing to use their personal savings, including money set aside for pensions, to provide initial capital for their businesses.[28]

Aside from business loans from banks, venture capital is a path that a lot of start-ups go down for investment, but again, unsurprisingly, the odds are stacked against Black women in this funding avenue.

In America in 2018 alone, there was $85 billion invested by venture capitalists.[29] Of that only 2.2 per cent went to female founders, and less than 1 per cent went to female founders 'of colour'. If we look at the stats around tech funding between 2009–2017, as an example of a single sector, we can see that Black women founders raised $289 million in venture capitalist/angel investment. Which sounds good. Until you realise that is out of a total of $424.7 billion invested. Meaning that Black women received just 0.068 per cent of total investment.*[30]

I have just one more bit of bad news, sorry to be a bummer. Trust me when I say I'm feeling it too. Whilst investment seemed to spike in 2017, the gap in revenue between white and non-white female-owned businesses has been growing. In 2007, businesses owned by white women

---

* What's super, *super* interesting about those numbers is that of that $289 million raised in the eight-year period between 2009–2017, close to $250 million was raised in 2017 alone. We don't have the data from 2017 onwards, yet – but I'm waiting with bated breath to find out if that huge jump is a one-off spike, or the start of Black women having venture capitalist/angel funding pathways opening out to them.

had an average revenue of $181,000; by 2018 it had jumped to $212,300.[31] On the other hand, businesses owned by non-white women started with an average revenue of $84,100, which by 2018 had dropped to $66,400, with those owned by Black women having the largest gap.[32]

I wrote a piece last year about the *Sunday Times* rich list – there was only one Black woman on it, and she was on it because she had founded a business with her husband, who is white, and you wonder – would that success have been possible if it had been just her? There are rooms that he would be able to get into, he would be able to access the capital needed to grow the organisation. I do think it's interesting that we don't yet have that. And that's not for want of trying, or lack of ability – it's the lack of the ecosystem that you need in order to be able to scale businesses, and it means you need to have a different set of tools in order to navigate the system. It was fascinating. When I was going through the list of all of the names I thought, 'How? How have we got here?' when you could list tens of white women who have founded businesses. I think you have to be worth a minimum of £100million now to be on that list, and not one Black woman. Not on her own, anyway.

For me the thing that I'd love to see even more than a Black actor or musician, which is all well and good, is a Black business-woman – because we are entrepreneurial by nature and there is no reason why there are not Black women at the highest level of business, and that, I think has to be the next frontier. And then you've created jobs – and you create cultures that are completely different to the kinds of cultures that we're trying to challenge, and you show that they can be successful.

– *June Sarpong*

## What's causing the funding gap?

Black women are, as a group, deeply involved in their communities, and often start businesses with those community interests at heart, or make businesses that fill the gaps for services that they want or need – from lifestyle brands to hair or skin care, or training and educational services that have been overlooked up to that point. These propositions, with the expert knowledge of a founder who is a part of that community, and knows how to talk to and access potential buyers, should be no-brainer investment opportunities. However, that's not how things usually pan out for these Black female entrepreneurs. Businesses like these, which speak to the personal or community needs of traditionally overlooked groups, by their very nature, require some insight, knowledge or imagination on the side of those holding the purse strings – or at least a willingness to really listen to the lived experience of the founder and understand the market need that their new product or service is filling. I say imagination because, as an industry, venture capitalists tend to be a largely homogeneous group (white and male), who have historically invested in products designed to help people like themselves, and businesses founded by people similar to themselves.

Black women may have to spend more precious time in investment meetings proving their credentials and the need for their business and product, than people pitching products and businesses that investors are more inherently familiar with, and with the need for.

Female entrepreneurs have long lamented their difficulty of accessing funding through traditional paths. There are more stories than I can count of women in pitch meetings being asked if they were on the pill[33] (we don't want to invest if you're going to go off and have babies – you know what female founders can be like, type of vibes). Similarly, trying to pitch businesses that they knew would make a difference to women's lives, that typically white, male investors just weren't interested in or didn't see the need for – such as products for children or women's health.

This is something that June Angelides MBE, founder of Mums in Tech, heard over and over again from the women in her programme who were looking to raise investment. Speaking of one of the experiences of one of the cohort who had founded an app to help parents to find baby classes, she told me, 'She was saying that when she was raising investment, she really struggled to get the male investors to understand why parents needed an app for that. They just did not get it. She's one of the many women who came to me and said that an investor asked them if they wanted to have more babies or if they were going to lose focus on their business if they wanted to grow their families, and I thought, "That's just such a ridiculous question to ask, and you wouldn't ask a man in a funding meeting whether he was going to have a family." These are the questions that you'd hope a woman wouldn't ask if she were sat across the table.'

Black women have this same experience of people not understanding their needs or proposals, but with products and services that can be even further removed from the typical VC's (Venture Capitalist) lived experience, and with the intersectional invisibility of not looking like the traditional, or idealised, image of a successful entrepreneur. This lack of understanding of the needs and perspectives of people outside of the lived experiences of most investors is something that motivated June, after winding down Mums in Tech, to step into the VC space, as an investor for a family fund in the UK.

June is a Black female exception in a very heavily white male industry. In 2017 Harvard Business School released the Diversity in Innovation report, looking at the make-up of VC firms from 1990–2016, which found that during that twenty-six-year time span, the industry had been somewhat 'preserved in amber', showing little, if any, of the progression of other industries.[34] They found that under 10 per cent of people working in the space were women, and under 1 per cent were Black people of any gender, despite the fact that both women and Black people had a much higher percentage representation in educational programmes that often serve as funnels to careers in this financially rewarding sector. The fact that the VC world is a pretty singular group is no great surprise or coincidence.

My personal mission is to have visibility for founders from under-represented backgrounds, and for them to feel comfortable to come into a room where I'm sat as well, because previously there wouldn't be many people who look like them across the table. I'm conscious that hopefully that gives them that extra reassurance that they're being listened to and heard.

I think the angel world in general can be quite a closed and quite a secretive network of high net worths, who don't usually publicise that they're actively investing, so you do have to know someone.

And I think that's also the world of venture capital – it's who you know. Speaking of privilege, I think I am privileged in that I had exposure to this world in a way before, because I worked at Silicon Valley Bank and I kept close to a lot of entrepreneurs and VCs that we worked with then, so I sort of had a way in. But, ordinarily, I think it's very hard to get into the world of VC if you don't know someone in it. Not many firms will advertise on their website that there are roles – very often we have WhatsApp groups for VC including a Ladies of VC one, and a lot of the times they're asking people, 'Do you know someone?', so really, it's a closed network.

I think how venture capital has evolved, I guess it started with people who had access to large pools of capital, and I think the reality of it is that the people who could start funds came from a lot of wealth. There's that wealth that has been intergenerational, and so it's just been a case that parents have passed that to their kids, and if you've had a better start then it's just easier. You've had a chance maybe to go to Oxford or to Cambridge, and your friends have done something similar, and so you just carry on, and I think that's what we've seen. For a lot of the VCs, it's been in their families, and they've been encouraged down that road because their parents were bankers, or they already had disposable income – extra income – so they could slowly be dabbling in investments, and they've seen that growing up. What you're exposed to makes a huge difference.

*June Angelides, MBE*

*June Angelides, MBE is a Banker turned Entrepreneur turned Investor, best known for starting coding school, Mums in Tech. Named by the Financial Times as the 6th Most Influential Tech Leader and by Computer Weekly as one of the most Influential Women in Tech. June recently received an Honorary Fellowship at the Institute of Engineering and Technology and was awarded an MBE for services to women in technology.*

The singular nature of the industry is something that June has been actively working towards as part of a group called 10x10VC, which when it began was a group of ten Black investors (all that they could find at the time in such an overwhelmingly white industry) which mentors people considering a career in the field, and offers advice on first steps. It started as a WhatsApp group and as Angelides explained, 'slowly we started inviting people in. We had a breakfast and started chatting about, "How is it possible that there are only ten?" It was very bizarre. And we just started speaking more about it, and people started getting in touch and getting added to the WhatsApp group, and it's really been about having like-minded people to talk to. I think that's been quite powerful. It's a case of actually, we're here, but it's our duty to educate and make sure we're not the only ones, but that there's some continuity. We need to open up doors, and I think there's that consciousness that we want to open up this world to more Black people and mixed people that want to get into venture capital that haven't had the opportunity or been welcomed in.'

The homogeneity of the VC investment industry isn't only a problem because of the lack of representation of Black women in this well-paid industry but because of the fact that investors are much more likely to invest in businesses founded by people who share their gender or race. In fact, being from the same race increases the probability of working together by 39.2 per cent, stacking the odds even further against Black women who share neither race nor gender familiarity with the majority of potential investors.[35]

N.B. Just as building personal relationships with people different to ourselves makes us less likely to buy into stereotypes about people at a group level, the personal relationships of people working in investment plays a role in the types of hires they make – and thusly the people who are in a position to control investment capital and those who are able to access it. Similarly, to men who have daughters suddenly starting to think that maybe feminism isn't such a bad idea after all, research has shown that when existing partners in VC firms have more daughters than sons, they are more likely to make a female hire.[36] These areas are good for business – VC firms who made a 10 per cent increase in their female partner hires saw an average 1.5 per cent increase in overall returns each year, and 9.7 per cent more profitable exits, which is pretty hefty considering that overall only 28.8 per cent of VC investments end with a profitable exit.[37] There isn't yet research on whether having close relationships with other marginalised groups, including non-white groups, makes the likelihood of more diverse investments increase.

Homophily is the tendency for people to be drawn to, and trust in, people who are similar to themselves, feeling (usually subconsciously) that their similarities offer shortcuts to personal connections. This is shown in many areas of life, from marriages to friendships, working relationships and informal networks.

This is something that Lauren Cohen, Andrea Frazzini and Christopher Malloy, when researching the article 'The Small World of Investing', found also to be true in decision-making around who to invest with, and in: 'A direct implication of this "birds of a feather" phenomenon is that venture capitalists prefer to hire, invest in, or co-invest with those that are similar to themselves in characteristics such as gender and ethnicity.'[38]

We're underestimated quite a lot, especially being a Black woman in business. It's hard. I find it really hard. Especially being a solo Black female entrepreneur. There was one story when I was early on in the business and I went to this guy – he was quite senior in a FTSE 100 business and I went to him to ask him for funding. When I met him, he really chastised me and was like, 'Oh, you're an underdog, maybe in a few years' time you'll be at a certain level'. It was just very, very patronising. It's especially hard if you're solo. I think if I had known I maybe would have got a co-founder. Because being a solo back female founder is so tough. It is really, really tough, and you know what people always said to me? They always told me to get a white co-founder, a white male. That's the advice I've been given, you know – 'If you really want to get the big bucks, get a white, male co-founder and he can just be silent, just to bring in the money.'

— *Vanessa Sanyauke*

Having shared characteristics between a business owner and a potential investor does make the likelihood of an investment happening higher, but it isn't necessarily a recipe for a fruitful relationship. In fact, it can be damaging to the investment's outcome. Homophily reduces the likelihood of an investment's success, particularly early-stage investments.[39] A lack of diversity in the investment team reduces the chances of success between 26.4 and 32.2 per cent.[40]

However, this information doesn't seem to have sunk in yet, and we're still seeing the investors who control funding pathways placing value, consciously or subconsciously, on shared characteristics and comfort rather than the business proposition, or the fact that the less homogenous teams make for better outcomes.

In this closed industry, the lack of diversity damages both Black women's chances of success, and the performance of investments.

## Setting your rates

Regardless of the business, or the funding that Black women are or are not able to secure, every product or service needs to set their rates, and get buy-in from potential customers or clients.

> I think it was tough, I had to prove myself because I was a Black woman running a business and working with corporates. I had some clients who were supportive and some that were quite sceptical in the first year, so I felt like I had to work extra hard to kind of prove my worth. I definitely figured out that I was severely undercharging for my services and coming up much, much cheaper than businesses that wouldn't deliver the kind of quality that we were – and I still experience it. I know that if I was a white man and I gave a ridiculous price I wouldn't be questioned, but being a Black woman, and a Millennial, we still get questioned over 'Why is this and why is that?' Even now that I'm seven years in I still hear, 'Oh I don't know, I haven't got the budget' and I think now I'm just more confident to say, 'Well, thanks, but no thank you,' but you know, when you're starting out and trying to grow your business full time, you'll just kind of take anything.
>
> – *Vanessa Sanyauke*

In order to make sure you're not short-changing yourself, do your research and set your rates in line with comparable businesses. This can be an intimidating thing for business owners to do, especially in the early days where your instinct is to do everything possible to make your new business a success, and giving discounts and building up favours feels like a good way to do this.

The problem with this approach is that once a rate is set, it can be difficult to unset it. When I was COO, I started by doing an audit of the P&L, and it quickly became apparent that there was work to be done. The rate card had never been formalised or checked against industry benchmarks, so that was one of the first tasks I gave myself – setting competitive rates. The founders were nervous – knowing the value of your own work is hard when you're close to it, and there's a fear that overcharging (or even charging correctly) will mean that your work will dry up and everything will fall down around your ears. Let me first promise you that this isn't true. If you have a good product, businesses won't run away from you charging a reasonable market rate. In fact, it can even change their perception of your business from something low-value and disposable to something valuable. Getting an external pair of eyes is helpful, whether it's an adviser, a non-executive director or simply a new senior hire – they're able to objectively assess the value of your product or proposition, and help you to make sure you're charging fairly for it, for both sides.

The second thing I found in my financial audit was that we had a number of small legacy accounts that were doing more harm than good. The work that needed to be done on these accounts was unexciting and the team couldn't work on them for too long before losing interest and becoming dissatisfied with their roles. The clients had known the business since it was tiny, and so didn't treat it with the respect it now deserved, and they were paying a fraction of the rate that other clients paid despite having a higher cost of sales. It was clear that the clients that contributed to a fraction of the businesses profits, whilst costing the most to run and making the team unhappy, weren't going to be able to continue existing in its current form. They were resistant to the new pricing structures, and wanted to continue to get the same work that they always had, for the same rock-bottom price. In the end, I was able to convince the co-founders of the business I worked for to drop the clients entirely, despite their concerns. The result was an almost 200 per cent increase in turnover in a twelve-month period as we were able to stop spending time and effort on low-yield projects, and focus that same time and energy in the more profitable and interesting clients.

### Structuring conversations about fees

Each industry is different, but the two key takeaways I learned from leading financial conversations was not to let a client control both sides of the conversation, and to be prepared to walk away if something couldn't work. Your time, your knowledge, your skills and your expertise is all invaluable, and not something you should ever feel pressured to give away for free.

If you're setting up a business, whether it's a side or your main hustle, the first question I'd always want you to ask first of all of any and all potential clients is, 'What budget did you have in mind for that?' Not, 'Do you have a budget for that?' Simply flipping the question in this way and asking for an amount, even a ballpark one, sets the expectation that your time is valuable, and you should be fairly compensated for it. Whilst 'Do you have a budget for that?' entertains the idea that the answer could be 'no.' 'What budget do you have in mind?' leaves less room for ambiguity.

The one thing I'll never agree to is a client controlling both sides of the conversation. 'I have £10k, and for that I want XYZ' simply doesn't fly. They can set the budget and you can use your pricing structures to confirm what you can offer in return, or they can tell you the level of service they need and you can quote them a price. But no client should be one-sidedly driving both the price and output of your work.

Where possible, share rates in advance. It's very normal to have different rates for different clients, within reason. A multi-million pound international company can afford different rates to a small start-up or charity – don't be afraid of reflecting that in your rates.

If you don't learn your worth – or if you do, but keep giving discounts on it – you'll still be in the darkness under the concrete ceiling, but one that you've had a hand in building for yourself. And I want more for you than that.

## OK, so how are we getting out from under the concrete ceiling?

I think we can all agree that under the oppressive weight of the concrete ceiling, it isn't the best place to thrive, so with that in mind, what can we do to get out and into the light?

### Get comfortable talking about money

- Since the gender and race pay gaps come together to keep Black women in the darkness, we have to start shining a light on our financial situations. Start with your Lady Gang, your partner, your friends. Look up industry and role benchmarks on sites like Glassdoor that filter by level and city. The first step into the light is finding out if you're being fairly compensated. Money isn't everything and different industries get paid different amounts, but there's no way that within the same industry, or within the same company with the same levels of experience, you should be getting short-changed because of your gender and race. None at all.

- Same goes for if you chose to branch out on your own – look for investment groups that are specifically set up for racially marginalised people or women. If you can find one that specifically invests in Black women in your industry, go for it with everything you have.

- Once you have a business up and running, don't give discounts on yourself. If your product is good, people will pay the standard industry rates for it. Work with outside eyes to get advice on your pricing structures – don't let imposter syndrome push you back under the ceiling.

I think I'm open enough now online that brands don't even call me or my management if they're not talking money. It's just not happening. And I'm never going to ask someone to do something for free – it's never going to happen, so you can just shelve that idea. No, there are no freebies here. Paying people fairly, especially brands who make your fee in a minute at a checkout sometimes, it's just not going to fly. It's also cool to be in a position where I know the usual fees for these kinds of things – so I'm not trying to get anyone else short-changed either. You're not going to say, 'Oh, you know, 15 quid for the day and some sandwiches' because no, just piss off. Make it make sense. You know? I really believe in that.

– *Candice Brathwaite*

## Be prepared to move to get what you want

Black women are promoted at lower rates than white women, or men. With this in mind, be prepared to explore opportunities in other businesses in order to progress. Businesses aren't people, they're not families, and you don't owe them anything. If they're not valuing you by promoting you in line with other employees (when you're ready and deserve it), then you shouldn't feel bad about taking your expertise elsewhere. Companies that deserve your talents won't underpay you or make you feel guilty for advocating for yourself.

## Know when to stretch the truth

If you decide to move on to a new company, and work with a recruiter to make that move, know that you can stretch the truth. Since we're historically underpaid from our very first roles, if a recruiter asks, 'What were you on in your last role?' or 'What are you looking for in terms of salary?' feel free to embellish. I've only ever seen two job-application processes that have asked for salaries and said, 'We check this'. Before you start applying for roles, do some personal benchmarking, look at websites with industry averages, speak to any industry bodies you can, look at job ads that list salaries and position yourself accordingly. If we ask for too little, based on what we've been told we're worth from our previous salaries, the gap will not only follow us but continue to grow with us.

## Use informal networks

Research has shown that Black women were able to be less affected by workplace discrimination when they successfully used networking strategies, and were able to use these networks to move to positions of greater power in their careers.[41] In fact, Black women's opportunities to progress from a worker to a supervisor rose by 39 per cent when making use of the assistance of her network. Even more impressively, the same research found that the opportunity to progress from a supervisor role to a manager increased by 500 per cent when Black women effectively used their informal networks.

It's amazing that the communities and networks that we as Black women build up through our lives and our careers are able to shield us from some of the mental impact of discrimination, but once again, it shouldn't be falling to us and our communities to take on this challenge.

It's clear to see that whether in traditional employment, or setting out on our own, the hurdles that Black women need to overcome to reach the top of their careers, and to be paid fairly for doing so, are manyfold. But they're not insurmountable. Being in the darkness, under concrete, can feel lonely and cold and isolating, and this is exactly why we need businesses and investors, to not only be aware of the advantages of having more diverse teams, at senior levels, but to work proactively to make those changes in their own workplaces.

Those of us who are able to, against the odds, break through the concrete ceiling can also consider ways that we can keep the pathways behind us open, through mentoring, sponsorship, and education and investment in the next generation of Black female talent. If you can't be what you can't see, then let's make sure once we're there, we give them something to see.

Starting Something of Your Own

Candice Brathwaite

**CB:** I have to admit, I got my first job – and I can't believe I got to do this, I think it might be the only privilege I've had in my working life – through nepotism. My dad was a partner of a really great law firm; I was 15 and he was like, 'Oh come and be the evening receptionist' – for 12 quid an hour! When you're 15! I was making cake. And I was doing it all of the summer holidays so I was rolling in the dough. It's actually hilarious. So, I left there and I went travelling, and I came back only to try to raise money to travel again, and just kept having to do these really . . . I mean, the jobs weren't shitty. Being a receptionist isn't shitty but I think the lack of respect given to people in front-facing service roles is really ghastly, man, ghastly.

And I remember, I was the receptionist at a popular agency at the time in Brixton, and apparently a package came in. I never saw this package. A white woman partner at the company accused me of stealing. I called my mum, completely in tears, because I'm being pulled into this meeting, and my mum comes marching down. And my mum was a single parent at the time, and I, as with most Black people from a really young age – and this something that I want to get across - was helping contribute to our housing costs (that is a really common thing, and it's not discussed enough). And then, just out of pride, my mum marches into the office and drags me out of the meeting and is like, 'Fuck you, fuck you, my daughter wouldn't do that.' And even as she was pulling me down the stairs I was like, 'Yeah, but

how are we gonna keep the gas topped up?' or whatever. Two weeks later they found the package. And I only found that out through a Black mate who was interning there. No one has ever picked up the phone to me, no one has ever apologised. And God, what was I, like 19, 20? And that was a massive wake-up call for me. I was like, 'Right, as a Black female in the working space, you are dispensable to these people.' And I didn't know how – I never know how – but I knew in my gut that the bulk of my working life would see me working under no one. No one. In that moment I was like, 'Girl, one day this isn't going to fly. And you just need to hold onto that nugget.' I didn't know what it would be, or what I would do, but I was like, 'One day, you will answer to you and only you.' Because that incident with the package, in the mind of that snooty woman, all she was concerned about was where her running leggings had gone. But in my mind, it was so layered. It was like my age, my sex, my race, all of those three things combined meant that I had stolen it. I felt that sting really early on.

**SW:** It's really interesting that gave you that motivation to say, 'You know what? Actually, I'm just going to do this for me.' Black women more than any other group start their own businesses, because why would we spend our time making those people money, when we could be making it for ourselves?

**CB:** I think that data [about Black women being entrepreneurial] is in our DNA. We all know the stories about the women who were hellbent on freedom during slavery. Or hiding rice in canerows. Like, when you just think of the logistics, and the art, and the deception. Actually, it can be no other way. For as long as the world has been trying to keep the Black woman's face in mud, we have been doing *bits* at trying to come up for air. So, it never surprises me to know that Black women are the ones who usually decide to go it alone. Of course, because we get that we are usually the masterminds behind situations. Even if we are working in nine-to-fives, it's usually our ideas getting stolen or someone trying to pass our work off as their own – these are not new things. That gets tiring.

And so for how long does the world expect us to be disrespected, and be underpaid at the same time?

And be grateful for it.

Again, it's so rooted in everything we've ever been through – it's that 'yes massa' mentality. Like, 'three bags full, sir, thank you'. Like no. No. I'm tired. Because I see so many white people, most specifically white women, doing sweet FA. For millions. *Millions*. Doing the bare minimum! I look at these businesses, I snoop at these business plans and I'm like, 'Are you shitting me? Are. You. Shitting. Me?' because the moment that an investor finds out that my mate's Black, then oooh, that pitch deck better be airtight.

So, I've now got to a point where, to protect my mental health, there are some people I don't even have conversations with. There are some things I choose not to see, because if I were to see everything, or point everything out, I would just forever live in a state of anger, so I'm like, 'Actually, I'm not gonna read that. I'm gonna unfollow you.' It just doesn't even register, because I'm like, at the same time, as angry as I am at them, and the system, I'm also like, 'You have no idea. You have no idea.' And if I could make money producing shit, maybe I would. But the only people I'm interested in having a conversation with are those who are willing to use their privilege to make the less privileged lives easier.

# Aja Barber's Favourite Thing About Being a Black Woman

Aja Barber is a writer and personal stylist in London whose work focuses on intersectionality and the fashion industry. Aja's writing can be found in the *Guardian* and *Eco Age*.

> I like how Black people love. I love Black people. When I think about the internet and what it would be without Black women – there would be no good memes. There would be no good jokes. I think of a world and an internet without Black people, and it is ten times less funny, ten times less fun, ten times less warm. The things that I have learned about what I do and am able to do – I wouldn't be able to if it wasn't for other Black women who uplifted me and pushed my work out there and shared me with their readerships – ten out of ten, I give them credit for allowing me to grow. I just love how Black women look out for each other and take care of the world. And they shouldn't have to. They shouldn't. It's so unfair, but yet we still do it. Because that's Black women, and that's what makes us wonderful.

# CHAPTER 8

# IS ONE ENOUGH?

'I am no longer accepting the things I cannot change, I am changing the things I cannot accept.'
ANGELA DAVIS

Female representation in businesses has come a long way. Whilst it's still not the norm for large companies to have an equal number of women to men on their boards, it's easier than ever to imagine, and find examples of, companies with more than just a singular successful woman in a decision-making position. But picturing the same with more than one successful Black woman? More than one Black woman who's made it all the way to the C-suite or the board? That's much more difficult.

We don't regularly see singular Black women in those positions, so the idea of seeing multiple Black women in these positions simultaneously seems unattainable currently. In 2019 only one in five C-level leaders was a woman, and only one in twenty-five was a 'woman of colour'.[1]

The temptation is to say that change is slow, it takes time, and as momentum builds, representation in these roles will normalise and the gap will close. However, the reality of it seems that the opposite may actually be true, and we might actually be seeing a regression.

In 2009 Ursula Burns was the first Black woman to become the CEO of a Fortune 500 company when she took on the role at Xerox, a monumental achievement. After serving as CEO for eight years Burns stepped down in 2017. Many had hoped, or even expected that her appointment would be instrumental in opening the door for others like her, and that when the time came for her to move on there would be other Black women leading Fortune 500 companies. The reality was that when she stepped down the number of Black women heading up those organisations returned to the level it was when she joined – zero.[2] And that is where it remains two years later.

In the last chapter we looked at the ways in which white women encounter the glass ceiling – the experience of reaching a certain level in their careers and then encountering some invisible, limiting force which stops them from climbing any higher. Black women face a double barrier – they are likely to not only look at leadership positions and see only men, but also to see only white people. The message they receive is that for them to really succeed they need to be exceptional, and exceptional by its nature doesn't come in twos.

## What's wrong with being the Onlys?

I speak from personal experience about the discomfort of being an Onlys at any level in your career, and one moment when my Oneness, my visible difference to everyone else, sticks in my mind most of all is this.

I was in a senior stakeholders' meeting with clients at the advertising agency I worked at, a meeting to discuss the project with the clients I knew, and their wider team I hadn't met yet. Like most advertising agencies, it was a very white space, and the clients worked in banking, so again, not exactly a Cyndi Lauper video. I'd previously mentioned to HR that there were no Black people in the entire agency of around 300 people, male or female, with a title that included 'head of', 'manager' or even just 'senior', so that should give you a rough idea of the level of diversity the company was working with.

I had worked hard to be invited to this meeting; I knew my numbers and my project plan back to front, I had spent hours prepping and planning, and the night before I had considered and decided against straightening my hair. This might seem trivial, but as many Black women know, simply having natural hair in a professional setting can be seen as an act of defiance in itself. I was still relatively junior in my career and had been wearing my hair natural for several years at this point, so I knew very well that having a natural afro would make me stand out even more in the white environment I worked in, and not necessarily in a positive way. And so for this important meeting I had considered straightening it to help me pass under the radar somewhat. However, even though I'm a Black woman, I'm mixed-race and have very light eyes and I can't deny that this proximity to whiteness has given me a lot of white privilege. I decided that if I straightened my hair to feel more comfortable in that meeting I would be, in reality, trying to 'pass' – to tone down my Blackness in ways that other, darker-skinned people didn't have the option of doing, and that didn't feel true to who I was or who I wanted to be.

I arrived to the meeting late – a man who was more senior to me had sent me to do some photocopying for him and despite that not being my job, and him being aware that this last-minute task would make me late to a meeting that he was also attending, I didn't feel in a position to say no. By the time I got to the room the introductions had been completed and people were finding their seats to get going. When I walked in, I was greeted by my client gesturing towards me and saying, 'Aaannndd here is our diversity'. That was my only introduction, I didn't get a name or a title, and because doing someone else's photocopying had made me late I literally didn't get a seat at the table.

I pulled up a folding chair at the back of the room and sat there, feeling embarrassed to have been pointed out in that way and to not have had the chance to have an identity beyond Other and Only. And that's where I stayed for the whole meeting; silent, embarrassed and belittled, until I got asked to go and make some more copies (really).

Once the meeting was over and the clients had left I spoke to the man who sent me to the photocopier as well as to the creative director and HR, and all they could say were the common gaslighting favourites: they were sure they 'didn't mean it like that', or I should 'learn to take a joke', or that 'it really wasn't a big deal', and so nothing happened and nothing changed. Those new clients still don't know my name.

This is a more explicit example of Oneness than usual. Microaggressions that Onlys face are usually just that – they're micro, but they're no less damaging in their aggression.

The experience left me feeling small and embarrassed, like I had been put in my place, and despite my hard work that place was much lower than I had anticipated. I felt that no matter how hard I worked I would still be limited by how other people saw and thought of me. This experience, in various forms, happens to Black women on a daily basis, and personally I'm tired of it.

Businesses have a responsibility to build an environment that by its very nature rebuts the idea that there is only space for one. If your company has people of all genders and backgrounds at all levels, particularly leadership, and fosters a collaborative and supportive environment, where progression paths, salary bands and development plans are clear and transparent, then people can see each other as collaborators rather than competitors, and invest in one another and the business for better outcomes for all. But how?

I can understand that it might sound tantalising, being the only senior Black woman. You could think of being the only Black woman in leadership in a company as an achievement – indisputable proof that against the odds, it was *you* who was able to succeed, leaving your competition in the dust and pulling your seat right up to the table. I've met several people who feel this way – they had to work hard, no one ever gave them anything, and if other Black women can't pull themselves up through their careers by their bootstraps that's no one's fault but their own.

The term 'pull yourself up by your bootstraps' is, by design, ridiculous – don't let anyone tell you to do it, or make you feel bad for not being able to. People use it to mean 'to succeed on your own without any help'. Firstly, that in itself is deeply misleading – whether it's your family structure, generational wealth, or simply the race, gender, body or country you were born into, everyone comes from somewhere and basically nobody is an entirely self-made success, though some people do have to work a lot harder than others in ways that aren't always obvious. Secondly, pulling yourself up by your bootstraps is literally and physically impossible – when the term was first used it meant 'to try to do something completely absurd'.[3] Like trying to go it alone instead of building up a support network of people who want you to succeed.

Structural bias in hiring and promoting means that as women progress through their careers, moving up in seniority, the number of other women being promoted alongside them shrinks and shrinks, typically leaving them with fewer and fewer women available to collaborate with.

According to the 2018 Women in the Workplace study, although women achieve more bachelor's degrees than men, women of all races are less likely than men to be hired into entry-level jobs, making it more difficult for them to get started in their careers.[4] This gender disparity doesn't end at entry-level positions, and it becomes even more pronounced when we add in race as a consideration. Which we always must. The study shows that 36 per cent of entry-level jobs are held by white men, but when we look at those who hold the title of manager, this jumps up to 46 per cent, and then 68 per cent when we look at representation in the C-suite. In the exact opposite experience to Black women, as white men progress up through companies they become less and less scarce, and see themselves increasingly represented in powerful, aspirational positions. The exact same optics that make it hard for Black women to imagine their futures in these roles tell white males that these positions were made for them.

In 2018, all other groups experienced the opposite of the funnel white men experience. As the funnel became wider for white men on their journey to better-paid, more senior roles, it narrowed for everyone else – women from marginalised racial backgrounds in particular.

If we believe the adage that you have to see it to be it, that the next generation of Black women need to see success modelled for them in order to believe they can achieve it, we're in for trouble. Unless we all take action. Particularly those who control the hiring and progression pipelines.

## It's lonely at the top

For those Black women who are able to move through the ranks of a business, the experience can be unexpectedly isolating. There become more and more occasions when they look around rooms, meetings and whole offices, and realise they are the only one like them. They have reached Oneness. (Reading that back, it sounds like a good thing – maybe like spiritual enlightenment. Trust me, there's nothing good about this type of Oneness.)

The experience of Oneness is isolating and lonely, and results in a huge amount of pressure and dissatisfaction for those who become Onlys. Women of all backgrounds who are Onlys report increased instances of bullying and microaggressions. They have worked hard to get to where they are – but the reality isn't meeting expectations. Research has shown that women who are Onlys have much worse lived experiences at work with 80 per cent facing microaggressions at work versus 64 per cent of women as a whole.[5] They are more likely to have their abilities challenged and be subjected to unprofessional and demeaning remarks, and twice as likely to be subjected to sexual harassment in their careers.

Women who are Onlys in their environments are 150 per cent more likely to think about leaving their jobs, as was Candice Brathwaite's experience. 'I moved to a different department every six months because of the way the role was structured, and the department I was moved to had no people of colour. And still I always tell people, "Oh, you know, I just found the work–Mum balance wasn't working for me." But I think that's partially a lie. I think that environment depleted me somewhat. I was like, "Oh, I can't do this every day" and so I left.'

Even though a staggeringly high percentage of Onlys suffer micro- or macro-aggressions at work, being the only person who looks like you can be deeply draining and uncomfortable even when there's nothing else going wrong in the working environment.

Even when things are going good, it's still hard to be the only Black woman. There was a job I did in France, and the crew were amazing, they were really lovely people, and the cast was really lovely, but, I'm telling you, even when it's nice like that, being the only Black person on set does something to you. You can't help but feel lonely. I thought, 'Is something wrong with me?' Nobody's being bad, nobody's being mean. Nothing. Nobody was being tricky. And yet I would still go home and I was like, 'This is not . . . right,' and I spoke to a few friends and I was like, 'Being the only Black person on set is really hard.' What it does is make you feel really lonely, and what it does is unmask the – I'm just going to say it – the racism in the game. Because, I mean, this is France, you can't tell me there are no Black people that can be on set – you can't. So it just was quite, sometimes it's quite – all of the time – it's quite upsetting when I'm the only Black person on set. On a personal level it makes me feel lonely, and on an existential level, if you like, it makes me feel, 'Oh, this game is rigged, for sure.'

– *Destiny Ekaragha*

An additional unexpected negative outcome for Black women when they find themselves as Onlys is the added weight of visibility, which means many Black women feel that they can't be their full, authentic selves at work. Black women in these positions find that they stop being invisible, the state that they most often self-report as feeling throughout their careers, and suddenly become *hyper*visible. They find that they are much more likely to stand out, and to be seen as a representative or proxy for all Black women. They report feeling heavily scrutinised, held to a higher standard, constantly on guard and left out – all of which has an impact on their mental health.

> When we fall, we fall and break our necks. We're not allowed individuality. No one ever says that to white people. White people aren't failing their whole race if they screw up. A lot of White people are allowed to change their minds and their positions, and people are still willing to listen to what they have to say. I don't have that grace extended to me as a Black person. I feel like people are kind of looking for a reason to see a mistake and be like, 'Aha! I knew I was right! I'm never listening to a Black person again!' No one ever feels like Black people are owed an opportunity to stumble in a public way and then come back.'
>
> *– Aja Barber*

Aja is far from alone in these feelings, as Naomi Ackie explains: "I think the main fear when you are one of very few existing in an elitist environment, is that anything you do wrong can send you packing – which forces people into "behaving well".'

This is a real gut punch – after working hard and succeeding against the odds, Black women who finally reach the heights of success in their careers are the left to experience the isolation and unhappiness of Oneness, and the unprotected exposure that causes, and so feel they are forced to consider leaving the careers they've worked so hard for.

## Why is this a business problem?

> Here's why it's important for me to not be the only Black woman at work. We spend most of our time at work, so you want it to be somewhere where you feel comfortable. I know people will be like, 'But just because you're the only Black person doesn't mean you can't feel comfortable', but there's that form of sisterhood that you get when you bond with somebody because they understand your experiences, and you being more comfortable means that you can

speak up more about things that might actually be beneficial for the company – that other people who aren't Black people, or Black women, can't see.

If you're there by yourself and you try and talk about this issue, they can brush it off because it's just you saying it. But if it's more than one person saying it then they're more understanding. I think the point I'm trying to make is there's more proof in numbers. So, if you have more than the token Black person, or the token Black woman, and you've got a number of them there who can support each other before coming to you with an idea that they have, or an idea of how you can approach something, just that way of them being able to be comfortable in that space is very important.

So, if you as a business go above hiring the token Black person, or the token Black woman, and you've got a number of them there who are appreciated for their skill, who can support each other before coming to you with an idea that they have, or an idea of how you can approach something, just that way of them being able to be comfortable in that space is very important.

*– Lopè Ariyo*

As I've said, people who are Onlys are 150 per cent more likely to think about leaving their jobs. Finding, hiring and training new people in a business, especially at a senior level, is a time-consuming and expensive endeavour – retention, although it can be difficult, is a much smarter and more time- and cost-effective way to work with valued team members. It is a much savvier business that can recognise these difficulties and build them into their talent support and development pipelines, rather than have an ongoing churn of talent becoming dissatisfied and leaving the business, taking their skills and experience with them.

If you're a business leader, and you've not spent much time before thinking about the racial make-up of your business, only to be looking around now and realising that you have a much more homogeneous workforce than you had noticed, you might quickly discover that even this first step of recognising the issues to fix can be difficult. But it's essential.

It's important to understand that in companies where intersectional racial and gender equality has been overlooked, asking Black women to share their thoughts and experiences can leave them in a position of feeling exposed, and worrying that they could face penalisation for sharing their thoughts. As Aja Barber said, 'There's always a moment when you're in the minority in a company when you're asked what you think and you have to make the call of, do you tell them what they want to hear, or do you tell them what you actually think?'

> Just the everyday microaggressions that you experience being a person of colour are a lot to deal with. I think it's even more exaggerated when you're in the huge minority, and often I feel like it's very difficult to have a voice and to be able to speak your mind.
>
> – *Natalie Lee*

The best way to end Oneness and the perception of there only being space for one type of person at the top of a company is for businesses to truly invest in creating an environment where a range of people are not only recruited, but are also invested in, retained and promoted equally and without bias.

We all like to believe that we live in a meritocracy, and so hard work and talent lead to success. But then why is it so difficult, when a friend asks about a summer work placement for their child, to give them the details of the blind applications process that all other applicants will be screened through, rather than immediately saying yes? If they are the most talented, the most deserving, that will make itself known and they will naturally float to the top of the meritocracy pile, right?

Rewarding people you like, have good personal relationships with or a social investment in (like the child of a friend) is easy. It's quicker to develop a shorthand and natural rapport with somebody who inherently understands your cultural context and frames of reference, and to feel comfortable in their presence. There is a lower chance of friction as everyone rubs along harmoniously, part of a well-oiled machine. The problem is that smooth running and no friction is not where great work, new ideas, creativity, or even profitability come from.

There is a bias known to psychologists as the fluency heuristic – it means people perceive information to be 'truer' or 'more beautiful' if it is presented in a way that is easier for them to access or (and this is the important part) is already familiar to them.[6] How does this relate to diversity in the workplace? Simply because people naturally accept ideas, suggestions and feedback as being more intuitive, more beautiful, truer, when they come from a person who is more similar to themselves. People with shared backgrounds and experiences are likely to have similar outlooks on the world and therefore approach problem-solving in similar ways, which makes their shared experiences smoother. This smooth and intuitive communication results in a natural desire to associate with people similar to yourselves; this is called homophily. Homophily can feel good, if you are part of a majority group, because it has the benefit of making people feel comfortable and giving them a sense of belonging. When we build more diverse groups we don't have this fluency to the same extent, because we are asking people to interact with those who are different to themselves, in terms of race, gender, sexual orientation or background. People who don't share our background are less likely to have an exact replica of our cultural references and fundamental beliefs. They are more likely to express views that can be challenging or contradictory to our personal outlooks and assumptions, potentially creating discomfort by challenging us to more deeply integrate our own positions and biases, which more homogenous groups don't require.

Knowing this, it might seem that hiring diverse groups of people is a recipe for disaster, unhappiness and friction within teams – something no business is looking for. Therefore, it may feel intuitive, when you're in a hiring position, to offer the role or the promotion to someone who feels comfortable to you – someone who you have or can imagine having shared experiences with and who feels unchallenging, 'a natural fit'. It's worth remembering that comfort doesn't usually breed greatness, so much as stagnation.

It's our responsibility to find overlooked and under-heard voices and experiences and bring them into the conversation to challenge the status quo. In doing so we challenge our teams to understand and anticipate different perspectives, and to integrate one another's ideas, to make them the best that they can be.

Uncomfortable as it might be, it's a very worthwhile exercise which can lead to better-performing teams and overall better financial success for the business. A 2009 analysis[7] published in the American Sociological review which looked at 506 companies found those with higher rates of diversity of race or gender had greater sales revenue, more customers, and higher profits.[8] When teams are less comfortable and challenge each other to reach the best ideas possible, not only do the results speak for themselves, but the problem of Onlys goes away. Two birds, one inclusive hiring policy.

When considering this it's important to remember that we are *all* made up of multiple, simultaneous, overlapping facets of our identities, and that we never pull out only one section or segment of a person to interact with. Instead we are always our whole selves. And so, we can't overlook the barriers that people with additional layers of marginalisation face, such as gender non-binary people and members of the LGBTQIAP+ community.

I think a lot of employers want a diverse workforce, but they're not making their workplace a desirable place for minorities to work, and they're not au fait with the experience of Black trans women. You can't expect minorities to be applying for your jobs, or to feel comfortable in your workplace, if you haven't put in the right procedures or precautions, or put into place the right environment and the right feel for those people to come on board. You wouldn't create a culture within your workplace that's very much a boys' club, and expect women to be applying for the jobs, because that's just not going to happen as women want to feel supported. So, if you want trans people in your workplace then you need to make sure that everybody is on the same page with treating people with respect. Things like putting pronouns in email signatures just levels out the playing field for trans people and makes it less of a thing. Like if someone is getting misgendered on email, it makes it so much easier to show a sense of solidarity within the workplace if everyone has got their pronouns on there. It's like expecting a trans person to wear a name badge but expecting no one else to. Making small changes like that can adjust the culture of the workplace and make it so much more appealing for minorities to apply.

*– Munroe Bergdorf*

## Reducing the number of Onlys in your workplace

The fact that businesses need to do better isn't news to anyone. For years and years people have been talking about the unfairness of the system, and the ways in which systemic bias disadvantages marginalised people. Many companies have talked a good game, they've said all of the correct things, have made the right postures and gestures, and so far it's all largely led to a lot of nothing.

After Stephen Lawrence, who wanted to become an architect, was murdered in a racially motivated attack in 1993 whilst waiting for a bus when he was just 19 years old, among other things an annual award and a foundation were set up in his name. However, the industry which he dreamed of joining has not made the necessary changes to become more inclusive, and in fact the number of 'BAME' architects in the UK has fallen in recent years despite several public commitments to increasing representation in that space.[9]

The same is true for advertising, the industry in which I have spent the majority of my career. Diversity has been a 'hot topic' for a number of years, with various pledges and benchmarks put in place to increase racial diversity, as in architecture. However, the industry's body language is not matching its words, and in 2020 it was reported by the IPA that not only had the targets set been missed, but that 'BAME' representation in UK agencies had dropped, year on year.[10]

The time for talking is over. The time for action is now.

I'm only about actions now – I actually look at people's work and I'm like, 'Was a Black and brown person involved in this? Was a woman involved?' I'm trying to do that a lot more because I want to feel safe at work. I want to double-check – I double-check everything because I'm over the walking on eggshells thing. I don't want to live my life like that. My work is most of my life – I don't want to spend most of my life second-guessing and worrying. I don't want that. I don't want to be the only Black person in the environment where I'm working. I don't want to be the only woman. I just don't want that. So now I'm just asking all of the relevant questions to make sure that doesn't happen – because the job is hard enough and I don't need all of that extra, extra stuff.

– *Destiny Ekaragha*

## The recruitment pipeline – what if the talent is just not out there?

I want to be clear that when I'm advocating for building a more diverse and representative workforce in an organisation, I'm not proposing a quota system – I can see the potential good intentions of having quantified, pre-set targets but I don't think quotas are the way forwards. At all. I believe that quotas lead to tokenistic hiring, schisms and hard feelings on all sides. People who are used to seeing themselves represented at every turn feel hard done by when quota systems are put into place and begin to make the – wrongful – assessment that less deserving and less qualified people are taking roles and opportunities that are 'rightfully' theirs. (The very epitome of entitlement.) At the same time, marginalised hires, brought in under quota systems, are left to worry about the legitimacy of their place within the organisation – and no one wants to feel that they were hired to fulfil a quota or be a statistic on an annual report. Everyone needs to be secure in the knowledge that they, and everyone around them, are there because they are the best person for the role.

So, I'm not in favour of quotas, but I do want to find a way, outside of that system, to make sure that businesses are able to be, truly be, the meritocracies we'd like to believe they are. At the moment, we've been taught to work from the collective understanding that society, and by extension, the workplaces that we are part of and have built in our society, truly are meritocracies – that they're set up to reward merit, which allows the best and the brightest to rise to the top, no matter who they are or where they come from. This idea of talent and ability being the only things needed for everyone to have an equal chance of success overlooks the systemic and structural racism that we know is ingrained in the very fabric, and foundations, of Western society. It relies on the idea that our world, our businesses, and the policies they have built, developed and protected are equal and accessible to all.

At the moment, that is simply not the case – the closest I think we come to it is when individuals or organisations describe themselves as 'colour-blind'. Just like I don't think quotas are the way forwards, I don't think racial colour-blindness is either. In fact, I strongly believe that claims of colour-blindness are very, very damaging.

When people claim to be colour-blind to race (you know, the people who say, 'I don't even see colour, someone could be green or purple for all I care, I'm colour-blind, I'm post-racial'), they are generally trying to say that race doesn't, or shouldn't, matter, at least not to them. They are saying that they treat everyone in the same way and would never even take someone's race into consideration when making a hiring decision in their business.

This is an idealised version of the world, and it's not representative of the world we currently live in. In my experience, it is almost always white people who claim colour-blindness and that in itself is a privilege.

In the West, white are the only group of people who don't have to think about or be reminded of their race, and the role that plays in their lives, on a daily basis.

When you say race doesn't matter, you're ignoring the daily hardships and othernesses of people who aren't like you, people who move through the world being immediately perceived as different. Non-white people, women, and particularly non-white women need to spend significant time and energy to simply be acknowledged or taken as seriously as cis, het, white men. Time that those men simply don't need to invest on proving their own humanity.

Colour-blind thinking may have good intentions, but in practice it delegitimises the lived experiences of marginalised people and overlooks the fact that different people, through no failing other than the colour of their skin, have a harder time accessing different positions and industries. The basics of intersectionality.

Acknowledging that you're not colour-blind (and no one really is, in the 'I don't see race' sense) is hard – it requires admitting to yourself that there's an issue of inequality that needs to be solved, and hard work to be done in solving it. It also requires acknowledging your own conscious or unconscious bias, which is uncomfortable for everyone, especially when race is involved. No one wants to feel like a racist.

Growing up, we've all been taught that good people are not racist, and racist people are evil, it's black and white, and so admitting your own biases can feel scarily close to having to see yourself as part of that second group.[11] But everyone has biases, and we need to understand and acknowledge them in order to see the impacts they have, and begin to go about counterbalancing for them.

> I don't agree with the idea that people don't see colour – I think everyone sees colour, and I think that might have an impact on how people interact with you as a Black woman. It's like we're invisible sometimes. It's like they see us but we're just irrelevant. I think that's the way we're treated.
>
> – *Vanessa Sanyauke*

Once we admit that we're not colour-blind we are able to look around our companies and the make-up of them, and question just how they were built and on what assumptions.

One of the most common complaints I've heard from people running companies where people 'just happen to' look like them is that 'diverse talent' isn't out there.

It's not that they're self-selecting with a bias towards people like themselves, it's that they're choosing the best of what's on offer – and that's all one type of person. By coincidence. It's not their fault that they just happen to all be from the same race, the same part of the country, and have gone to the same three to five universities. It's not a bias because they *hadn't even noticed* that the candidates all looked the same. In fact, if they were to go out of their way to diversify their hiring, they would just be filling a quota, hiring less talented people to meet some kind of PC nonsense, and *that* would be wrong.

I want to take a moment to be clear about something. Individual people are not diverse. You cannot hire a 'diverse person'. People are individuals, they are single entities, and no single entities can be diverse or homogeneous. What you can and must do is build diverse teams. Referring to individual people as diverse only serves to further other, and tokenise them.

It only takes a moment of interrogation to realise that it's simply not true that the talent pool of marginalised people is too shallow. The talent is undeniably out there: 44 per cent of Gen Z and 40 per cent of Millennials self-identify as 'Non-white', creating a rich and varied talent pool.[12] As Black women are a growing group who are underrepresented in professional fields, but overrepresented in educational attainment and qualifications, they are also overrepresented in the available pool of talent available to hire. The talent is out there, they're just not finding their way in or being welcomed.

The recruitment pipeline is the first touchpoint to be aware of when considering the people who will become part of your team – whether that's a self-selecting group of people who have applied directly, or people who have come through the filter of a recruitment service.

As a business leader, when working with recruiters it's important to set out your minimum standards. Your non-negotiables. I've had so many conversations with recruiters who have promised to find me the 'right man for the job' or referred to the company I was leading as a 'thirty-man office'. It's taken a while, but I have now developed a three-strike system; if I have to remind anyone that gendered language is unacceptable (it betrays an underlying bias about the person who will fill the role – I see it much more often from men, and *especially* when I'm recruiting for senior roles) on three occasions, I will end our relationship. It's as simple as that. If, after being reminded on multiple occasions they *still* can't use gender-nonspecific language, they are showing me that they have a conscious or unconscious bias. With that in mind, I can't trust that they're showing me, or are even able to attract, a good representation of the talent available without it being skewed by their own prejudices. I also can't trust that they're speaking about my company to potential new hires in terms that I'm comfortable with or endorse. Similarly, if I'm working with a recruiter and they don't show me any viable women or racially-marginalised candidates I won't work with them a second time. Again, it shows a narrowness of thought, and a limit in their professional network and outreach. I can't directly control the people they show me right away, but I can choose who I give repeat work to and who gets a commission from me, and I make that choice actively and consciously.

If I'm working on a role directly, not through a recruiter, and I'm only getting homogeneous applicants through, then there is some kind of disconnect between either the image or reputation of my organisation, the job spec or the places I'm posting that spec that is either not reaching, or not resonating with the widest groups of people that it can. And should.

## Developing a diverse recruitment pipeline

One of the things that I've learned to utilise (when I'm looking at potential places to work) is LinkedIn and Google. It sounds really silly but if I'm applying for a place, I'm looking number one at what their work culture is, and for me the ones that are more progressive (for lack of a better word) tend to have pictures or images of what their workplace actually looks like, and who's in their workplace. And although the people there probably don't appreciate it, I think looking at it from the outside when you're trying to come in is very useful. Twitter is one of my best networking tools, even more so than LinkedIn, because a lot of the time you'll find that people tweet about their experiences of where they work, and if they're the kind of people who you actually get along with, it's very easy to ask them for advice about how to get in there and what their actual reality of that workplace is like. But yeah, those have been great tools for me in terms of actually finding out what it is to work there and if there are actually other people like me there.

– Lopè Ariyo

- Have a public statement on your website outlining the commitment to diversity and inclusion in your business – this early touch point can show marginalised hires that they are valued, and shows hires from more represented backgrounds that this is an important value to you. When you mention the other values and culture of the company during interviews and onboarding, include the D&I statement as standard to everyone, and not just women and racially marginalised people (in the same way that information around the parental-leave policy, pension and everything else should be shared universally, rather than being siloed into groups depending on their life stage, marital status, etc.). It is a collective responsibility to ensure that your company's body language matches its words, and a company can't be committed to diversity and inclusion without everybody in the team at all levels knowing about it and how it impacts their rights and responsibilities.
- If you work with an internal talent, recruitment or HR team, make sure they understand, are invested in, and champion the value of diversity in the company. This group of people need to be the leaders in this area, they need to be fully aware of the business's plans in this area, and able to communicate them comfortably and confidently.
- Make sure you have achieved sustainable pay parity – now that there is a requirement in the UK for all companies with 250 or more employees to report any gender pay gaps, savvy job hunters will look at those reports and make an informed decision about joining your organisation or going to a competitor. It is likely that this requirement will be extended to race pay gap in the next few years.
- Be conscious about where you're posting roles, as different groups of people, depending on level, background, and pre-existing industry knowledge, read different publications and job boards – even within industry groups. Work with industry bodies and organisations to align on the best ways to reach traditionally excluded groups.

- Make sure the spec uses gender- (and race-) neutral language. You don't need to use pronouns in the spec such as 'he will . . .' or even 'he/she will . . .' The word 'they' is a non-gendered singular way to refer to an individual.
- Seek accreditations from organisations like Stonewall, Investors in People, and Creative Equals to show your values. They are simple ways to show a commitment to equality in your organisation.
- Have a zero-tolerance policy for gender or racial discrimination within the company, and stick to it.
- End job listings with the simple line: 'We strive to be an equal-opportunity employer and welcome applications from people of all backgrounds.'

### Establishing pay parity and salary banding

One reason Black women consistently give for leaving roles and companies is the feeling of being undervalued. Feeling valued at work can come from all sorts of things, including personal relationships with colleagues and managers, support and the type of projects people are given to work on. It can also come from knowing that you are compensated with a fair and equal salary for the work you do and value you add.

I'm aware that a lot of the information I've shared about the race and gender pay gap is from American sources, and so it might seem like a purely American problem – but I can assure you that that isn't the case. In fact, in the UK, according to the ONS analysis of median earnings, which compares people of the same level of education living in the same region, we see white male graduates aged 26–29 working in London earned on average £7,398 more than white female graduates and £15,473 more than Black female graduates working in the capital during 2016 alone.[13]

But this doesn't have to be the case, and we, as people who run businesses, can change this. When we hire people, we are in control of the salaries we offer, and we are in the unique position of having an overview of other salaries in the business – information that applicants and employees don't have. I implore everyone with the ability to make sure that your company achieves and maintains pay parity. It can seem intimidating, it can take time, but it's worthwhile, and it can be broken down into a few simple steps:

1) **Start with definitions.** What does pay parity mean? A simple definition would be that pay parity means ensuring that employees who do the same role, at the same level with the same contracted house, in the same location, are paid within a certain pre-agreed band, regardless of age, race or gender.

2) **Do an internal audit.** Audit all of the titles in the company, and all of the salaries of the people with those titles. Are they all within a reasonably narrow band of one another or are there any outliers? This is your starting point. At this point you may discover that there is a pay gap, but don't worry – we can fix it.

3) **Do an industry audit.** There are tools available to allow you (and your employees) to gauge average salaries by title, location and industry. And in many sectors, governing bodies and even large recruitment companies publish annual salary surveys, broken down by level, title and permanent versus freelance. For industries where annual salary surveys aren't easily available, both LinkedIn and Glassdoor have great tools to achieve the same manually.

4) **Draw up bands.** For each of the roles within the business, establish a maximum and minimum salary anyone with that title will be paid – this is the role's salary band. Make sure you're conscious of which roles develop/get promoted into which, and build a clear progression through the salaries in those groups to reflect that. The job roles in some departments may be more technical or specialised in their skillsets, and may require higher compensation than others. This isn't an issue so long as this is mapped out and reflected universally through that department to reflect those skills. Equal pay isn't about all roles being paid the same, it's about all people within the same level of the same role being paid within set parameters across the business.

5) **Make any necessary adjustments to existing employee compensation.** If there are changes to be made, now is the time to make them, usually by increasing the salaries of those who have been historically underpaid in their roles to bring them into the newly established bands. This is the most difficult period, but once this work has been done the system is established for all new employees and promotions going forward.

6) **Be transparent from the start.** When you put out a job post, include the salary band available for the role. Not only do cryptic terms like 'competitive salary' mean you risk wasting time on both sides by attracting people with misplaced expectations, it also begins the relationship with a taboo and establishes secrecy around salaries. When you interview someone for a role, instead of asking about their current or previous salary, ask their salary expectations and if they come in below banding, let them know. I've done this for people I'm hiring, and had it done for me, and it feels amazing on both sides. The value that another business put onto an employee, and their previous employee salary structure, doesn't need to be a part of your negotiations, or inform your belief of the value a new hire can bring to your business. The employee should be able to put forward their salary expectations, having seen the banding on the job listing without being constrained by their previous employer.

# Being Unafraid to Fail

## Daniellé Scott-Haughton

*Daniellé Scott-Haughton works as a scripted comedy and drama Development Executive at Balloon Entertainment, where she works with underrepresented, emerging voices.*

**SW:** I'd love to hear your thoughts about the pressures of Michelle Obama's mantra 'When they go low, we go high'.

**DSH:** I've worked in TV for four years now, in scripted editorial work, and it's a very small company – there are six of us, four are whom are in the editorial team. I am the only woman in our editorial team, and I'm the only Black woman in the company. I was two years into my job here, and I had just been promoted as a development executive, when my boss and I went to LA to sell our shows and speak to networks. We went for dinner in Malibu (this sounds so fancy, I swear to God it's not) and he was just like, 'I need you to stop being afraid of making mistakes. I am never going to fire you for getting things wrong – I'm going to fire you if you don't try.' It was a really big turning point, in terms of looking at my personal background and experiences I've had in and outside of the professional setting, where the fear of making mistakes has created this debilitating state where I'm not actually able to get things done. I think that the superwoman complex affects Black women, where we feel as though we must constantly be working, and we're not allowed to make mistakes. We also have inbuilt into Black womanhood, into the design of Black womanhood from the lens of white supremacy, the idea that we are easily disposable. If you're easily disposable, the best way to avoid being disposed of is to never make a mistake. But what that does is it strips your humanity away, it strips your ability to grow away, it strips away your–just that confidence that everyone should have in themselves, I think that Black women deserve that.

For me, it was so funny having that broken down to me by a white man – because he could see I was absolutely distraught when I made a mistake, really beating myself up, and he saw the ways in which that was getting in the way of me doing my work. The quote that I always go back to is that 'racism is a distraction' from Toni Morrison, and it's to keep you from doing your work – and because that comes from a racist place, that idea that we're not allowed to do anything wrong, it was affecting my work. I had already had mental health challenges, so that, compounded by racist ideologies in my head, that at any moment I was going to be let go, and I was going to fail, and I should never fail. But I was a junior exec, I was going to make mistakes, you know?

**SW:** It's really interesting that your white, male boss recognised that and had the insight, and the language to say to you, 'Don't worry about this' and the empathy to say, 'This isn't going to cost you your job'. It's really great. I don't think too many Black women who I've spoken to have had that experience.

**DSH:** No, no, I am extraordinarily privileged in that way, but it also comes with its own challenges. Because we have that level of proximity to each other, on an almost familial basis, it means that sometimes mistakes are made on both sides – and so that level of empathy and forgiveness, I have to also learn how to extend it too. I take that as a responsibility because I work in an environment that is conducive to my Blackness, that acknowledges my Blackness, supports my Blackness – because I don't leave it at the door when I walk in. I am Black and woman and queer and all of that together, and so the work environment that we have allows us to acknowledge each other's differences, make mistakes, say the wrong things, do the wrong thing, whichever side it's on, and allowing growth to happen.

**SW:** Until you mentioned it, I hadn't thought about the responsibilities that come with working in that way. I was like, 'Oh it's really great that you've got that', without taking the time to think about what it is that you have to give back. As the only Black woman in your company, is that a comfortable position to be in – to say, 'Actually, when you said this, this is how it made me feel and these are the implications of that'?

**DSH:** Yeah, but it didn't come straight away. It was something that we grew to be able to do. But I've always felt comfortable in my workplace – I mean, my hair's only been touched twice, which is a miracle! And both instances were

from people who were outside of the company. That environment where we were allowed to make mistakes and be open, it didn't come naturally, and it was something that we grew as a team. And because of all of the advantages and privileges that I am afforded working there – that's why I'm OK to have these challenging conversations with my employers because I feel as though that's the only way we're going to continue to break down barriers. It is hard work, but it's never too much – because I'm always thinking about the baby version of me, who's coming up. I'm always thinking about the other person, and I'm wanting to make sure that their journey is going to be easier. I don't want anyone to go through what I have, I also want to extend my privileges to others.

I think there are some barriers to understanding that when you have underrepresented voices in your company, you have to create the opportunities for them to grow, and the learning curve is steeper than it would be with other people whose families are in the industry, who have grown up around structures that kind of mirror the one that you're creating. But if you have somebody that has just raw talent, and a potential, that means that you're going to have to facilitate their ability to grow into the role that you have given to them, and a lot of that is about understanding and patience, and also learning . . . how Black people talk. And I mean, you can't apply that in a blanket way, but I think my boss is learning to understand the ways in which I communicate, and so he doesn't get his back up when he hears something that he doesn't understand, instead, he just asks me 'What do you mean?'. That's a big thing that we've both had to learn to do. I think it's that understanding of one another that has been absolutely vital in creating the kind of working environment that we have – and that we're still learning and growing.

# Destiny Ekaragha's Favourite Thing About Being a Black Woman

Favourite thing!? Everything! I always say that if reincarnation is real, I'd always come back as a Black woman! Even with all the pain, even all of the suffering, even with the difficulties that we have to face, I would always come back as a Black woman. I love being a Black woman. I love being a woman. I love my Blackness. I love the Nigerian ancestry that my Blackness comes from. I love the culture of being a Black African woman. I love the in-jokes that globally, Black women can understand. We're so similar, even with all of the different cultures, I love everything that comes with it. But mostly I think what I love about being a Black woman is that we have been tested. And even with that test, we still come out as wonderful and as magical and as beautiful as we are. We remain triumphant. And to me, there's nothing bigger or more beautiful or more precious, and more valuable, than that. Nothing. Nothing. We have been tested and we triumph every time. Every time. Everything down to the way we look has been discussed and, like a scientist came out and said he's *proven* that Black women are the most undesirable women on the globe. *This* is what we face every day, *this* is what affects our relationships. It affects how we feel about each other, and ourselves. We are universally, probably the most loved and unloved people on the planet. It's sad to think about it. And yet, we triumph. And we triumph as fabulous women. We're like, 'Yes, I will rock my hair this way! Yes, I will buy that handbag! Yes, I will take over your shit, because I am that!' And that, for me, is what makes us wonderful. I love being a Black woman, I wouldn't change it for the world. Even having told you everything I've told you about how hard things have been, I'd never, never change it.

# CHAPTER 9

# IS DIVERSITY THE SAME AS INCLUSION?

'I was going to die, sooner or later, whether or not I had even spoken myself. My silences had not protected me. Your silences will not protect you . . . What are the words you do not yet have? What are the tyrannies you swallow day by day and attempt to make your own, until you will sicken and die of them, still in silence?'

AUDRE LORDE

I s diversity the same as inclusion? If your company is racially diverse, does that mean you, by default, have an inclusive company? Is inclusion a natural by-product of diversity?

The answer to all of these questions is very simple. No. It isn't, it doesn't and it's not.

I think that this is something that businesses have been slow to learn, and slower to act on – so to be perfectly clear: not only is diversity not inclusion, diversity on its own isn't enough. Not by a long shot.

There's a Verna Myers quote that is often used to outline the difference between diversity and inclusion: 'Diversity is being invited to the party, inclusion is being asked to dance.'

I remember the first time I heard it, 'Oooh,' I thought, 'yep, that's great – that's it, she's nailed it.' But, as time has gone on and I've had more time to think about it, I'm not sure it quite hits the spot.

Don't get me wrong – it's a great starting point. But I think, if we're all in agreement, we should really push the comparison a little further.

The problem is that in both of Myers' scenarios, being invited to the party and being asked to dance, you lack any autonomy. In both situations, you are left waiting for the invitation from someone else. You are not creating your own space or shaping the activity, you are on the outside, or in the corner like a wallflower, waiting for someone else to invite you in. It's a good start, but it's not quite good enough. It's not inclusion.

Maybe diversity is being asked to the dance, whilst inclusion is picking the song, or even making the playlist? Or, maybe diversity is being invited to the dance, and inclusion is being on the party planning committee.

Diversity, being invited in, is a start but it's not an end. In businesses, discussions around diversity are usually held between hiring managers and HR officers, who focus on bringing in the right number of 'diverse applicants' to interview and maybe even hiring a few.

Diversity, when it's thought of in these terms, all too often stops with a foot in the door, once a hire has been made. It doesn't take you up the stairs and into the boardroom. It doesn't give you a voice in shaping the future of the team or business, or even keep you in the building for very long. Diversity says, 'You got in, that's enough, great job us, and now job done. (Our job, that is – you're going to have to keep working, but just probably not here.)'

If you're looking for my definition, it would be this: diversity is having a range of people present in your working environment. Inclusion is treating, valuing and listening to them equally. Catchy, right?

In an inclusive environment all team members' experiences, expertise, perspective, ideas and contributions are considered and valued equally, and they're taken into account when the organisation makes decisions about how it operates and what its collective beliefs are.

## What's the problem with not achieving inclusion?

Companies that haven't grasped this nuance between diversity and inclusion, and so haven't put in place active practices at all levels to address and increase their performance around inclusion, are in for a bumpy road in the next few years as the face of the labour market changes.

In both the UK and US, there are already large populations of Black women, which will only continue to grow. In the 2000 Census, Black women and girls made up 6.4 per cent of the total US population.[1] In 2016–17 Britain's Black population was around two million people, or just over 3 per cent of the total UK population.[2]

More and more people are identifying as non-white in one way or another – in 2018, 44 per cent of Gen Z self-identified as 'non-white' (growing from 40 per cent of Millennials and 28 per cent of Baby Boomers).[3] This is the current and next cohort of employees being hired into businesses, and before long, we will be the people looking to progress to management and leadership positions. And businesses need to be ready for that if they want to remain relevant and successful.

This new, more diverse workforce not only looks different, but has new value-driven expectations of their employers and the brands and businesses they shop from. We respond positively to companies that can demonstrate values in line with our own. Values that we have developed through navigating the world with more varied personal identities than previous generations have had.

This values-lead decision-making puts race very firmly on the priorities list for Gen Z. In fact, 72 per cent of Gen Z, when asked about their workplaces, say that they believe 'race equality is the most important issue today.'[4]

Another important shift is in generational attitudes – Millennial and Gen Z talent aren't looking for the same thing in our employment as our parents were. A job for life not only doesn't really exist anymore, but it also sounds more like a trap than a reward for a generation of side hustlers and multi-hyphenates. There's no more corner office to aspire to – our offices are open plan and we spend more and more time working from home – especially now we're all adapting to life during Covid. Businesses which don't grasp this generational change in expectations are already starting to find themselves with disengaged employees. A recent Gallup study of employees across 142 countries found that only 13 per cent of working people world-wide classed themselves as engaged at work.[5] Interestingly, they also found that the management behaviour most likely to improve engagement was 'demonstrates strong commitment to diversity', particularly among those born after 1980 – the Millennial or Gen Z age groups.[6]

Gen Z and Millennial cohorts have led the way in holding brands and companies to account. They vote with their money, spending with those that resonate with their social and ethical values, and boycotting those that don't. It would be short-sighted to not think that the same rigour of consideration would be applied to the companies they choose to work for.

> I don't even really have the want to exist in a space knowing that I can't bring people [like me] across that river. There's a little floodgate that is opened in different industries to let people in, and when that gets filled to capacity – which happens very quickly, with one or two – it's closed it again for the foreseeable future.
>
> – *Naomi Ackie*

Businesses need to learn and adapt, quickly, to become places where these new generations of employees can not only get a foot in the door, but can feel safe, welcomed, listened to, and supported to achieve their full potential. Those businesses that can't achieve this, or can't achieve it quickly enough, will not only suffer from being seen to be non-progressive, but they will suffer consequences in terms of their ability to attract and retain top talent, and ultimately their profitability and relevance.

We've seen many high-profile examples of businesses making tone-deaf, outright offensive decisions or products, which make us throw up our collective hands and cry out, 'But who do they have on their teams!?' Do you remember H&M's 'the coolest monkey in the jungle' gaffe? How about TRESemmé's negative characterisation of afro-textured hair that saw their products being removed from shelves across South Africa, or Prada's figurines that had to be pulled due to their striking resemblance to golliwog blackface dolls? When we only have homogeneous teams, there isn't the same integration of ideas from the widest possible number of viewpoints, which leads to unnecessary and avoidable mistakes slipping through, and finding their way into the public consciousness – causing damage to brands.

We already know that there is a real advantage in having diverse teams in your business, and especially in nurturing that talent to progress to senior and leadership roles. A 2017 Cloverpop study found that inclusive leadership teams make what they define as better decisions 87 per cent of the time, and decisions made and executed by diverse leadership teams delivered 60 per cent better results.[7]

Companies in the top quartile for racial and ethnic diversity are 35 per cent more likely to have financial returns above their respective national industry medians.[8] This is notable in comparison to companies in the top quartile for only gender diversity, which are just 15 per cent more likely to have financial returns that were above their national industry median. Race and gender diversity together are good for business. But only if you can engage that talent and get them to stay. Which is where the work on inclusion has to come in.

We've spoken about how, too often, well-meaning, 'colour-blind' people put in place well-meaning 'colour-blind' policies and practices. Whilst these may seem, on the surface, the fairest way to do things, they actually ignore the realities of intersectional experiences that groups like Black women face. To borrow from the 2017 Lean In and McKinsey Women in the Workplace report: 'Many companies also overlook the realities of women of colour, who face the greatest obstacles and receive the least support. When companies take a one-size-fits-all approach to advancing women, women of colour end up underserved and left behind.'[9]

One thing that we see over and over again as a result of diversity without inclusion is Black women leaving organisations after a relatively short timeframe. This isn't surprising when we look at the things that

Black women self-report whilst at work. 44 per cent of African American women, compared to 30 per cent of white women, interviewed for a 2015 study reported feeling stalled in their careers.[10] 46 per cent of the college-educated Black women surveyed said their ideas aren't heard or recognised, and 26 per cent of Black women stated that they feel their talents aren't recognised by their superiors, compared to 17 per cent of white women.

Whether the decision to leave is made themselves, due to feelings of a lack of a voice or support, or taken out of their hands with claims of a 'bad fit', 'poor communication style' or 'bad vibes', it's easy to see how working in an environment where you feel overlooked and under-supported would create an environment that doesn't encourage Black women to stay in roles.

I can speak to this from personal experience of having had my own HR issues (in a company with no real HR team) when a new, junior member of the team complained of my 'bad vibes'. Here's the context – I had been flown from the London HQ to the small three- or four-person satellite office which was struggling. Badly. Work wasn't getting done, inter-office communication was a mess and clients were showing the first signs of discontent. I was essentially sent over to be something between a sticking plaster and a spy, something I should never have agreed to take on, but at the time it was what I was asked to do and I misguidedly obliged. I was to spend two weeks there, meeting clients and going to meetings and putting on a happy 'there's nothing wrong here' face, whilst also, and most importantly, observing the office and the team in it. How was it running? What time were people getting in? When were they leaving? What were they actually *doing* all day? (Races in the corridor on wheely chairs, mostly, as it turned out.)

It was the worst working experience of my life.

When I arrived I discovered the office was in a shambles; team members due to arrive each day at 9 a.m. were turning up at 3 or 4 p.m. if at all, meetings were being missed, and the little work that was being done was so low in quality that the team in London had to take on the burden of redoing it the following day.

All in all, everything you hope and trust isn't happening in a remote office with no real senior oversight, was happening. It was my job to be pleasant, affable, but somewhat distant – observing and reporting on, but not taking part in, bad behaviour. I was asked to model best practice, in the hopes that somehow through osmosis the rest of the team would follow suit? It made sense at the time, kinda.

It was the most hostile environment I've ever been in. People would completely ignore me when I spoke, or start different conversations over the top of what I was saying. They would take lunches several hours long together, over times we were meant to meet, and were generally hellish. They treated me so badly that I cried every night of the two weeks I was there, and woke up at 4 a.m. every morning to have calls with the UK office, sharing my findings and troubleshooting solutions.

As the time went on, I reported back countless instances of behaviours that would simply not have been tolerated in the UK office. I made formal reports, had one-to-one meetings with the office's three people (during which one screamed at me, and another told me that I 'just didn't get it, because I had no idea how hard it was to be a pretty blonde white woman)'. I made a fully actionable roadmap to recovery plan to get the office back on its feet. All agreed to by the founders, who were saddened, but not surprised, to hear of the state of affairs.

The day I got back, exhausted physically and emotionally, we went into the boardroom to talk implementation, 'But, just before we do – we wanted to let you know that we were disappointed to hear back from someone on the team that you had a "bad vibe", we wanted to discuss this with you.' It was a gut punch – I had given up two weeks of my time to go into a hostile environment, where people had treated me awfully and screamed at me, and now we were going to be focusing on my 'bad vibe'.

There was a long conversation. I kept pushing for more – more detail, context, examples of this 'bad vibe'. There was nothing more: just those two words, with nothing to back them up, had the power to invalidate my weeks of work, and discount the importance of all of my evidence-based feedback. Thinking about it all this time later I still feel worn out.

This story is in no way unique, comments about Black women's 'vibe' or 'attitude', or a thousand other unquantifiable, intangible terms are used to diminish and belittle Black women's work, and our experiences. Feedback of this type is impossible to pin down, to argue against or to prove wrong without your pushback being seen as the perfect case in point example of you, indeed, having the bad attitude you're being accused of. And so, if you find allegations like these being made against you, without proof, or the possibility of a fair right to reply, I'd suggest you start weighing up your options and planning your escape as soon as you're able.

## What happens when Black women are forced out?

As we've seen faced with businesses not suited to properly supporting or progressing them, Black women are opting out to start their own businesses – only to find themselves in situations that still aren't to their best advantage. This is a lose-lose situation. Companies have lost the talent of a team member who may have unique and valuable skills and underrepresented perspectives which the business can benefit from. They need to go through the process and expense of recruiting and re-training a new team member, and they risk further attrition by not demonstrating behaviour that will motivate growing Millennial or Gen Z teams. The Black women who have opted out often find themselves in less financially rewarding, and less secure positions, but at least they don't need to worry about being singled out for their identities.

Some companies hear 'diversity and inclusion' and think it's the 'in' thing to focus on now. Many are being forced to look at gender and BAME representation more seriously than they would have in the past because legally they have to report on the gender pay gap and soon they'll have to do the same for the race pay gap. Many businesses are still saying, 'Oh no, we don't have an issue – we just can't find the talent when we're recruiting, they're just not applying.' And of course, it's absolute rubbish. Black women and men are applying to jobs, and they're just not getting through to the first or second round because of bias, racism and discrimination.

However, some companies are seeing the data around more diverse teams making more money by helping to sell more products or services. It's visible in a lot of sectors that women are not coming through the ranks and so some companies are starting to realise that if women aren't coming up in the pipeline they're going to end up with no women at some point. It's a threat to their survival.

Having said that, many are not supporting women internally. Some businesses still don't understand that sponsorship is the key to getting women into senior positions – assigning them to key projects, advocating for them, putting them forward for things and setting out a career path so that they don't lose talent – that's really what's going to change the outlook for women in the workplace. Black women need to be encouraged. If within a year you're not getting the support – you've got to keep it moving. That's a scary prospect especially because we're disproportionately likely to have caregiving roles but you've just got to take the risk and carefully plan your route out.

*– Vanessa Sanyauke*

## Achieving inclusion as well as diversity

Making sure you recruit a diverse range of people and are paying people equally will help to make strides toward a more diverse working environment. But it's important to understand that left on its own, diversity doesn't necessarily lead to inclusion. Without putting in the work to build a top-down intentionally inclusive space, the investment in developing a diverse pipeline and hiring well is wasted. What is more likely to happen is that you will bring talented people into a space where they feel ostracised and Othered, and instead of a well-unified team you actually end up with separations, schisms and factions.

The crux is that diversity without inclusion is nothing more than tokenism. You bring people in but don't give them the chance to deeply integrate, or to have any fundamental say in their environment. You don't empower them to drive change or to iterate improvements – and so before too long they end up feeling that they are only there as a ticked box or a statistic to make others feel better about how 'progressive' they are. This type of 'diversity' is easy to do, since it's much easier to invest in diversity than inclusion because diversity is quantifiable. It's countable and lives in numbers and statistics, and that makes it so much more convenient to report back to the board or shareholders on and to show improvements in. This is not the same for inclusion. It's much easier to show how many racially marginalised candidates you interviewed for a role, how many you hired, how long they stayed and what percentage of your total work-force they make up, than to show how well integrated they are, how invested they feel, how included they are, and how listened to they feel. Inclusion is hard, it deals in feelings, emotions and relationships, it's ephemeral and personal, but it's also the only thing that makes diversity worthwhile.

If Black women don't feel included in a real way, if they're always pulled to the front in company photos, and featured on the website, but overlooked in the day-to-day of the business, the likelihood of them remaining and growing with the business is reduced and the possibility of attrition is much higher.

## Making an inclusive space

To successfully achieve inclusion as well as diversity, businesses need to adopt real equality as a core part of their DNA, to understand that it's a responsibility, rather than an optional extra. This commitment and belief needs to be shared with and by all members of the company, and as an equal expectation for all. It needs to be communicated from the interview stage for all new joiners, and everyone must be aware of a zero-tolerance approach to *any and all* non-inclusive language or behaviour.

A temptation that a lot of businesses succumb to is to silo diversity and inclusion, making it the specific remit, or problem, of a small number of people, usually a self-selecting, opt-in group of staff from underrepres-ented backgrounds who take on the burden in addition to their day-to-day job roles. Whilst I think that these moves are usually well intentioned, I think they're also misjudged.

When you silo the responsibility for diversity and inclusion to a small group of people, you are doing two things: firstly, you're letting the majority of the business know that this is not a core business priority. It's just something that those people over there are doing (for free, on top of their existing workload), which you are tolerating rather than championing as an essential value or responsibility of the company. It says this is not real work, so we don't need to invest time, budgets, or training in this area. It doesn't recognise the time and effort that is required to self-educate on the topic in order to be in a position to teach your colleagues, and the wider business.

> Doing work around diversity is a real double-edged sword because it takes time that takes you away from other work. People want us to do the work for free, without realising that we weren't just born with this knowledge – we've acquired it from years of lived experience and hard conversations, and should be compensated for our work, and our knowledge.
>
> – *Aja Barber*

Secondly, it further reinforces the idea of Otherness, making people more aware of their differences, and putting those who are the focus of the activities in a subordinate position. The underlying message of siloed diversity and inclusion groups is that 'these poor people weren't talented or successful enough to make it to where you've got to on their own, so now you need to sacrifice some of what you've got to help them. Else you're a racist. OK?' And that's not good for anyone.

Inclusion needs to form a part of standard business practice at the very highest levels – it can't be something that junior members of the team, who have relatively little power and influence, are left to push forward. In the UK, stats show that employers are more likely to make senior leaders accountable for delivering on gender diversity, equality and inclusion strategies than for ethnicity strategies.[11] Only 57 per cent of organisations have a race champion at board or equivalent level, yet 67 per cent have a race champion at senior manager or HR professional level. In order to make this a change that sticks, we need to have increased commitment from the very highest levels – from board-level stakeholders.

Having the responsibility in the hands of a senior manager or HR person is better and more effective than in the hands of a more junior person, simply because they are better positioned to make change. But having it as a shared responsibility at the changemaker level of board or chair is best of all, as they are the people responsible for the strategic growth and direction of the business.

## Focus on development and progression, not just recruitment

Once the first piece of hard work of hiring diversely is done, it's time to build on it. This approach was used at global consultancy firm Ernst and Young (EY), which they later turned into a case study.[12] They used a data-driven approach to get a clear picture of their workforce, to measure diversity and map for inclusion.

EY looked at their existing team structure and they found that 20 per cent of people currently at manager level were 'BAME', and so expected that one out of every five promotions from manager to senior manager would be someone from a racially marginalised background. They explained that this worked on a 'comply or explain' basis, which was not something I was aware of before, but is now something I suggest to the businesses I work with. It simply means that if an area of the business didn't meet this one in five expectation, their HR team would gather feedback on why those candidates had been unsuccessful and use that feedback to understand gaps and support in the implementation of processes and strategies to close that gap. This has included looking at the way that work is allocated, making sure that people from all groups are given access to glamour work in order to showcase their skills and potential, rather than being judged on their characteristics, background, or their manager's preconceived idea of what a leader, or path to leadership, should look like.

In their first two years of implementing this comply – or – explain framework, EY reportedly found that promotions have become more representative and their teams have become more inclusive. Their team at the most senior level rose from 3 per cent 'minority ethnic' to 8 per cent.

They are quick to point out that these structural changes, and the resulting increased inclusivity in the team structures, was only made possible by buy-in at leadership level, where they were supported in uncovering and addressing unconscious bias, and by those who were in a position to make promotion and appraisal-rating decisions.

## Inclusivity training

Training can also be very helpful, but again it has its own dangers to bear in mind and consciously avoid. When training around topics like unconscious bias is optional, the people you attract to these sessions will most likely be those already engaged with and sympathetic to the cause. This isn't to say that these people won't receive a benefit from the training, but it keeps the people who didn't engage unengaged, and overlooks the fact that the people who aren't in the room are most likely those who have the most to learn. However, making these sessions compulsory is also not a catch-all solution. When training like this is a requirement, there can often be a backlash from people resistant to change, who may see it as a waste of time or even propaganda or agenda-pushing.

In my experience, the best solution to this is to have a company-wide commitment to training on a range of subjects. Topics could include skill development in relation to specific job roles, health and well-being, company culture, team achievements, unconscious bias, and diversity and inclusion. The training should be regular enough to be habit-forming (sorry to businesses that think a single lunchtime session on diversity is going to solve everything, but we all know that's just not going to happen) but not so much that it distracts from day-to-day jobs. When all training is compulsory and on a wide range of rotating topics, rather than just diversity and inclusion, it can have a lower barrier to entry, and lead to higher uptake from the widest team.

## Listen to feedback

This sounds simple, and it is, but it's overlooked *so* often that it's worth saying it again. If you're in a management position, and people tell you what's happening, you *have to* listen. Leaders and managers rarely see the true dynamics of their teams, and how they interact when they're not there, and so relying on feedback from a wide range of people is essential. It's really easy to fall into the habit of only really listening to feedback from a small number of your team – usually those who don't complain too much, whose ideologies most closely align with yours, or those who you've developed close personal relationships with. Doing that is like bringing to life all of the worst parts of being on social media – everything you already thought is echoed back to you and nothing new gets a chance to break through.

Make places and structures where team members can feed back, in person or anonymously, on their experiences in the workplace. And then act on that feedback for positive change.

The 2019 Diversity and Inclusion Study by workplace website Glassdoor, which surveyed over 5,000 people in the UK, US, France and Germany, found that 42 per cent of Millennials reported either witnessing or experiencing racism in their workplace, which is three and a half times the rate reported in those aged 55 and above.[13] Similarly, almost half of Millennial employees reported having experienced or witnessing gender discrimination, versus just 17 per cent of over-55s. As we know, Black women sit in the intersection of those two forms of discrimination, and so are doubly vulnerable. I don't know if these stats mean that these instances are necessarily becoming more prevalent; I suspect that they mean that our cultural understanding around different types of discrimination has increased, and younger people are more attuned to spotting unfair and inequal work practices which may have previously been overlooked or accepted. Who you ask questions to, and who feels they have the right to speak up in a safe space will hugely impact on the feedback that you hear.

The problem here is Millennial and Gen Z employees are currently the youngest members of our workforce, and therefore most often the most junior members of companies – which can mean that often times their voices can go unheard.

Speaking out when something is wrong is hard and intimidating, and takes a lot of bravery, especially for new or junior employees. Someone who has come forward with an issue has likely not done so lightly – take the time to really listen to them. Follow up with next steps and solutions, to make sure they feel listened to and protected. Failing to not only hear but listen to and act on issues raised can make marginalised people feel doubly unsupported and unprotected.

### Make zero tolerance mean zero tolerance

Most businesses understand the importance of having zero-tolerance policies when it comes to racial discrimination, which is great. What's not so great is, as we've already seen, it has been found that despite most UK employers having these policies in place, 25 per cent of 'BAME' workers reported being the victims of bullying and harassment at work, and only 45 per cent of businesses have carried out investigations or reviews into bullying or harassment in their organisations.[14]

Zero-tolerance policies only work if they're enforced and acted upon. A company's body language has to match their words – and a policy that's never enforced is nothing more than a PR exercise.

### Make an environment where people can be their full selves

One of the things I've been proudest of doing. in businesses where I've been in a leadership position, is consciously working to create environments in which people can come to work as themselves. In truly inclusive workplaces, people's individuality and differences are celebrated, rather than dampened or downplayed. This idea was first given to me by a wonderful ex boss who explained the intentional steps she had taken in setting up the business she founded – mindfully creating a space where people felt safe and encouraged to be their full selves was part of the fabric of her intentions when designing her business, not an afterthought tacked on at the end. It meant that the company was founded and led by her, with the grounding principle of respect at all levels, and not just internally – it was also, importantly, something that was laid out clearly to all clients and potential new hires. We were all part of the same team, on the same journey, and we were all going to get there by working with, not against each other. Always.

As well as making an environment where people feel safe and respected for who they are just being the right thing to do, I'm going to share two good business cases for setting up your business in this way. The first is the ability to reach a range of audiences. If you have a wide range of people in your business, and those people are able to speak freely and authentically about their experiences, and have those taken into consideration, you're more likely to create work that deeply resonates with a wider range of your audience or consumer base. As people have a stronger affinity to brands which authentically align with their views, the potential for developing brand loyalty grows as people are encouraged to contribute openly.

The second advantage (aside from lessening the rate of churn through a business from underrepresented and marginalised team members) is simply building a staff of people who can dedicate their time and thoughts to the work at hand. If a safe, comfortable and inclusive environment has been made, top-down, then your team aren't using half of their brains, or their time, to self-police or worry about subduing some part of themselves. They can simply be, and invest that time that would otherwise have been spent worrying into their working days.

This, as a process, is long and ever evolving. It involves having a very clear idea of your business culture and values, and reaffirming them regularly, from someone's first interview to their last day with the business. It involves being open and authentic in who you are and encouraging your team to do the same without fear of repercussions. It means letting your team know that you see them as real, fully rounded human beings, and that all of their identities are safe, protected and respected within the business.

Being the only one – it has felt deliberate, I think it's done on purpose, and it's done so that there's not so many of us that we tumble the system, as it were, or make it too normal. Tokenism allows a space for industries to be congratulated on the bare minimum, the lowest standard ever, and get away with still upholding the same structures. Ultimately if you bring in more marginalised people, and in my case if you bring more Black women into spaces, the foundation would have to be changed. Without doubt.

One example, on a filming set, is when actors have to change their hair. If we look at a lot of hair and make-up crews, they are all white. So, if you bring on 50 per cent actors of colour but still have a crew of all white artists, who are not trained in styling the hair of Black people in particular (because they were never required to take the lessons that they should have when they did their other hair and make-up training), then you have to diversify the crew. If this change in the power structure happened, it would enable Black hair and make-up artists to move up, and we would have more heads of departments who were people of colour.

> Then we're looking at a work environment where it really is very diverse and inclusive. The foundations are different and people are being given opportunities that generations down the line can allow us to make our own economies, bigger than what's already there. That would tip the balance. So, I think that's why the tokenism thing happens. I'm just not able to believe it's just all out of ignorance because it's been going on for too long for it to not be somehow thought through. The world that we live in makes me suspicious and extra cautious about how I move in it.
>
> *— Naomi Ackie*

### Don't give up!

Implementing these changes can be difficult, and it's unlikely to be smooth sailing from start to finish. I've had experiences that have felt absolutely impossible and soul-destroying. I've faced pushback at all levels, and have had moments of feeling like change is impossible and I'll never be able to make the progress I've been hoping for.

There may be a bedding-in period where not only do your efforts not seem to be making things better, things might actually feel worse. There may be pushback and resistance, success might seem hard to find.

I'm happy to say that, even at times when they've felt like they would, these low moments don't last forever, and the reward is most definitely worth the struggle. When people who are used to being overlooked see and feel that the investment in them is more than just lip service and is a core part of your business, they notice and they invest right back. It's a beautiful thing to see.

As a change-maker in a business, your role is to take the wider team on the journey of progress alongside you, keeping them motivated along the way.

### What can Black women do?

I didn't want to end the chapter without having some proactive steps that Black women can take, after all that's what we're here for. But I do want to be clear – the weight of making these changes and seeing them all the way through does not sit on Black women's shoulders. Those who already have power need to be the trailblazers in this respect – doing the legwork and changing the systems from the inside out.

Black women who aren't in leadership positions can't force inclusion. It's not a case of us working extra hard or leading a committee or taking on any of the other emotional labour burdens that are often pushed in our direction. It simply can't be changed by our efforts alone.

It can feel overwhelming, maybe disheartening – having identified something so important, only to be told that it's out of our hands. We, as a group, are used to striving, pushing and advocating for what's right. We're change-makers who have often historically taken on the groundwork that has led to societal changes (even if this is later overlooked when the history is retold). Being told something is out of our hands is just about the worst thing to hear.

But don't worry, things aren't hopeless, not by a long shot. We can still use our voices, and we can vote with our money – not just the money we actively spend, but the money we help businesses to earn through our labour and contributions.

One thing that anyone, of any race or gender, at every level, can do to show that inclusivity is important to them is simply to ask and call it out, from the start. In the same way that you wouldn't leave an interview without having discussed salaries, benefits and culture (please, please always discuss these things!), even though it might feel weird the first time you do it, make sure that inclusion also becomes an essential part of your standard interview questioning. The further forwards you move in your career, the more you come to realise that it's true – you really are inter-viewing the company to see if they're right for you, as much as the other way around. You are valuable talent who businesses would benefit from having on board, and they're just as keen to impress you.

Before interviews, look up if the company has published its gender pay gap (which is now compulsory for larger businesses in the UK), or anything about its race pay gap. Pay attention to what you find: this is the company showing you its beliefs before you even step through the doorway. They're giving you a glimpse into who they really are, and as Maya Angelou told us, 'When someone shows you who they are, believe them the first time.' If the gaps are huge, and don't show any improvements year on year, is this a place you're sure you want to dedicate your time and efforts to? Are you sure they're going to have your best interests in mind? This is something that is totally reasonable and acceptable to discuss during an interview, whether good or bad. If the gap is large ask them why they think this is the case, and ask them what's being done to narrow it. If it's already narrow, or they've achieved parity, congratulate them, ask in the interview what they think they as a business have done to achieve that, and what they're doing next.

Don't only ask what success looks like, but how it's measured, how it's quantified, who makes promotion decisions and based on what. When they talk about their culture, pay attention to the words they use and the examples they give – does it align with your values and identity?

The more we ask these questions, the more they're normalised, and the more businesses understand that these are factors that talent are bearing in mind when making decisions about where to take their skills.

# Working Towards Inclusion

## June Sarpong

**SW:** I'd love to hear about the work you're doing in your role as director of creative diversity at the BBC.

**JS:** Well, the work that I'm doing in that capacity, there are two reasons why I decided to take it: firstly, I've been on the receiving end of the things that haven't worked within our industry, and within the BBC, and secondly because I had assurances from the top that this was something that they were really committed to, and they were going to equip me with the resources to actually, *really* be able to get stuff done. And so, although we're at the beginning of this work, I do think that there is a willingness to change in a way that maybe there hasn't been in the past. And I think, for them, it's not a question of wanting to, but it's a question of not necessarily knowing how to. And so we have a number of things that we're working on, looking at how you diversify the creative process, how you measure progression rates of diverse talent, and how you put systems in place to remove some of the barriers that have held them back until this point as well as where you need to try and find ways to accelerate that process because it hasn't been a level playing field. It's exciting, it's early days so I'm hoping that we can get things done.

**SW:** Why does on-air diversity and inclusion matter?

**JS:** I think a couple of things - there's a wonderful quote from the children's rights activist Marian Wright Edelman, and what she says is, 'You can't be what you can't see' and I would add

to that 'unless you're exceptional'. And by mere definition of the word, the majority of people are not exceptional. We know representation matters - there's a reason why in order to keep up systems that are unequal and unfair you've always had one particular ideal that has been pushed out to the whole of society. And there's a reason why - it's because representation matters. So, if our idea of leadership is a posh white man, if our idea of beauty is a young white woman, and so on and so on and so on, at the end of the day that keeps a certain system going. And so, to be able to unpick that, it's really important to be able to present wider and more accurate alternatives - because, as we know, there are myriad stories that are interesting and can connect with wide audiences, and often when those stories are given a wider platform they do well. So I think the BBC, in order to truly represent its audience, and to be able to survive and thrive, it has to get this right. I mean, if you look at the changing demography in this country - mixed-race people are one of the fastest growing ethnic groups and actually, if you look at America, by 2030 brown and Black people will be the majority in that country. The world of ten years' time is going to be very different to the world that we're in now, and for any organisation that wants to be around then they have to get ready for it.

**SW:** I wondered if you'd be willing to talk about any instances in your professional life that have been impacted by you being Black and female?

**JS:** Ooh, yeah, I mean, where do I start? There have been so many, there have been loads. Well, one of the main ones was when I was at MTV, and at the time I had a show with Richard Blackwood that was one of the highest-rated programmes on the network. During this period, MTV had something called MTV Girls (you could never get away with that nonsense now, but that is what we were called) and MTV did a photoshoot with a magazine at the time, and it was a cover shoot with all of the MTV Girls and I wasn't included. So the first I heard of this shoot was when I was walking past the news stand and saw the cover. I think I was about 20 or 21 at the time, so I was completely heartbroken. Then what happened was – I mean, if it was now there'd be a social media storm – the viewers started calling up MTV to find out why I wasn't in the shoot. So obviously this then caused all sorts of issues within the leadership. In the end it all worked out – I was assigned my own person for press, the following year I had lots and lots of activities, and renegotiations were very good. I think that actually, sometimes those moments are a reminder that there's still a lot of work to be done in terms of the inequalities that exist, but also that you don't have to accept it. And these moments can act as teachable moments for those that were doing it, you know? The person who decided to keep me from the shoot honestly thought that he was doing something that was helpful to the organisation, and that actually the audience wasn't ready for, even though our show was one of the highest-rated at the time.

And then there were loads of times – lloooaaaddss of times – where I'd be promised something, we'd agree something and then last minute it wouldn't happen. And you'd always *know*. I think it's one of those things where you intuitively know, and I say this to a lot of my white colleagues. *You know*. There's a feeling to it, and it's very hard to articulate, but anybody of colour knows what I'm talking about. You know when something is as a result of your race, or when something is just because maybe you weren't good enough or whatever else. There's a difference. And there's a sixth sense that goes off and makes you say, 'OK, I know what that is.' And so, yes, these things happened lots and lots and lots and lots.

**SW:** The fact that it is a feeling we all know, but that it's not like someone shouting a slur across the office, where you can go to someone and say, 'this happened to me' – it's so intangible, ephemeral and so hard, almost impossible to prove, and I think that makes it so slippery, and I think that's deliberate.

**JS:** Yes, very much so. It is. It really is. But it's real, it's not imagined. And the results show us it's real. You know, when you look at the levels of success, if you look at the levels of wealth and everything else, it's all clear that something is going on. So it's not imagined, and it's a horrible thing to have to deal with every day of your life.

**SW:** We speak a lot about diversity and not enough about inclusion – do you have any thoughts about creating inclusion alongside diversity?

**JS:** Well, I think inclusion is everything. Because the problem is if you don't have this inclusion piece it means that people can't be themselves, can they? And therefore, they can't give you their best work, and it then means also *because* they can't be themselves, *because* they can't give you their best work, chances are they're not going to succeed. And so, the inclusion piece is so important, but the problem we have is that often, those who are designing the inclusion have no idea of what it feels like to be othered, so how can they know? You can only see things through your lens, so the process of designing for inclusion itself needs to be inclusive. And that you actually have to make sure you're bringing in people who can fill in your blind spots. For example, I'm an able-bodied woman, so there are things that I just wouldn't even consider that somebody with mobility issues has to grapple with on a daily basis. I need them to tell me because I won't know, and it's not for me to tell them what they need. And so actually when talking about inclusion it's so important that that process is inclusive too.

**SW:** I think it's important that that process is not just inclusive – which is essential and often overlooked, but that it's also respected and paid. I think much too often marginalised people are asked to take on those things as added, unpaid extras on top of their workloads.

**JS:** Because if someone is coming to fix your finances you're paying them, aren't you? So it's about what we prioritise, isn't it? You set goals and targets for things that are a priority because you want to meet them by a certain point, and I think there has to be the same with this – because if it matters to you you're going to make sure it's documented and everyone knows what they're working towards.

# Diversity without Inclusion

## Munroe Bergdorf

**SW:** Do you think that speaking about race and gender has caused any professional difficulties for you?

**MB:** Oh my God, 100 per cent. When I first started speaking about race, and I was fronting a beauty campaign at the time, it was a period when we were *kind of* speaking about identity, but not really. It was a bit like an *identity lite* kind of way - people wanted your representation but didn't necessarily want you to speak about the realities of what it's like to be, say, a Black transgender woman. So I think that when I first started to speak about the realities of being a Black trans woman, but also working in the fashion and beauty industry, people found it very confusing. They were like, 'Oh . . . erm . . . we're not used to actually speaking about the realities, more just you just being there and being visible', and I think that in speaking about race I wanted to take visibility and then just turn it on its head. To say, actually, visibility doesn't keep us safe - speaking about our experiences and asking for solutions keeps us safe.

So I think that not just me, but this whole wave of intersectional feminism especially, within the British media, and all media in the West - but especially in the British media at the moment, I think that we're all saying that visibility is all well and good, but it has to be structurally behind the scenes as well. You can't just have people in front of the camera being diverse, the whole workplace needs to be diverse, otherwise it's just tokenism - it's just a show.

I think that with every single year that's come since that tipping point around 2015, when I really saw things starting to change, for trans people anyway, and then the intersections within identity, and Reni Eddo-Lodge's book *Why I'm No Longer Talking To White People About Race* - I just think that as time goes on we're really pushing the envelope and saying visibility is not enough, we need structural change, we need institutional change, we need allies.

This involves everybody!

The problems are there, and the problems have involved all of us, and the problems are the reason that we're here, so you can't speak about diversity without questioning why there is a lack of diversity. You can't speak about visibility without asking why there is a lack of visibility. There's always cause and effect, and those have involved us all.

# Naomi Ackie's Favourite Thing About Being a Black Woman

"Oh gosh. Ooh, I love being a Black woman. My favourite thing about being a Black woman is that I feel attuned, and especially perceptive to the world around me because of my standing in the world, and I think that makes me wise and sensitive. Over the years I have seen aspects of the world and people that seem to be kind of invisible to others, and I think the cool thing about being a Black woman is that I can observe it all through a unique gaze that not everyone has access to. I was raised to "play the game", to code-switch and think ahead. That's something that I've started to really enjoy – the versatility that it gives me, and the power that I feel brewing within me. I think the idea of the strong Black woman is overused and some-times dangerous, but I do think that when you have lived in a world that isn't for you, and you can still make a space for yourself, in the way that Black women are doing and have done for centuries, and you are aware of that lineage that you come from – that's a power that we have in ourselves that when unleashed in the right way can be as rejuvenating as it can be destructive, and I think those things are not mutually exclusive, they go hand in hand. Because we need to deconstruct and rebuild at the same time."

## CHAPTER 10

# THE GLASS CLIFF

'I am a Black feminist. I mean I recognise that my power as well as my primary oppressions come as a result of my Blackness as well as my womanness, and therefore my struggles on both of these fronts are inseparable.'

AUDRE LORDE

**W**e've spoken about the glass ceiling, and the concrete ceiling, but what about the glass cliff?

In 2003 *The Times* published a story with the headline 'Women on board: help or hindrance?' The article suggested that women leaders have a negative impact on business performance and concluded in no uncertain terms that women on the board were, in fact, bad for business.[1]

The article's reasoning for women being a hindrance was the fact that after companies appoint women to top roles, such as CEO or board member, the performance of the business (in terms of revenue or market value) was likely to decrease. And they were right, the trends of business performance do indeed back up this pattern. So that seems pretty straightforward, right? We, women, had stomped our silly stilettoed feet right into the boardroom, then realised we had no idea how to actually run things, and left a big old mess for the sensible men to come in and clean up for us. Sorry, chaps!

When women make it to the top, companies fail, and so it's clear to see that women are bad for business, or at least bad at running them. It would be easy to think that, unless you understood the glass cliff, and spent a little bit of time looking at how these companies were performing *just before* the female leader was appointed.

A 2004 study looked at the performance of FTSE 100 companies before and after the appointment of new board members.[2] They found that when there was an overall period of stock market decline, companies that appointed women, or racially marginalised men, to their boards were more likely than others to have *already* experienced a consistently bad performance for the previous five months. This bad performance could take a number of different shapes. It could be that these companies had gone through a reputational scandal, where the tarnish could be transferred to tarnishing the new leader, had a PR issue, or suffered a hit to its share prices or profits – in some way, the companies were in a moment of crisis *before* they turned to a female leader.

These findings are backed up by another piece of research which looked at a data set of Fortune 500 companies over a fifteen-year period, and they also found that marginalised people (women and 'ethnic minorities' in their study) were much more likely to be promoted to CEO in companies with an already weak performance.

So, what the *Times* article didn't take into account is the glass cliff. When a company is *already* in trouble, or underperforming, they are much more likely to bring in a female leader, or a man from a racially marginalised background to try to clean up the mess. These businesses are already on a downward trajectory before these people were brought on board, and so the chance of success in this role is significantly limited, and the chance of them falling off the cliff is much higher than usual.

Knowing that the odds are already stacked against them, it would make sense for internal team members and investors to give these new marginalised leaders every helping hand possible to make sure they are successful in their mission. But no, by now, we all know that's not going to be the case, it's something close to the exact opposite.

A report from global consultancy firm Pricewaterhouse Coopers (PwC) in 2013[3] found that after being appointed, female CEOs were more likely to be forced out of their positions than white males, at a rate of 38 per cent of women compared to 27 per cent of white men.[4] Despite the companies that appoint these women to senior roles being much more likely to already be in trouble, the women who take on the roles are given much less leniency in failure. If they don't fall off the cliff, they're likely to get pushed right over the edge.

The reason we need to go into this is 1) because it's bullshit and we need to understand and recognise that, and 2) because all of these things together have a real impact on how we as a society view the suitability of anyone who isn't a white man to successfully take on a top role.

This stacking of elements that make it much harder and less likely for female or racially marginalised leaders to succeed feed into our internalised images of what a 'good' and 'successful' leader looks like. If people who aren't white men are usually only appointed when there is already a downward turn, and are more likely to fail, the narrative that we as a society receive about what happens when someone other than a white male is appointed to run a business is unlikely to be inspiring.

It seems that businesses have come to realise this – it has been found that if a woman or racially marginalised person is appointed, and business performance continues to decline in such a way that they end up leaving the company, they are more likely than not to be replaced by a white man.[5] This replacement is seen as a signal to investors and employees that the company is going back to business as usual, something that researchers term the 'saviour effect'.

Since white men are less likely to be pushed out of CEO positions, they are then given more room to fail, or to succeed, which allows time to turn what might have seemed like a failure with a rocky start, into success stories for themselves, and to reinforce the image in wider society of white males as the natural leaders of businesses.

Two things may seem strange here: why are businesses in crisis more likely to offer these roles to women and racially marginalised male leaders, and why are they going ahead and saying yes to those offers?

Businesses might look for women leaders in difficult periods because women are often seen as caregivers and nurturers, valued for their 'soft skills'[6] – which can be useful to a business in a time of uncertainty or crisis, especially if the wider team is feeling stressed or demotivated. It may be that women are even hired without the expectation that they will actually resolve the business issues (and so not given the tools or time to make those changes), but to be good managers of people, guiding the teams within the businesses through patches of rough water.[7]

Kristin Anderson, psychology professor at the University of Houston, said in an interview with *Psychology Today*, that she believed that a potential reason for employing women in these roles, when the likelihood of failure is higher, is that women in business 'may be seen as more expendable and better scapegoats'. She went on to suggest that 'organisational leadership might believe that putting women in high risk positions is a win-win strategy: if a woman succeeds after being placed in a difficult position, then the organisation is better off; and if she fails, the woman can be blamed and the prior practice of appointing men can be justified and resurrected.' All whilst the business receives the glow of being able to position itself as forward-thinking and open to all.

As we well know, women and racially marginalised people are usually promoted to board and C-level at much lower rates than white males – and this might explain our willingness to accept these much riskier roles with much lower chances of success. It simply might seem like the only chance someone is ever going to be offered – and who can blame someone for shooting their shot.[8] Even if it's a long shot.

I say all of this to give some important context to what people with one area of marginalisation are experiencing as they take on leadership positions, and the state that businesses are likely to already be in before they are offered the role. It's important to remember that this is a landscape faced by white women and racially marginalised men, but what's the experience like for those with intersectional marginalised identities, like Black women?

What happens when against all of the odds, a Black woman has made it to the peak of leadership? She's pulled up a seat and taken her place as a member of the board, or the CEO. She's ready, and you're ready. Having a Black Lady Boss is going to be amazing, right?

The first thing to look at is what the make-up of the company she's going to be managing is like.

A quick look at demographic sizes shows us that most companies in the USA, at least, are likely to have a lot of white male employees, and these white males are more likely than any other group to be in senior or management positions. According to the 2019 Women in the Workplace Study, at entry-level, white males make up 35 per cent of the workforce, rising to 45 per cent at manager level, 51 per cent at senior manager/director, 57 per cent at VP, 64 per cent at senior VP and finally 68 per cent of the C-Suite.[9]

Not only is 35 per cent the highest starting percentage of any group listed, white males are also unique in being the only group, at all, whose representation grows as they progress in seniority, whilst representation for all other groups shrink.

As a comparison, the same study showed 'women of colour' making up 18 per cent of entry-level employees, which immediately shrinks to 12 per cent at manager level, 9 per cent at senior manager/director, 7 per cent VP, 5 per cent at senior VP and crashes out at 4 per cent of the C-Suite.

'Men of colour' start at 16 per cent representation and fall to 10 per cent by C-Suite, and white women enter the workforce at 30 per cent, which reduces to 18 per cent by the top rung, making them the second most represented group at the most senior level, following white men.

It seems reasonable to say that a Black woman who made it to CEO level, in a company that's likely to be already struggling before her appointment, is likely to find herself managing a significant number of senior white men.

## Having a Black, female boss

Not only is there likely to be increased external scrutiny for Black female leaders, there is likely to be increased inspection and surveillance from inside the company, by senior white male managers.

Let me explain what I mean. As a society we are all unused to seeing Black women as the image of a leader. Leaders, at least successful ones, are usually presented as both white and male. When someone who doesn't fit that image on either count is brought in, people who are themselves more in line with the traditional image are required to do some mental gymnastics. This mismatch of experience and expectation can cause people to be more unsure and questioning of Black female leaders' decisions, choices and directions.

This layer of added internal and external scrutiny forces the CEO to have to work doubly hard to not only make and implement processes and systems, but to get positive buy-in from the team she's managing. Twice as hard for half as much, anyone?

A piece of research looking at management structures discovered something that I found shocking – when a female *or* 'ethnic minority' person was appointed to a CEO position, white male upper management (so, as we've seen, the majority of senior managers) tended to feel less able to identify with the company as a whole. These men did not see themselves mirrored back at the top level of the business, as they've become used to, and so they felt less attached to, and less invested in the business overall. That's wild.

What's more, because these white male senior managers identified less personally with the business, they were less willing to provide help or support to their colleagues (a big part of a manager's role), particularly marginalised colleagues.[10]

I need you to let that sink in for a moment, because it's truly out of this world.

When white men worked in a company where a leader was appointed who was not also a white man, where they were *anything other than that at all*, they felt less connected to the company overall, and stopped performing an important part of their jobs – helping their colleagues – particularly if those colleagues were also from a marginalised group. And this is when the leader in question is *either* racially marginalised *or* female

– so we can only presume that this risk is higher and the outcome more pronounced for those with visible intersectional identities, like Black women.

I've always imagined that as a Black woman myself, having a Black female boss (which I've never had in my whole career, though I have been one to others) would be great. Like, *really* great. I imagine a trickle-down (gross) or halo (nicer) effect, whereby more junior people with marginalised identities would benefit from a female marginalised leader and the doors she'd be able to open for them – especially as we talk so much about needing to see it to be it. To learn that it may actually be damaging to more junior marginalised team members because of lost support or mentorship is devastating.

But why would this happen? Why would white male managers lose their investment in the company after the appointment of anyone other than a white male to the top positions? After all, many marginalised people have *never* worked for someone who shares either their race or gender, let alone both.

As a society, we have traditionally gained a lot of our social standing, and our perceptions of ourselves and others, from the work we do (though I suspect as career paths become less linear, this may well change for Millennial and Gen Z employees). Marginalised CEOs are, in some ways, untested water. Knowing what we know about the probability that they will be appointed at times of uncertainty, and forced to resign more often, they may be perceived by white male managers as risky bets for the future direction of the company, and by extension for their own future prospects, reputations and careers. If this is the case, a natural risk aversion strategy would be to create some distance between themselves and the business destined, in their minds, for failure. Separating yourself and disinvesting may be a self-preservation strategy, to attempt to mitigate any fallout from a lack of success being shared by, or blamed on, themselves. The problem with this is that it can become a self-fulfilling prophecy – a company with disengaged senior managers is not likely to be one on the fast track to success.

Another reason might be linked to the fact that people have strong self-identity ties to their race and gender. This may be, as is the case for many racially marginalised people and women, a feeling of being inside of something (actively feeling Black, and/or actively female). For non-marginalised groups, in cultures such as ours where maleness and whiteness are usually viewed as the blank canvas things start from, the feeling of *not* being a part of something is equally strong – the feeling of not being 'other'. This is the fluency heuristic at play again.

The impact of this bias can be really clearly shown by the fact that people who are used to holding majority/well-represented positions have an increased tendency to think that people who are unlike themselves who have reached positions of success have achieved those positions because of 'special treatment'. And so are quick to dismiss that success – after all, we could all be successful if we'd had the same opportunities handed to us. Studies have shown that white people tend to hold the belief that Black people who are successful have been so at least in part due to affirmative action or positive discrimination. Men also often put women's successes down to the same. This gives them further reason to believe that not only do these people not deserve these roles, they are poorly equipped to execute them.[11] Again, Black women are subject to double jeopardy in this regard throughout their lives.

> I remember getting into drama school, and I had a really close friend who was an actress too, who is a white girl. When I got in to the Royal Central School of Speech and Drama and she didn't she went, 'Oh, you know you only got in because you're Black, right?', and then she was like, 'Haha, only joking.' I never spoke to her again, obviously.
>
> And then let's jump ahead to *Star Wars*. I get the part on *Star Wars* and people are saying 'Oh, she's only a diversity hire.' I've just had to get used to it. You've got to get used to it, the fact that actually whatever space you're in is going to be politicised. I'm like a walking billboard for people's prejudices and I need to get comfortable with that and use it to my advantage – because if people are going to be scared, let them be scared.
>
> – *Naomi Ackie*

When white male managers see someone unlike themselves promoted to the most senior role, they may lose investment because they instinctively underestimate their new boss's performance potential, and presume that the company will fail under their watch and guidance.

It would make sense, in this case, that those white male managers would try to counteract this by investing *more* time and resources into training and supporting their teams, including marginalised team members, but this is often not the case.

As I said, I've never had a Black female boss, but I have been one. Knowing what I know now, I feel compelled to think back to those roles, and wonder if me holding them made things more difficult for precisely the people I most wanted to empower. I can't be sure, of course, but I really hope not, and here's why I think we might have just got away with it:

## Avoiding an overabundance of white male managers

So, now we know that white, male, senior managers lose investment when someone unlike themselves is appointed to the top role in a company, and they stop fulfilling their job roles by helping more junior members of the team, particularly those who are racially marginalised. We know this is a problem that bites hard simply because in most companies most senior management is made up of white males, and those junior to them are more likely to be women and/or racially marginalised people.

In companies where I've been part of senior management teams, it's most often been in a senior operations role, such as COO or director of operations – this means that the areas of hiring, retention and progression have fallen firmly into my remit. I've been responsible for them from start to finish, from their structure to their function, and ultimately their success. I have worked hard on hiring and promotion policies, ensuring they were clear and transparent to all staff members, and applied fairly. This meant that unlike a lot of other companies, we managed to avoid having a disproportionate bloat of white men (new collective noun, anyone?) in senior and middle management roles. This meant that all levels of the business, including middle and senior management teams, were made up of people from a range of different backgrounds and gender identities.

In a business that has been able to achieve more diversity at all levels, disengagement may still take place but it's likely to be less damaging if:

1) Senior management is made up of people from a range of backgrounds. In this case, disengagement is likely to touch a smaller number of people. Those people this disengagement does impact will stand out more, and their behaviour can be addressed, in the same way that any underperforming or unengaged team member would be – with a reminder that supporting more junior team members is a significant part of a manager's role which we expect them to continue performing.

2) The mid- and junior levels of companies are also more diverse. In most companies, those in more junior roles are more likely to be women or marginalised people. Again, if we diversify our hiring pool, and smooth out the paths to progression, a white man is just as likely to be managed by a Black woman as the other way around. Since there is no evidence that groups other than white males are negatively impacted by the appointment of a female or marginalised leader, we are again limiting the scope for this disinvestment, and simultaneously limiting the number of people who are likely to have support taken away from them.

## A commitment to inclusion from the top down

From the first time I interact with a business I might end up working with, or for, I make sure that my commitment to diversity and inclusion is clear, and I ask them about theirs. Before they meet me they see the line 'I am committed to diversity and inclusion in the work I create' at the top of my CV. Whether it's as a member of a business's senior leadership team, or as a producer creating an advert and casting the people who are shown in it, from the very first meeting, potential employers and collaborators know exactly what I'm about.

But a potential new employer knowing what I'm about isn't enough – it leaves the choice solely in their hands. I need to know what they're about too if I'm going to be able to make a good choice about working with them, or not. Before meeting people, I always make sure to look at any published information online about their race or gender pay gaps. I look through their websites at pictures of the team – do they all look suspiciously similar? Are there a small number of visible racially marginalised people who always seem to be conveniently placed at the front of group shots? I always make sure to dedicate a good part of any meeting or interview to asking them about their commitment to diversity and inclusion – finding out if it's an official policy, written and shared internally and publicly, as well as what their next steps are for continued investment in the area.

I feel confident in saying I do my best to go into new opportunities with my eyes open, but I can also say that the way I've done it hasn't always been perfect – and I've always lived to regret not following my gut. Take, for example, one of the first roles I took on after becoming self-employed. It was with a small creative advertising agency, where me joining would double the total number of Black people on the team. Not just the leadership team, mind you, I mean the whole team. Everyone who interviewed me was white, almost everyone was male. As usual, I made a point of asking about diversity and inclusion and was told they knew the agency wasn't there yet, but they were planning to tackle it this year – hopefully with my help.

I was dipping my toe in the self-employment waters. I think (hope) that under any other circumstances I would have made my excuses after that first meeting, and cut my losses. But leaving a PAYE role for the uncertainty of self-employment is a big step, and the allure of the security of having something lined up was too tempting.

I lived to regret accepting it almost immediately. Within my first two weeks in the company, someone was outrageously racist to me at a work event. I knew it wouldn't go fantastically well when I had to raise it to my boss, the founder and CEO of the business. 'I don't want to have to sort this out,' he complained, 'you're causing me problems I don't want to have.' I pointed out that I actually wasn't trying to cause problems, but outright racism was not something I should be expected to just brush off, especially since in my interview they had asked for my help to become a more diverse and inclusive business. 'You can't blame me for this,' I told him, 'I can't stop being a Black woman, that's not going to go away.' 'No,' he said, 'but you can stop talking about it.'

The business lacked a commitment to diversity and inclusion. Me making a complaint was seen as a worse offence than someone being outright racist. I didn't follow my instincts and bore the brunt of my decision.

On the whole, though, my questioning and forthrightness about my beliefs has steered me in the direction of good and progressive companies, where I hope that my presence has been a boost to other more junior, marginalised teammates, rather than a hindrance.

## Millennials and Gen Z for the win

I was young when I transitioned from head of production to chief operating officer in 2018 – just 30 years old. I was made chief financial officer of our American corporation when I had just turned 31. I'm not saying that I wasn't good enough for the role, (I certainly was), but I do suspect that if the company didn't have such a young team overall, and such faith in their skills, this opportunity might not have come my way. I'm so glad it did.

I know some people complain about Millennials at work, but my experience couldn't be further from that, and it's the final reason that I hope the times that I've been a Black Lady Boss have been a positive experience for my team, particularly female and racially marginalised team members, rather than something they had to work against.

It's impossible for me to overstate how much I love the changes that Millennials are bringing to the world of work. We're shaking things up and really setting out our stall for what we will, and won't, accept from our employers. As Gen Zs age into the workplace, in this regard, they're looking like Millennials+, with an even better idea of what they can do, what to accept, and when to walk away. The team I managed were, on the most part, young, ambitious, career-focused and the most open-minded and tolerant group of people I've ever had the pleasure of working with. They understood intersectionality, and had a wide range of influences that played into their own, individual self-identities, and were conscious and accepting of each other's.

The number of Gen Zs and Millennials who identify as non-white has skyrocketed from their parents' generation, not to mention their grandparents'. This means that the number of people entering workforces who solely identify as white and male will start to decrease, and in progressive companies like the one I was lucky enough to work in, this is already starting to happen. If more people have growing intersectional identities, perhaps they will find it less difficult to keep remain motivated by, and to see themselves reflected in, leaders outside of the white male archetype we have come to expect.

Those who don't personally identify as non-white are much more likely to have friends and family members who do. My hope is that marginalised people, like Black women, become less 'other'-seeming in the more progressive minds of new generations, who will find it less difficult to remain mentally, emotionally and professionally invested when they see them take over the leadership of businesses.

# Funding a Feature Film

## Destiny Ekaragha

*Destiny Ekaragha is a BAFTA award-winning director who was named BAFTA breakthrough Brit in 2014. Her award-winning feature comedy* Gone Too Far! *premiered at London Film Festival. Destiny directed* Danny and the Human Zoo, *written by the acclaimed comedian Lenny Henry, primetime UK television* Silent Witness, *international drama including* Riviera, *and most recently the second half or the BAFTA-winning season 2 of* The End of the F\*\*\*ing World *for Netflix.*

**DE:** I've seen the ceiling as concrete many *many* times. But I found it not to be helpful, because even though you're right, it is dark and it is concrete, I'm not the most creative in the darkness. I'm not the happiest person in the world in the darkness. And I start to falter in the darkness. So, even though that is the reality of the situation, I've found it wasn't helpful. So one of my very very bestest friends in the world, she said 'racism is a distraction', quoting Toni Morrison, and the moment she said that to me I started to sort of live in that. Racism is their problem. It's not my problem. It's what they're trying to do to me. So, therefore, it's distracting me from doing my work. It's distracting me from going out and forming relationships. It's distracting me from living my life. Remember that it's a problem they have that they're trying to impose on you. It's not something that you've created. It's not even something that I myself would dismantle. It's something that they have to do. They have to do that shit. So, in the meantime, I need to love my life. And so, I find the way that I'm able to get through all of this is by seeing, visualising what it is that I want to achieve. I'm not looking at the concrete ceiling, or the glass ceilings anymore. Because I believe that I'll smash through them. I think there has to be some

sort of belief there – that's the gift *Gone Too Far* gave me. If ever there was a concrete ceiling to smash through, it was that one. Only two Black women prior to myself had made a feature film that had been cinematically released. And that's in cinematic history, which is insane. And I'm glad I didn't know that when I was making my film – I thought there was bare – why wouldn't there be? I just didn't look into it, I was focused on my own journey. It was a journalist who told me, and I couldn't believe what I'd heard. So for me, knowing that I'd broken through that, nobody can tell me anything. I have to focus on my own journey, and I'm hoping that whatever door I manage to slide through – because the door is never open, it's just like a slight crack that I just kind of do *The Matrix* through – I'm hoping that many other Black women can come and do *The Matrix* through that as well.

I'm not going to sit here and tell you that I'm busting doors open, because I'm not. I don't believe that I am. If that was the case, there would be 10 Black women with films out in the cinema already. You just reminded me that that film was 8 years ago, and there should be 8 other feature films directed by Black women as standard now, by 8 different Black women, but there aren't. There aren't. So, I'm not busting down no doors. I might be cracking a couple, but I don't even know if they're even staying cracked open, so I just think I have to focus on the work. Focus on what it is that I want to achieve, and believe that I can achieve those things, and so far that's how I've got to where I am at the moment.

**SW:** You've spoken about the difficulties in getting funding for your first film and I wondered if you were able to speak about that

**DE:** *Gone Too Far* was written by Bola Agbaje. It's based on a play that she wrote, and it's important for me to say this because the play won an Olivier award. Talk about having to prove ourselves as Black people. If your play has won an Olivier, you've done it! There's an audience there, you've won the highest accolade you can possibly win, we're done. Right? You'd think. But no. I got attached to the project maybe two years after it had first gone into development, and so Bola had been at it for a while. When we got together and we were going into these production companies to try and get funding, to try and get development money, some people would say it's not for us, and that's fine, that's great actually because the no's were quite quick and preferable to drawing it out, but we also got some people having problems with the story – the film version deviated from the play a little bit. We wanted to make it more of a comedy about friendship, about identity and coming of age, the bond between brothers and the bond between friends, so we changed some of the darker stuff. And some of the notes we'd get back from production companies were along the lines of 'oh, shouldn't the brothers be angrier? Shouldn't they want to stab each other?' Truly! That was a real note from a real person in the industry, 'shouldn't the brothers want to kill each other? I don't understand why they don't want to kill each other – he should be really angry at his brother because he had to grow up in Nigeria' – like Nigeria is this horrible prison place, 'he had to grow up in Nigeria whilst his brother got to grown up in London'. Obviously, you have no idea about life in London or in Nigeria, and why the fuck would they want to stab each other? What are you talking about? But they literally heard 'Peckham' and straight up went to gang violence: Peckham, Black, boy, hoodie. Do you know what I mean? And that's why it was very important for Bola and I to dismantle that, because I grew up on these estates, I'm a product of the environment that I grew up in, but I'm in the room with you; that should tell you that if everyone was just stabbing each other we'd all be dead. Those weren't the only things happening on my estate. People were getting on with life. People were doing things. There was a sense of community, so I just found it not only insulting but upsetting.

And then the notes came in and some people were like 'it would be really difficult to sell because it's an all-Black cast'. It was so frustrating, people weren't allowing us to not only tell the story, but to do our jobs. This is our job, and people were actively stopping us from doing it. Stopping us from earning a livelihood because of the stories we wanted to tell. Bola will always be my sister for life anyway, but one thing that bonded us even more is that we refused to change the film. We refused to add white leads. We refused to make the story darker. We refused. We refused. We stood our ground that this is the film, and if you're not on it then you're not on it - it got to the point where after many tears had been shed we thought 'if God wants this film to happen, then it will happen. But we have to stop fighting now, and we have to move on.'

And the moment that we moved on, someone recommended we do a reading, suggesting 'the industry is never going to read this script and understand what's going on, they're just not, but if they hear it they might get it a bit more.' So, we did a reading at the Royal Court, and it turns out most people still didn't get it! Some of the notes we got back were, 'there's a lot of talk about race in the film, maybe that should go?' Someone else mentioned 'maybe there should be a party at the end, or something?' because apparently that's all Black people do. I didn't know, but apparently that's what we do, we love to party, you know, just randomly. This is the industry. This ain't people from road. But Chris Collins, may he rest in peace, gave a note saying 'this film is really funny, I don't understand why it's not being made', that was his note, and he was at the BFI at the time. So he invited us for a meeting at

the BFI with Ben Roberts, who was the new head of funding. I went to meet with Chris Collins and Ben Roberts, and Ben had the same view as Chris - this is a funny film that should be getting made. I remember saying to Ben, 'What do you mean you liked it? You read it?' He replied 'Yeah. . .' I asked, 'and you understood it?' '. . . What's not to understand? It's just kids in London . . .' he said. I mean, *he* was looking at *me* like I was mad, but you have to understand this was like two and a half, three years of no's. This was over a period of three years, five for Bola, and so I just didn't understand what was happening in that room! They were both very white men, who I didn't know at the time, telling me that they understood this script, and so in that moment I was like 'Wow, we're not aliens!' - I'd been going into these rooms feeling like a fucking Klingon, it was almost like I was someone from Mars trying to sell our culture from another planet! This is London! It's just kids in London! But that's how they would make us feel. So, once Ben said that, he followed with 'I think we should make the film, I think we should make it in October.' I was just lost for words. And then I blacked out, because I don't remember the rest of it at all. Chris's version of the story is that he took over the meeting because I stopped talking - and I must have because I don't remember anything else that was said. I don't even remember coming out of the building. I just didn't understand. I think my mind was like . . . what? When Chris Collins said 'we're making a film' I couldn't even believe it. I thought that the rug was going to be pulled out from under me, but I figured that getting a crew together was going to be a really good experience, so I may as well do it before they took the film away – because I was sure of it. I was sure. Until about two weeks prior to filming and Lizzie Francke invited myself and Bola and there were Lindt chocolate in the middle of the table, and I thought, 'This is it. This is when they tell us that funding has fallen through or some other excuse' but instead she asked,

'Oooh, are you excited about October 22nd?' and I just asked '. . . What's happening on October 22nd?' Now it was her turn to look really worried. '. . . Erm . . . well . . . you making a film . . . you start shooting!' and I was like, 'Oh yeah, yeah, of course, of course,' you know when you start playing it off? Like 'Of course! Of course!' and inside I was thinking, wow, this is actually happening, this is actually going to happen.

And then I made the film and it was wonderful and it was hard and it was a triumph. It was literally a dream come true.

# Nana Bempah's Favourite Thing About Being a Black Woman

Oooh, that is a question that I have never been asked before. You know what I think it is? I think it's the culture. Or the sauce. There's something so special in having this deep culture and rich history, and understanding that my ancestors came from all of this, and passed it down from generation to generation. The food, the music, dancing, the expression, culture – it's all so special. And I have to say, I don't see that everywhere, I just think it's really, really special. And you know, for the longest time growing up I didn't realise just how much of a vibe it was, as it was just normality, but now I go to family gatherings and I really appreciate the way we are expressing and dancing, the way we eat and how we communicate with each other, and I just – I love all of the things, and I think it's a fantastic thing to be part of and have it running through my veins. And if you know Ghanaian culture at all, you will know that the women play a massive part in all of that. When I think of my grandma and the way she just ran the show and made things happen, and the same with my mum who is the absolute queen when it comes to these events – they are just so instrumental in creating all of this. I come from a line of amazing women and hope that I can pass this forward to my daughter.

# CHAPTER 11

# WELCOME TO THE LADY GANG

'Abandon the cultural myth that all female friendships must be bitchy, toxic or competitive. This myth is like heels and purses – pretty but designed to *slow* women down.'

**ROXANE GAY**

One of the most common pieces of advice that crops up over and over again in discussions about climbing the professional ladder is 'use your network'. It's the simplest, most effective way to progress, make new relationships and strengthen existing ones – and it's pretty undeniable that it works. I can't count the number of times I've worked with people who are on work experience, doing internships or in entry-level jobs, who have had a personal connection to someone senior in the company. These connections, usually fostered by people's parents rather than themselves, open doors that would otherwise have been shut. These connections give people a first step on their career ladders, add a line to their CVs, and provide references who can be called to help with their next step, and the next, and the next.

I'm not saying that this is the path that every person from a non-marginalised background takes to begin their working life, by any means. Nor am I saying that anyone with these opportunities to shortcuts shouldn't try to make the most of them – I know if I'd have had them, I would have at least given it a go. What I do want to say, though, is that from the start, this challenges our idea of meritocracy and shows that the playing field we're all on isn't quite as even as we might like to believe. These connections and opportunities are not available in the same way to everybody.

Historically Black people, and all racially marginalised people, have had serious limitations to the types of industries and roles that have been open to them, not by chance but by design, through segregation and outright discrimination. The legacy of this historical imbalance means that even now it is not unusual for a young Black woman to be the first person in her family or social circle to have gained access to a traditionally exclusionary space. This lack of precedence means that often there is no one whose footsteps she can follow in, making it hard to know who to reach out to for that same support in getting that all-important foot in the door that other people can take for granted. I don't believe that marginalised groups are less willing to use their networks for personal success, but that through no fault of our own, we lack a professional network to call on in the first place.

For the Black women who are able to have the opportunity to get a foot in the door and a job at their dream company, the impact of that early disadvantage of not having a network doesn't go away, it just shifts slightly. Without the advantage of joining a company already staffed with people you have a pre-existing connection to and understanding of – a pre-built support network of sorts – Black women often struggle to find both role models or sponsors during their careers. The impact of this is made worse by the lack of robust external professional networks available in a lot of industries, outside of the traditional old boys' clubs, which are, by their very nature and design, exclusionary.

Not having the sponsors to bring you into a new company or industry means that if you do manage to get in on your own, there are fewer people to advocate for you, or protect you when mistakes happen, and things don't go according to plan. In the UK, as the McGregor-Smith Review, 'Race in the Workplace', found: 'There is discrimination and bias at every stage of an individual's career, and even before it begins. From networks to recruitment and then in the workforce, it is there. BME people are faced with a distinct lack of role models . . . they are more likely to be disciplined or judged harshly.'[1]

In my early career in advertising, I definitely felt this lack of a group of people to call my own. I had made it in, seemingly by chance, and stayed in by pure force of will, but what next? My parents couldn't offer advice at the start of my career – my dad is a retired gravedigger and crematorium operator, my mom is a cleaner – they had no idea how I should approach a salary negotiation, craft an outstanding CV or deal with a difficult client or, as the case was more often, a difficult colleague. My friends outside of work were as junior as me – they didn't have an old boss to call to get me a favour, a placement or a reference. My friends from university most certainly didn't have salary benchmarking information for me to compare against; we had graduated in 2008, the year of the financial crash – jobs were hard to come by and money was taboo, not something to be compared or discussed.

If I wanted a network, I was going to have to build my own. So, I built my Lady Gang.

I know, calling something a gang can sound intimidating, but don't worry – nowhere on earth is safer than in the company of your Lady Gang. You could call it finding your tribe, horizontal mentoring, a group glow up, or anything else you like. To me the non-threatening, unassuming qualities of the word Lady, alongside the strength and collective power of the word Gang, really perfectly sums up what this whole thing is about – but I'll come to that in a moment.

First of all, let me tell you about my personal Lady Gang, what we do for each other, and how you can harness the same power by finding and collaborating with the best people in your life.

## Lady Gang

These are a group of people of all races, backgrounds, genders (I know the name suggests women, but the power of your Lady Gang really does lie in its diversity) and stages in their professional lives who you invest in, and who invest in you right back. They are your personal board of directors, they are the people you turn to for advice, and who champion your successes just as much as you do theirs. They want you to succeed, they help you to succeed. They celebrate your wins as much as they let you know when you've got to stop that bullshit. They are an extension of yourself and they mirror your shine into the world, and you shine right back onto them.

This is a concept inspired by the wonderful Aminatou Sow and Ann Friedman – hosts of the podcast 'Call Your Girlfriend' and inventors of Shine Theory. They are amazing, and well worth looking into!

> I'm really fortunate to be surrounded by other people running media companies with a clear purpose and a focus. And in this strange time, I think it's just been so amazing to have that support network to be able to stress-test ideas and talk about issues or things that are going on for us in our businesses that are tricky. It's great to have that network – there are so many people that I'm just so inspired by and, you know, who I'm fortunate to be able to have conversations with and share ideas with, I think that's brilliant.
>
> – *Liv Little*

## What's the point?

Work, life and everything else is too tough to do alone, or to always be in competition with those closest to us. Mentoring is great; I've been a mentor several times and have found it hugely rewarding and hope I've done some good. But the reality is there's only so much that someone who is removed from your immediate cohort and situation can do – advice can be limited and overly general, and the power dynamic of mentor and mentee can be quite unbalanced. Without specialised schemes, which have limited space and availability, good mentoring can be hard to find and Black women often report feeling hugely under-supported in their roles, lacking sponsors, advocates and guidance.

Particularly early in their careers, Black women can suffer from intersectional invisibility, a term which means that two marginalised parts of our identities (being a woman and being Black) compound one another to make us doubly invisible.

When people are asked to think of a Black person, they usually think of a man, and when people think of a woman, it's usually a white woman they picture. Black women's two marginalised identities layer on top of one another in invisibility – instead of being recognised as belonging to two marginalised groups and being doubly supported, we are overlooked as a member of *either* and afforded the protections of *neither* group.[2]

Black women's lack of representation means that despite being physically hypervisible – often reporting that they are the only woman who looks like them in the room when in a professional setting – we are cognitively invisible. We often find ourselves left out of consideration spaces in conversations around pay rises, promotions and even simply praise.[3]

Doubly unfortunately, this invisibility tends to only last until things go wrong. When things don't go according to plan, or mistakes are made, Black women lose this invisibility and again find themselves becoming hypervisible. This is when intersectional invisibility becomes double jeopardy, meaning that Black women are more harshly punished for on-the-job mistakes.[4]

When things are going well, you're invisible; when things are going badly, you're in double trouble – it can feel like a no-win scenario with no one in your corner.

So, let's get in each other's corners. I think it's time that we looked to our peers and informal networks to give us the support we need, and for us to give it back to them.

> I have a few different groups of friends who do similar types of work to me – most of it is friendship based on our WhatsApp group chats, where we go to say the things we can't online, including questions like, 'Does this sound right?' And so with that, my friends who are mostly writers for different publications or novelists, a question might be, 'Hey, this publication offered me this amount of money, does that seem right?' or 'Oh, actually, if you speak to this editor or that, then maybe you can get that commissioned'. I've found it extraordinarily helpful – these groups have been invaluable in lifting each other up, and really creating a space where you get to know like-minded people. And it's really, really nice when you see somebody who you've introduced a friend to, for work, which has gone well and they say 'Your friend did an amazing job!' because you know that you are strengthening each other, and creating these bigger ecosystems that are going to mean that for the rest of our lives, we have that network. I mean, God forbid someone loses their job – but even if that happened I don't feel like we'd be unemployed for very long, and that's mostly because of the support networks that we've built, which I'm eternally grateful for.
>
> – *Daniellé Scott-Haughton*

### So, how exactly does it work?

It's pretty simple – building your Lady Gang is about finding the best and most inspirational people you know and work with, and adjusting how you think about them. It's about deciding, instead of trying to one-up them, or tear them down, to see how you can best collaborate and work together. The beauty of it is, once you start working with people in a collaborative way, they notice – and nine times out of ten they reciprocate. Over time you'll find that dazzling 'competition' that you were wasting energy on trying to pull down now has your back, and you've got theirs.

It's no exaggeration to say that being intentional about forming and nurturing my Lady Gang is the best idea I've ever had. I'm lucky to be proud of a lot of things in my career, but my Lady Gang and the way we've been able to help and support each other over the years, and still do today, is the thing I'm proudest of building. Ever. And I want the same for you.

My Lady Gang has helped me move forward in my career in ways I wouldn't have thought (and probably wouldn't have been) possible without them, and I have helped them in return, gleefully – feeling each of their successes as personal wins. They have become my network when I couldn't rely on family connections or colleagues for an intro or a recommendation. They are basically my good reputation – the people who say nice things about me behind my back or tell someone looking for a collaborator how perfect I'd be for this project or that role. We know each other's salaries and let one another know if someone is selling themselves short or not demanding their worth. We practice negotiations together, so the first time we say that big scary number out loud for real at work, isn't the first time we've *ever* said it out loud, and it doesn't sound wild coming out of our mouths – and by the time we're doing it for real we've already heard someone we trust saying we're worth it. We read each other's CVs and remind each other when it's been too long since one of us has had a promotion or pay rise. If one of us is offered a project that we can't take on we will always make sure to pass on each other's details and make introductions if we know someone who'd be a better fit than ourselves. We have nominated each other for awards – making sure the world knows about the superstars in our midst, and I always know when I do a speaking event I will be able to look out and see someone there from the Lady Gang, being a supportive face in the crowd and clapping the loudest (and shouting, 'That's my friend!' – Rory, I see you).

I know I said Lady Gangs were a safe place, and they are, but I do have to admit that the origins of my personal Lady Gang first were in an act of defiance to an offensive company-wide email sent around the advertising agency where I worked at the time. We've come a long way since then but let me tell you how it all started.

On International Women's Day 2017 a managing partner of the agency I was working at (who had developed a habit of spotting when other members of staff had left their laptops unlocked and sending prank all-agency messages) sent the prank email that was to be his last.

The title of the email was 'Women's Weak' (Yeah? Geddit? Cool cool. A great start, I'm sure you'll agree), and the mail contained such gems as:

> *As you know, behind every good man is a good woman. I certainly know this to be true. There are some very good women way, way behind me.*

And:

> *If you're a woman, lady or girl, tell me your story of how your feminine weaknesses have held you back in your career or personal life, and I will give you £5 towards righting the wrongs that the cruel twist of genetic fate has handed you.*
>
> *As an added bit of fun, as a subversion of the norm – I will make you a cup of tea while you share your personal experiences. How quaint?!*
>
> *(You'll do the washing up though. There are boundaries.)*

As you can tell he was one of the great comedians of his time. Perhaps of all time.

I vividly remember the email landing in my inbox, along with the inboxes of the three hundred or so people who worked in the UK company at the time, and leaving me feeling somewhere between enraged and deflated. Ready to take action, but resigned to the knowledge that nothing I could do as a mid-level employee would ever make a change within a global agency. This was a man I worked with every day. I had met his family, we talked about his children, he seemed like 'one of the good guys', I liked him. And yet this was the joke that this seemingly progressive man thought would be funny to share with the entire agency – the majority of whom were much more junior than himself, on the one day a year set aside to celebrate women.

I don't know what it was about that moment but I decided that I'd had enough. I'd had enough of working in a company totally dominated by older white men, I'd had enough of running International Women's Day campaigns for clients celebrating women externally whilst senior members of the company quietly belittled their own teams behind closed doors, and I'd had enough of not having a voice.

I was lucky enough to work with some amazing people who, it turned out, were just as fed up as I was. 'I'll reply if you do,' we told each other. And so we did – in a string of reply-all public emails calling him out for his misogynistic, outdated thinking, and his impulse to share his 'comedy' with a wide audience of more junior staff who I'm sure he felt confident would never challenge him. A real power play.

More and more people jumped on the chain, sharing their experiences of working with him and calling out the agency's sexist tendencies. In response, other people, mostly older men, jumped on the chain, or broke off into little huddles of discussion around the office, to lament the loss of the 'good old days' before all of the 'HR nonsense'.

In reality, as is so often the case, the mails people sent in solidarity with the initial mail were probably worse than the first mail itself. It showed us all, laid bare in no uncertain terms, what other people in the agency thought, but had never felt they could express before. Suddenly they felt they had a platform, and in seizing it we were able to see exactly who we were working with, day after day.

It wasn't long, only a few minutes, before the COO told us all, very clearly, to stop replying, to move on, and essentially pipe down. We were effectively silenced, as going against the COO would have resulted in bigger problems than any of us were equipped to deal with at the time. We needed another way to show that we wouldn't stand for it – and somehow I became the leader of this small resistance.

I went out and bought a variety of plain T-shirts and jumpers, and came back to enlist the help of my superstar designer friend (Rebecca Petts Davies, OG Lady Gang member and the designer of my first book, *Anti-Racist Ally*), to block print some slogans. 'That's the good thing about agencies; all of the skills you need to put together a good protest under one roof. We made one or two T-shirts saying 'Feminist and Riot Grrrl, but far and away more than anything else we made was Lady Gang.' I had a pile on my desk and people from all over the agency came to take them, wearing them around the office for the next week, sharing on social, and showing their silent solidarity with the message.

We wore them to internal meetings, then client meetings, and eventually to HR meetings. The managing partner was told that there would be no more 'joke' emails from him and was put on probation. In the end, he left, and we stayed, but it didn't feel like a victory. Not really.

One reason I was conflicted was that I liked him. I still do. He had done and said something stupid and poorly judged, but I felt that the permission that it seemed to give to others to share their own sincerely held beliefs was worse than the initial email itself.

The other reason was that in reality, it was hard, and really uncomfortable – as using your voice (or using your T-shirt as it may be) often is. There were moments that I was pretty sure I was going to get fired. A creative director called me a 'storm in a D-cup' and warned others to be careful of me. I got a reputation for being a 'difficult woman' who 'wouldn't take a joke'. Which I was fine with. But I couldn't shake the worry that I might have done irreversible damage to my career. (This is a feeling I've had several times in my working life, and generally means I've done the right thing and taken a necessary stand, but until you have hindsight that can be hard to feel sure of in the moment.)

As well as being difficult and scary, it showed me who my allies were, who shared the same ideologies as me, and what strength we could have when we worked together. And that became the basis of building my Lady Gang.

These days, my personal Lady Gang has grown into something that's much more about support than protest. We work together for one another's good, and shout from the rooftops about our clever friends every chance we get. But if the need ever arises again, Bec still has the stencils and I have the fabric paint.

I had a group of Black women that are in the game – they're writers, they're producers, they're novelists, they're playwrights – and we talk to each other regularly. I can only speak from my own experience, but I can tell you off the bat that without that support from those

Black women I don't think I would have got as far as I have managed to get. And I cannot get anything or achieve anything without saying that first.

*– Destiny Ekaragha*

## Building a good Lady Gang

There are some essential things to remember when you're building your Lady Gang – let me share them with you:

- Everyone in your Lady Gang must not, I repeat *must not*, look like you and they absolutely must not all be women. My Lady Gang at the moment is mostly men, as a result of working in the hyper male-dominated advertising industry, but I'm not going to change the name of it, and they don't want me to. If your network is just people like you, you'll be shouting into an echo chamber. Consider that 'All BME groups are more likely to be overqualified than white ethnic groups but white employees are more likely to be promoted than all other groups'.[5] You need to be able to get a true understanding of benchmarking, average progression and professional development, to be sure you're getting your worth, and being rewarded at your true economic value. To understand that value you need to build close and trusting relationships with the widest possible range of people whose experiences you can compare to your own. You have to be open about your salary, benefits, bonuses, and your progression timeline with people you trust, and they have to be honest about theirs too. Knowledge is power, and without openness from a variety of people you'll never spot the race or gender pay gaps, or notice that you've been in the same role forever whilst other people have been promoted five times. There was outrage when people in Hollywood started being open about their salaries, and when the BBC started publishing the payments for their top presenters, not because of the amount that people were being paid, but because of the differences in those amounts between people based on their gender and race. Until people slowly started having these conversations, everyone was operating in their own bubble, without any visibility on their colleagues and community. Injustice and imbalance relies on secrecy and siloed information. The more light we can shed on other people's situations the more empowered we are as a society to push for and demand our worth. But we have to know our worth before we can demand it.

- Really, *really* invest. Your Lady Gang will only work if you are deeply invested, and everyone else is too. There can be no secret one-up(wo)manship, no deep burning resentments or quiet competition. Lady Gang relies on everyone really, truly pulling together, being proud of their amazing networks and telling the world about it every chance they get.

- Offer to help more junior people – some people who I befriended when they were at the start of their careers have turned out to be absolute superstars, so now as well as me being able to hook them up with gigs, they're also able to give me valuable roles, projects and intros. When you spot someone who is amazing, no matter their level, they will only continue to rise.

- Don't be afraid to ask for help from your peers. It might seem like admitting you need help with something makes you appear less professional and capable. The reality is that the *most* successful people admit when they need help, and the right people will want to help where they can. Admitting you need help is humanising and vulnerable and can turn a work relationship into a collaboration, and who doesn't want that? But remember, asking for help is a two-way thing, you need to be generous with your time in return; you have to kiss down, not up and help others to succeed.

> I certainly have a WhatsApp group of people who do similar roles to me, and I know there are people who have definitely recommended me for work, and vice versa. I often recommend Black women for work, because I often do feel that I am the token Black person when it comes to campaigns, and I sometimes do speak up about that, if I feel like it's a safe place to do it, and try and make a suggestion about how they could be much more inclusive.
>
> – *Natalie Lee*

## Being a good Lady Gang member

Being a good Lady Gang member is an active project – think of it as 'Ask not (only) what your Lady Gang can do for you, but what you can do for your Lady Gang' and you'll get the gist. The founding principles are true investment in other people's success and a belief that we are strongest together, so here are a few techniques designed to make things as effective as possible:

### A Lesson from the Obama administration: amplification

It's a scenario that most women are familiar with: there's a meeting going on, voices all around, and you make what you think is a great point, only to have it go totally unnoticed. It's OK, I guess not every idea is 'the one'. Until. Hang on. What's this? A man in the group has just said exactly the same thing, in the same way, only louder and as if it's his idea, and suddenly it's the best idea anyone has ever heard. Meeting over, Steve has cracked it. He's such a smart guy.

Whilst it's true that conversations move quickly and everyone gets cut off, interrupted or overlooked from time to time, studies have shown that not only are women interrupted at a much higher frequency in the work-place by both men and other women,[6] but that they also receive less credit for their ideas and can even be penalised if they choose to speak out.[7]

> Looking back at my first very senior role, I can see much more clearly how the things my male colleagues said were taken on board, and how the things I would say were just not taken on in the same way. I can also see the respect that I was given – or, more so, the lack of respect, which wasn't really based on anything aside from my age, race and gender. My thoughts and opinions weren't being taken on board, and so I had to come up with different strategies to get my point across because the default lack of respect meant that if I didn't use certain tactics to try to be heard, then I wouldn't be able to enact change.
>
> *– Nana Bempah*

Women who do try to assert themselves and have their voices heard, especially Black women, are often characterised by the persistent stereotype of being angry or aggressive. This characterisation is designed to limit credibility and authority, in the same way as calling a woman hysterical or hormonal. It gives people an opportunity to tone police, taking issue with the tone, or perceived tone of a complaint whilst ignoring the content. When we think of all of the ways that, over time, people have tried to diminish and belittle women's words and voices, it begins to seem that women being overlooked (and spoken over) in group conversations, and men taking the credit for their ideas may not be as accidental as it first seems.

Next time you're in a meeting with a mixed group of people spend a few minutes listening to the shape and patterns of the conversation – if you've never noticed it before you might be surprised by what you hear, or don't, coming from men and women.

In situations like this, when women are overlooked in favour of men making the same point, there are two key factors at play – gender bias (the idea that men have more good ideas more often, and so deserve more attention) and the simple reality that women's voices are usually physically quieter than men's and so easier to dismiss or, if we're being generous, 'not to hear'.

So, what can we do about this? This is a perfect example of how our voices are very literally louder together than individually, as the women of the Obama administration discovered. In the early days of the administration women in the top positions were outnumbered and felt that they had to work overly hard just to find a place for themselves in conversations and important meetings. So they started amplifying each other. When a female colleague made a point, another woman would repeat it, and credit the woman who had said it first. This eliminated the risk of the men in the room taking the credit for the idea, and reinforced the relationships between the woman as collaborative rather than competitive.

The additional benefit here is that when you start doing this for marginalised voices, the owners of those voices notice. You become a trusted person, someone who wants to help people, and in turn, someone who they want to help. Through the small act of actively listening, and showing that you value one another and one another's words and thoughts, you can begin to form bonds.

By the end of his administration, President Obama couldn't deny the strength of the voices, ideas and words of the women in his administration, and the women, through the power of collaboration, gained parity with men.[8]

### Useful phrases for amplification include:

- 'I think that's what Anna said a moment ago.'
- 'Sarah, could you give us some more details about how that would work?'
- When someone interrupts or talks over a woman making a point: 'That's a really interesting point, we'll come back to it in a moment, but I think Preeti was in the middle of saying something.'
- 'I think Michelle made a good point earlier that I'm not sure people heard – let's circle back for a moment.'
- 'Susie had the great idea of . . .'

### Know when to pass the mic

As I've got older and more established in myself and my career I've developed a much better understanding of where my strengths lie, and where they very much don't. My years of working have also given me the opportunity to have collaborated with people who are amazing in areas that I wouldn't have the first idea how to approach, and I'm proud to have a lot of those people as core members of my Lady Gang. This is great, because it means I have built up a network of talented and trusted people and I know that between us we can solve just about any problem that we're likely to have. It also means that when people approach me for projects or opportunities that aren't right for me, or if they ask me for help in solving problems I don't know how to tackle, me saying 'Sorry, no' can be the start of the conversation rather than the end. Sure, I could probably muddle through most things people ask me for help with, but why would I when I could keep doing the things I do best, and passing the rest on to someone I trust who can do the job a thousand times better than me?

Learning to let go has come at the same time as building up a talented and trustworthy Lady Gang, and I don't think that's a coincidence.

Part of being a good Lady Gang member is having an investment in knowing what everyone else can do, where they want to go, and helping to make connections any time you can. This means it's important to check in regularly with your network – you never know what amazing new skills they've learned and the new avenues they want to explore. Make a point of asking what people are working on now, and what they want to do next – you'll be surprised how often it will line up with conversations you're having in other areas of your professional or personal life, and how many times you'll be able to make them a valuable introduction to a new connection.

Doing what you do best and passing on the rest means that when people come to you for help on a project, a 'Sorry, I can't help you on this one', a dead end for you and the person looking for a solution, becomes a 'I'm not the best person to work on this but I know someone amazing who is'. You add value to your Lady Gang by making new introductions for work and experiences they otherwise wouldn't have got, and you add value to your wider network by sharing a new connection with them, one who comes with your stamp of approval.

Making good use of your Lady Gang isn't all about giving, though, it's also about not being afraid to ask for help and leverage connections when you need to. If you're working on a project and you know someone in your Gang has a great contact who can help you, just ask them for an introduction. More often than not, people like to be asked – someone coming to you as an expert in your field is flattering and validating. The answer won't always be yes, and that's OK, there may be underlying factors that you're not aware of until you ask, but most of the time people will be more than happy to make an intro – nothing reflects better on them than having a great friend they can introduce to new people. As we all know, people are known by the company they keep, and you're great company to keep.

## Dress rehearsals

Big life and career conversations can be scary, and the worst part is there's no dress rehearsal. Unless, of course, you make one. This has truly been one of the greatest things I've started doing with my Lady Gang – it's so simple but deadly effective.

Progressing in your career, especially as a Black woman, means having a lot of difficult conversations. As we've seen, statistics show that Black women are often overlooked for pay raises and promotions, and without people in senior positions advocating for us, the weight of the burden of progress falls onto us. That means understanding our value (which can be difficult in itself) and then advocating for it, which can, quite frankly, be terrifying. But don't worry – you've got your Lady Gang in your corner.

The first step is benchmarking. As I've mentioned there are great tools like Glassdoor, LinkedIn and industry salary surveys available to benchmark your salary by location, title and years of experience, but your fact-checking doesn't need to stop there. When you've built up your Lady Gang from a diverse range of people, you then have that group of people to call on to sense-check. Asking them about their salaries, benefits and the tools they used to negotiate them can seem weird at first. We've pretty much all been socialised to not ask people what they earn, but once you get into an open dialogue about these things the stigma quickly falls away and all that remains is the benefit, in both directions.

Once, when I was having a wobble about encouraging people to be forthright about their money – is it really the right thing to do, or just awkward? – I asked the group chat (mine is on Instagram rather than

WhatsApp, I love a GIPHY sticker) what they thought. 'Your willingness to be open about money has made me so much richer, so I'm certainly not going to tell you to stop!' was my favourite response, and so, we continue.

I know it can be jarring to simply ask someone what they get paid if it's a conversation you haven't had with them before, and so a gentler way to broach the subject can be centring yourself in the conversation and offering up the information as it relates to you first. For example, you could say:

- 'I've been stuck on £25,000 for almost two years now, and I've learned to do so much more in that time, I'm thinking about asking for a raise, do you have any ideas about what a good amount to ask for would be?'
- 'I've seen a spec for a role that seems great! The salary is £59,000 – I know you work in the industry, does that sound about right to you?'
- 'I think I'm underpaid, at the moment I get £36,000. I know you do a similar job, and I wondered if that was similar to what you get?'
- 'Someone is asking me to do a freelance project, and they're offering me £200 for it – they say that's industry standard. Is it in line with what you've been paid?'

All of these examples lead with openness and vulnerability from you and give the person you're speaking to the opportunity to be open with you in return, without forcing them to disclose if they don't want to. Personally, I encourage everyone to talk about money as much as they can, as openly as they can in safe, trusting environments, because the mystery surrounding finance is only beneficial for people invested in maintaining the status quo of inequity and imbalance, and truth lives in the light.

I found out we were undercharging and the only way I found that was by speaking to white women who had similar businesses. I've had quite a good support network of white women who understand the barriers we're facing and have been very open about how much they charge [to try to help address that]. When I found out what they charged, that's when I realised . . . wow. I also learned a lot from some of my other friends who are Black women in business, we're sharing stories and they're telling me what they've discovered – so everyone has been doing research and sharing what we've heard, and that's when I realised, by being transparent and asking them what they're charging, what their day rates are, that I found out wow, I'm seriously undercharging. I found out that I should have been changing twice what I've been charging for some programmes – and I was still getting pushback from some clients asking 'Why are we paying for this?'

– *Vanessa Sanyauke*

Once you have the information you need to know what you're worth, the next step is to practice asking for it. I say practice asking for it because that's exactly what you need to do – if you were going to give a big presentation for work you wouldn't just rock up and think, *I'm just going to wing it, no need to practice first*, and the same should be true of the things you do for yourself. Practice, practice, practice. That salary you want, the one you've put the time and energy into researching and you know you deserve, practice saying it, out loud, to people. Say it until it feels right, because the first time you say it the words will feel alien coming out of your mouth, or the way you express it might come off a little wrong, and that's why we're practising.

Ask a few members of your Lady Gang to run dress rehearsals of the meeting with you, from going into the room, to asking for what you want and negotiating any curveballs along the way, and what to do if you get what you asked for, and if you don't. You're much more likely to get what you ask for if you've taken the time and used your connections to find out what's realistic, and to practise asking so you sound and feel confident when you do it for real. When you're in the room you'll have the encouragement of all of the test runs you've already done in your head, cheering you on.

## Reminders of greatness

All too often the compliments that people give and receive, in and outside of work, are related to their physical attributes rather than their character, thoughts or achievements. Take a moment to think about the last compliment you gave to a co-worker, was it closer to, 'I was so impressed with the way you made that presentation? I learned a lot from it,' or 'I love your shoes' (or, maybe, in this new remote working world, 'Your Zoom background looks great!')?

Even though we've all been taught not to comment on people's appearance, especially in the workplace, it still feels like complimenting someone's shoes, hair or outfit is a lot less vulnerable than complimenting their work, values or bravery. It's also a lot less valuable. Nice shoes come and go, haircuts grow out, and bodies can change beyond recognition, with or without the approval of the people housed inside them.

When so much emphasis is placed on appearance over professional achievements, no wonder Forbes reported in 2018 that two-thirds of women in the UK suffer from imposter syndrome, that worrying little feeling that,[9] deep down, you're not good enough. It's the feeling that you may have been able to fool people up to now but it's only a matter of time before someone is going to realise that you don't *actually* know what you're doing and you're going to be found out in a big embarrassing mess for the fraud you've been all along. This is particularly prevalent among Black women who, as a group, have their achievements and credentials challenged much more often and suffer from more microaggressions than any other. Even the most successful Black women are susceptible to these feelings: as Maya Angelou said when discussing her success, 'I have written eleven books, but each time I think, "Uh oh, they're going to find out now. I've run a game on everybody, and they're going to find me out."'[10]

If even Maya Angelou felt that way, then there's a pretty great chance that the people we care about feel it too, and so I make a real effort to affirm my Lady Gang in ways that are not physical, but that show the real value that they bring to my life. It sounds simple, but affirmations can be powerful.

**Easy affirming compliments that aren't about appearance include:**

- 'You are so impressive.'
- 'I thought it was amazing when you . . .'
- 'You inspire me.'
- 'I'm proud of you.'
- 'I've learned [X] from you.'
- 'I value your opinion.'
- 'You have such good ideas.'
- 'You are so clever.'
- 'You are so brave.'
- 'I always know I can come to you for help.'
- 'You've made me so much more confident.'
- 'I would have had a much harder time achieving [X] without you.'
- 'You're such a good listener.'
- 'You've made a difference to my life.'
- 'You make me feel important.'
- 'I love how passionate you are about . . .'
- 'I'm so glad you're in my life.'
- 'Your support means a lot to me.'
- 'You have taught me so much about . . .'
- 'You are amazing.'
- 'You're so talented at . . .'
- 'You have great taste in . . .'

## Shining together aka the group glow up

It might sound selfish or overly simplified, but it's true – there's nothing that reflects better onto you than having a group of talented and impressive people in your close network who think you're great and have your back. You benefit from, and reinforce, each other's good reputation and all go on a glow up together.

As Lizzo (and The Killers) told us, when one of us is shining, we're all going to shine, and that really is the perfect embodiment of the Lady Gang message and mindset. We are collaborators, we are a team, we build each other up and never tear each other down. We reflect each other's shine back and forth, making it brighter and brighter until it's impossible to tell where the original spark came from, and it doesn't matter. When my successes are yours and yours are mine then we are all reflectors and we are all shining.

Really reflecting means making a big investment, the kind of investment which means showing up to support one another and celebrating together when things are good, but it also means doing the invisible work behind the scenes to make success possible for us all.

Being a reflector might mean recognising someone's greatness and nominating them for an award or writing them a recommendation or endorsement. It might be as simple as saying nice things about them when they're not in the room, or mentioning their name in a room of opportunity. It could be recommending them for a project or a piece of work, or just reminding them how much they're smashing it before they go in for an interview or a salary review. If you're at a more senior level in your career, shining together might mean using your voice and opportunities to spotlight a more junior member of your Lady Gang, or someone who has taken a career shift and needs a helping hand. Anything you can do to make life and work better for someone only makes their shine brighter, and yours in return.

# Setting Up Informal Networks

## Nana Bempah

**SW:** Would you be able to tell me a little about the community and organisation you co-founded, Pocc, and what led you to wanting to start it?

**NB:** Throughout my career I've had lots of highs, and I got to a place where I felt comfortable enough to take some time away from it for a bit, and that just gave me the space to be able to think about a lot of things that had happened up until then. When I came back, the instances of things happening that shouldn't have been happening were just so loud. Much, much louder than before.

I was working on a commercial for this brand, who like most had likely seen the success of what Fenty were doing, and decided darker-skinned women were worth investing in, and so released darker-skin tone shades. Because the time length of a commercial is limited, usually to 30 or 60 seconds, sometimes even 20, we were having to fit lots of short sound bites in from interviews with the women of different shades who featured in the film. Each original interview was around forty-five minutes long so there was a lot of material available – but for the Black girl they chose this one particular sentence. For the white and lighter-skinned girls it was all like, 'I'm fun' and 'I use my identity' and I do this and I do that, but for the darker-skinned girl they just chose this line, 'I'm a gangster'. And I thought, 'What? Why are you doing this?' and also because I was there at the actual recording of the interviews, I knew it was being deliberately taken out of context

and was not what she was saying. She was playing with her words, saying, 'Oh, when I dance some of my friends say I'm gangsta, hahaha, but I don't really think I'm gangsta. Maybe I am, maybe I'm not haha. I dunno.' She was just playing around, and that was not the essence of what she said during that forty-five minutes so to reduce her contribution to that was insulting and wrong on so many levels. It was exhausting, I'd been away, I'd come back and was like, 'Why is this still happening?!'

Another thing to this is, I'm not the authority on all Black issues, it shouldn't be like, 'OK, we've got a Black person on the job, so it's on you to save us from all from any faux pas', but if I am in the room I'm happy to speak my mind. And I did say something about this incident, and it was mad because the response wasn't, 'Oh my gosh, thanks so much for the insight, and for helping us not have a Pepsi Kendall Jenner moment'. It was kind of like, 'Oh really? But, you know, she did say it. And I think this brand needs to be edgy,' and I was like, 'Wow, so this is going to be a thing.' And also I think to myself, 'You know what? I'm not here to save you. I've told you something important and now you're looking to enter into a combative moment where I'm telling you that the brand has not ever spoken to my audience; you've never spoken to me or people who look like me. And now you're trying to speak to me and the first thing you want to do is have the person who looks most like me say 'I'm a gangster'? That's wild. How are you, as white men and women, trying to supersede what my experience is in this moment? I'm giving you insight, because I am that audience, and you're denying my experience through what you're saying. This is the kind of gaslighting we have to deal with. Wild.

Then there was another incident. I was at a work leaving drinks and this woman – a middle-class white woman – came along, and she hadn't seen my boss for a really long time. My boss, who was also her boss, had injured his leg from football so was on a crutch, and he was going away that weekend. And she said, 'What happened to your leg? This is awful.' He responded, 'Oh, I had an accident – pushed myself too far playing football, but it's fine,' and she says, 'What are you doing carrying that big bag around?' He answered, 'I'm going away this weekend, it's fine, I can carry it' and she said, 'But you can't be carrying that, hobbling around – you need a slave or something.' And I was thinking, 'Wow, this woman. Just wow first of all – wow with a big round mouth – because I'm wondering, how in this day and age do you even pull the word slave out of your mouth so smoothly like that? Like how do you not say, 'Oh gosh, you could do with a butler or an assistant,' or another word relevant to the situation. A slave – forced unpaid labour – I just don't know where she was getting these words from. Something inside me, a sense you get from decades of encountering people's racism, anticipated there would be more. So then this woman turned to me

and continued, 'Oh Nana, get his bags.' Wow. That's a situation I've got to walk away from because I'm not entering into that zone. I'm not engaging in that space. I'm just not. And this was after work, so not an in-work situation per se, but a situation with work colleagues where you're there, where chats and promotions and all of these kinds of undercover soft skill things happen and I'm just sitting there thinking wow, what am I doing here?

Coming back to this after being away from it I was just tired of the same old story. And this is only two of many, many incidents. So, Kevin Morosky, who I worked with for years, and had experienced similar madness, and I had a conversation and we just thought it would be amazing if we had a space to be able to talk about them. So we started a small WhatsApp group, knowing that this kind of thing must be going on in every advertising agency and people are just out there on their own, not knowing that there are other people out here dealing with it too – we just wanted to connect people together. So, I spoke to Black and brown people at another agency and I told them about what we were looking to do. They thought it sounded amazing, joined the WhatsApp group, we made everyone admins, and it just blew up from there. So now we're a community of about 700-plus of us, across the UK, USA and the Netherlands, working in advertising and the creative industries, just doing our thing. Helping and supporting, I'd say, first and foremost, and having events, getting together and really trying to boost one another. Then lots of things lead off from that – like collaborations and people approaching us for partnerships and interesting projects.

I've always had the thought that you can't sit back and wait for things to happen. If you want to make a change, especially on something which is so important, affecting your life, the lives of people who look like you and future generations, you have to stand up and make that change happen. I hear people talking about diversity this and diversity that, talk, talk, talk but no changes and no action. We know what needs to be done to create change so why not build it ourselves?!

**SW:** I know whenever I've been in agencies and tried to do anything around community-building, there was a lot of pushback from within the agency and the people who were running things. Have you had any pushback or negative feedback?

**NB:** This is the thing, because we remain completely independent, there isn't an opportunity for people to tell us what we can and can't do. I mean, there are disadvantages in that we're not supported or funded, and we're not being paid, like some organisations that exist within companies, so a lot of the things that we do and the campaigns we put out like 'Making Britain Great Since . . .' are things that we've pulled together ourselves through sheer hard work and talent. And there are absolutely challenges to that but what I will say is that autonomy is the best thing that we

could possibly have, just because we avoid having to go through any gatekeepers or blockers. Because the people who are used to being in control and having power, keeping others in certain positions which worked to their advantage, are scared. And they don't want to let what appears to be different or appears to be threatening through the doors. And they won't say these things out loud, and maybe they won't even vocalise it internally to themselves, but all of a sudden, they will find themselves putting barriers in the way in order to stop progress because that would mean a shift in power. I have spoken to people in the community who run initiatives within their own agencies, and they find them good at times, and yeah they get funded, but it's also frustrating at times. Because these companies have clients and there are certain things that can't be said and can't be done due to fear from management. But with us, if we want to do something and we want to say something, then that's what we're doing, you know? There's no one to tell us otherwise.

I think that if we can align and assemble ourselves a lot better, open up a bit more, and help and support each other as a community, then we're going to be stronger and help ourselves in the long run going forwards. For example, if you and I know each other, then I can say, 'Oh, I can put you in contact with X and you can put me in contact with Y.' But if we're part of a bigger community and I need to be in contact with Z over there then somebody else can put me in contact with them. So the bigger that network, the more we can help to support and lean on each other. It may not be a direct swap of I do this for you and you do that for me, it will be a general thing of all of us belonging to the community. We give to the community when we can and we take out what it is from the community what we need, and through that everybody should get the help and support that they need.

**SW:** I'm interested in the format of building a community that isn't one-for-one, but where you give what you can and take what you need. It feels like Pocc is the ultimate Lady Gang – a group of people all invested in one another, helping each other to shine and saying good things about each other behind each other's backs.

**NB:** Yeah! Absolutely! 100 per cent and I really do agree with that as a theory. I think that all too much, in lots of spaces, Black people and/or women are pitted against each other instead of working together. It's in the interests of those in power to sow the seeds of division in the masses as it maintains the status quo, ensuring those with less power do not unite to become more powerful through collective action. There is this old narrative perpetuated and upheld by white supremacy that there can only be one of us anywhere, i.e. we already have the Black guy on TV, or we already have one book by a Black person or have a Black model on our books so there isn't room for any more. You would never hear this said to a white person. This notion of scarcity breeds an environment of competition, as opposed to an environment of working together, support and collaboration. I think it's kind of subversive to try to work against that – instead of thinking of someone as the competition, reframe it so that you think of them as your sister or brother, whom you want to help. We're going to help boost each other. And it may take longer than going it alone or maybe not, but it's definitely a better route for your mental health and means we all win.

# Naomi and Natalie Evans' Favourite Thing About Being a Black Woman

Naomi and Natalie are anti-racist activists and educators based in the UK. They run a successful Instagram platform @everydayracism_ as well as being highly sought out professional speakers and soon to be authors.

"We love this question because there is just so much to love, yet it's one you're not often given the opportunity to reflect on. I think one of our favourite things about being Black women is the strong sense of community. There is a unique shared understanding that comes when we meet other Black women. You know what it's like to have to fight and you don't have to explain that. Our culture is also so deep and rich. We are connected to ancestors who faced so much oppression yet to us it represents so much more; resilience and grace; being incredible entrepreneurs, educators, spiritual leaders and creators. Did you know that it was a Black woman, Alice H Parker, who invented the gas heating using natural gas. This paved the way for the central heating system most of us use in our homes today. Black women also invented the GPS, 3D movies, conditioner, caller ID, home security systems and so much more. Black women have changed the way we live, and that spirit runs deep within us. We are so proud to be in a community that does so much and even when we don't get the credit we deserve, we are humble and graceful enough to keep giving.

Black women, we owe you the world."

## CHAPTER 12

# BE A GOOD ANCESTOR

'I tell my students, "When you get these jobs that you have been so brilliantly trained for, just remember that your real job is that if you are free, you need to free somebody else. If you have some power, then your job is to empower somebody else. This is not just a grab-bag candy game."'

TONI MORRISON

**W**e've spent a lot of time talking about the issues that Black women face in our careers, and looking at what we, and business owners, can and should do to mitigate and safeguard against these inequities and discriminations.

One of the things I've been certain from the very beginning that I didn't want to do in *Millennial Black* is to put the burden for change onto the shoulders of Black women who have not, due to structural and systemic racism, usually been put into positions that allow them to make real change. But as we progress in our careers, all being well, we do increasingly take on roles where we have the ability to ask for more, and better, not just for ourselves but for those who come after us. We have the chance to be good ancestors, and to show that we're willing to give people the same consideration that we ourselves would have wanted early in our careers.

I'm aware that not everyone feels this way – I've had conversations with some older Black women who feel that the odds were stacked against them due to their race and gender (true), and that since no one helped them, they shouldn't be expected to help anyone else.

To me, this is a very short-sighted view and one that will only serve to perpetuate the struggles and hardships that we're working to overcome, not for the good of an individual, but for Black women as a group.

I have also had several conversations with younger Black women who have spoken about times when they felt that the women who looked most like them, in businesses where they have worked have been the ones working most actively to hold them back. I mean, I get it. If you've built a career working in environments where you've both explicitly and subconsciously been told that there is only room for one, and you are lucky to be that one, it's not hard to see why lifting someone else up could feel counter-intuitive. It makes sense that older Black women, having fought hard to cut through systems built on misogynoir, would be reluctant to do anything that would feel like putting their positions at risk, or throwing their hard work away.

But we know that those fears are not only unfounded (there is more than enough room for everyone, businesses just have to have the desire to be inclusive, and smart businesses who want to remain relevant to younger audiences are starting to invest in this), they are damaging to those who uphold them, creating a culture of Onlyness, microaggressions and isolation.

We, Millennials and Gen Zs, know that there is enough room for everyone, if only businesses will make it. We know that the success of one Black woman isn't our failure and shouldn't mean the loss of an opportunity for us, but a chance to normalise and celebrate our successes, that are too often hard-won and long overdue.

I personally see this work of elevating and amplifying young Black women early in their careers as a non-optional responsibility, but also as a chance to widen my Lady Gang – making it more robust through my commitment to nurturing and supporting fresh talent wherever I can.

Here are some things that I think we can all do as we progress in our careers to kiss down, and hopefully throw a ladder back, helping more and more Black women reach what have historically been snowy peaks at the top.

## Recognise your own privileges

We know that as Black women we have at least two societal disadvantages in the workplace – the way that society treats women and the way that it treats Black people. (Being Black or being a woman are not barriers in themselves, but the social constructs that have been built up around both race and gender have turned them into disadvantages.) When we take a wider, more intersectional view, many of us will also be able to identify additional layers of marginalisation – whether it's sexuality, neurodiversity, class, physical disability or a whole host of other factors in the things that make us *us*.

Having these very real and important areas of marginalisation, however, doesn't mean that we don't have any privileges, and the more deeply we're able to understand and make use of our privilege, the more good we're able to do.

To use myself as an example – my privileges include, but aren't limited to, the fact that I'm an able-bodied, very light-skinned (colourism is real) woman. I have a platform and I'm able to express myself in a way that people will listen to (tone policing is also real), and I have been lucky to have a career that has made me financially secure enough to have taken time out to be able to research, write and share my thoughts.

And so that's what I do – I write and I speak and I post online to try to shed a light on issues that are important to me, because I'm aware that my voice can travel to, and be accepted in, places and spaces that so many people who are more marginalised than me can't access currently.

I think sometimes we work so hard that we lose sight of the reality of others. I have been working for eight years, and not all of that was an easy ride, most of it wasn't. There have been big gaps where I didn't work at all, or was working in a pub, but I think what's interesting in the idea of success is how quickly your perception of other realities change. The things that I used to kind of be bowled over by, even last year, have now become a normal occurrence. I have to acknowledge that I am privileged so I can put that to good use.

That's something that I've had to look at in the last two years – I was spending a lot of time pointing the finger outside of myself, 'That person's got a problem because they're this or that, and they need to think about this, and whatever', but actually when I think about it, what privileges do I have? I'm able-bodied, I live in a rich country, I'm fair-skinned. Right? I know that my dark-skinned Black female friends have a very different experience to mine. I mean there are so many privileges I have that I have to go, 'OK, wait, this is about me taking responsibility. I've worked very hard to get to this point, and even though I'm still trying to build whatever I want to build, at the same time I'm accumulating these privileges as I go along, so this same thing that I'm asking white people to do, and men to do, and all of that stuff, I have to ask the same of myself.'

What am I doing to help? What am I doing to perpetuate this system? How can I help? And the questions just keep coming. The more I work in it and the more traction I gain, it becomes clearly apparent that I need to find a path to give back in a way that makes me feel like I'm actually making a difference. Making a difference as an actor is OK, you can be in a film and win an award and all of that, but that has so much to do with the self and not much to do with anyone else. I think there are more practical ways in terms of accumulating money for others like helping with movements, and I will confess I don't know enough about it yet. I still feel like I'm trying to find that thing – that one thing that I feel like I can be of real use to. When I find it, I think that's going to be a lot of where my focus is, because in a way my confidence has grown so much in the field that I don't worry so much about, 'Oh, will I ever find work again?' I believe in myself to find work – OK, now that I've solidified that, maybe I can put that outwards in a helpful way.

*– Naomi Ackie*

Look for your areas of advantage, and the ways that you can leverage those to make a positive change in the lives and careers of those who are coming up.

## Establish your non-negotiables

I remember early in my career people would talk about job interviews being a two-way street, saying things like 'It's a chance for us to both find out if we're a good fit'. When you're starting out, looking for an opportunity and a break, this doesn't really feel like the case – the power feels like it's very firmly in the hands of the people making the decisions and holding the purse strings. Later on, though, there's a shift, and suddenly you're able to start pushing, really pushing, for the things that matter to you. Your non-negotiables.

Do you remember when, in 2018, Frances McDormand won an Oscar and used her acceptance speech to teach the world about 'inclusion riders'? The concept, developed by Stacy L. Smith in 2014, is that high-profile actors and filmmakers can use their clout to ensure that the projects they work on commit to including and showing usually under-represented people. I think it's a really great concept, and an example of someone using their position to ask more of others. But I don't think it needs to be limited to the film industry.

Here are some things that you can consider adding to your list of non-negotiables to ensure that businesses that want to work with you know what you believe in, and understand their responsibilities to up-and-coming marginalised talent. Think of it as a jumping-off point to spark ideas, and curate a list that feels personal and reasonable to you and your industry – this is a real opportunity to make sure that your body language and that of the businesses you give your time and skills to, match your beliefs. Your non-negotiables could be requiring businesses you work with to have:

- Salary banding
- A public diversity and inclusion statement
- Voluntary publication of gender and race pay gap stats, regardless of business size
- A commitment to interviewing at least the same percentage of marginalised people as representative of the local demographic, for example London's population is 40 per cent non-white therefore at least 40 per cent of interview candidates should be non-white
- Zero-tolerance policies around bullying, harassment and discrimination, which are actually enforced
- A formalised mentoring or sponsorship scheme
- Measurable targets for inclusive recruitment, retention and representation at all levels, with time-frames

## Mentoring and sponsorship

It's easy to feel like you're already doing enough, and I'm absolutely aware that asking overworked, underpaid Black women to take on additional unpaid labour is not the way forward, but I do think finding time to mentor or sponsor the next generation can be a hugely fulfilling, and valuable, experience. So many Black women have worked hard, paid their dues, and even found time to do extra-curricular things to help the cause, like speaking on panels and at events. Whilst those opportunities can be powerful, and I think fun, take some time to integrate them, look into them deeply, carefully and critically. Who are they reaching and what impact are they having? I have often felt that the conversations I've had, and enjoyed having, in those environments were preaching to the choir somewhat. The people who come along to hear a presentation or a discussion about race in the workplace are those who are already aligned with the cause, and in my experience usually young Black women desperately looking for some tools to break out beyond their concrete ceilings. These conversations can be validating and empowering to hear and be a part of, but I think there is a deep value in creating, and maintaining, one-on-one relationships with real investment, such as investing time into mentoring and sponsorship.

I feel that mentorship works best when there's a structure and process behind it, and so I recommend reaching out to organisations who offer that structure and asking to be paired. The organisation doing the matching should then be able to help you work together to identify aims, timeframes and to create a structure that will allow you to really maximise the good you're able to do together.

At work, reach out to marginalised and overlooked team members. It is so much easier to reach out to someone more junior to offer help or just say 'I see you' than it is to reach out to someone above you who seems too busy and important to ask for help. Reaching up to ask for help can feel impossible but reaching down is much easier.

## Think bigger

Don't feel limited by the constraints of the business you work for. Think bigger. Dream bigger. Create your own work, on your own terms, to uplift people, wherever you can.

Maybe we can build something completely new that has a far more inclusive ideal to it because we know how it feels to be unseen, and in my case, I know how it feels to be ignored. I know how it feels to think I'm ugly, that my body shape isn't right, that I don't talk properly, that I'm too loud when I laugh, all of that stuff – I know how that feels and I don't want to make anyone else feel that stuff. Hopefully I will bring that into the work that I do in the future to eliminate that from this new world that we're building – which I think we have the capacity to do, more so than we ever did. So now I'm thinking, 'OK, how do I make enough money, and make enough of a name for myself, to make a production company that opens the door for more people of many different backgrounds to exist in the same space?'

*— Naomi Ackie*

I guess what I want to say, when it comes to it, is that there's space for all of us. As we know from our Lady Gang, we're better when we collaborate. When we're the only person who looks like us in a space, our mental health suffers, our happiness decreases and we start looking for ways out. We're not the only ones who can make the change, and it certainly shouldn't all fall onto our shoulders, but there are still things we can do to make the process as smooth, and quick, as possible. We've already waited long enough.

Creating a Legacy

Vanessa Sanyauke

There have been instances where there have been older Black women in places where I've worked who I thought would have been my biggest supporters, I thought they would have mentored me, but actually they were the ones who bullied and blocked me.

Maybe it's because of being threatened about their positions, but they would give more support to non-Black colleagues in my team. That's what I've experienced before, and I think we do need to call that out. There is a big problem in terms of some older Black women not supporting younger Black women – we can't blame it all on white men and white women, as it's something I've experienced from my own people. Those that are in powerful positions – who are they bringing up and who are they supporting?

I think there's such a narrative in society that one is enough, and I think if you've been that One, then someone else can feel like a threat, rather than an opportunity. I feel like Millennials are different to older generations. We have our networks and we're more supportive, so there's hope.

It's not just about the individual, but also the younger generation coming up – you have to think about them and how it will be for them hearing more stories about people who look like them being successful – that's the legacy that you're going to create, and the impact it's going to have over time. That's really powerful.

An example of this is Diane Abbot. When Bell Ribeiro-Addy, currently the Labour MP for Streatham, worked with Abbot as her chief of staff, Bell campaigned to be elected as MP in the 2019 general election. Abbot publicly endorsed her. Abbot gets a lot of critique, but this is a Black woman actively championing the progression of a member of her team, who is now her peer. That's what we need to see more of.

We talk a lot about how white people need to be sponsoring Black female talent, but it can't stop there. Those of us who are in senior positions – what are we doing to sponsor and advocate for up-and-coming talent? I'd love to explore that. We need to be mindful of those in senior positions and the responsibility that comes with it. And I understand that it's hard enough being senior in a business – I know myself the emotional toll it takes on you. It's really tough. But try to find the time and the strength to help others, even if it's just one coffee, because that's so important – just to say, 'I see you'. Otherwise what we're going through is in vain.

# Candice Brathwaite's Favourite Thing About Being a Black Woman

Aah, it's just that drip. I can't even explain it. It's that sauce. It's like, you know when you see the Kardashians trying to buy our everything, and you just laugh because you know you will never have the sauce. You could have all the Black kids, by all of the Black men, but you will never have the drip. You can go to all of the plastic surgeons, but there is something about how a Black woman can speak, without even opening her mouth. The look. The sass. Sometimes I go on a Black woman's page on Instagram and I know I saw a white woman wear that exact same outfit yesterday, but it just didn't have that 'aaah'. And it's just that, because I know it's that zing that has got my foot in certain doors, or has made people pay attention, or given me the privilege of – and it's so mad saying it – having the first-ever book backed by a big publishing house in Britain about Black motherhood. It's that zing. Black women are always told to change or appease – straighten your hair, lighten your skin, be skinnier – I think a lot of Black women, especially younger Black women, don't even realise they're trying to pull that sauce away from you, but it is that exact thing that will get you everything you've ever dreamed of. So yeah, it's the *je ne sais quoi*, that *zsa zsa zsu.*

# WRAPPING UP

'Revolution is not a
one time event.'

AUDRE LORDE

So much has changed in the world, and in me, since I started planning this book as a proposal back in 2017.

My main hope for *Millennial Black* is, and has always been, that someone finds some comfort in it. That a Black woman who has struggled in her career realises that *she* is not the problem. You are not the problem. You, me, all of us are working in systems that were built without us in mind, often they were built to keep us out, and every success that we have is in spite of that. It's exhausting and it's daunting but wherever you are in your journey, don't let anyone gaslight you into feeling like you're making it up. Your experiences are real, and they're shared by people in all kinds of industries, however sorted or successful they might seem.

Black women are amazing. We are resilient and we are strong but we also need to allow ourselves to just be us. I hope you build communities and Lady Gangs, and surround yourselves with people who share your vision of success and push you towards it every day. I want you to win.

I also hope that this book – that all of the time and energy and emotional openness that not only I have put into it, but that the amazing Black women who have given their time to be interviewed have been able to share – is able to be a part of making real change. I hope it sheds light on issues and barriers that people who aren't from marginalised communities may not have engaged with before – either due to a lack of knowledge or information. It is not the job of marginalised people to open ourselves up and show the world the rawest, most painful parts of ourselves as a form of education, but I hope that what we've been able to share here, along with the actionable advice for making better, fairer businesses, will be able to reach people who can make real, lasting change.

I'd like to imagine a world where someone picks this up in the not-too-distant future and thinks to themselves, 'Well, there's no need for this book – this is all solved'. At the moment I can't imagine it but I can dream.

Millennials and Gen Zs – our career paths, our values and our aspirations are not the same as our parents' were. Both we, and our careers, are coming of age at a time of immense change that no one could have predicted or prepared us for. Not only has technology changed the working landscape, but we're also living through pandemics and social change at a rate and scale not seen before – and looking for ways to make it work.

I see you.

I know it's not easy. I know it can feel impossible and intimidating and all just too much. But it's going to work, and it's going to be OK, if you invest in your communities and get their investment back. We need people who run businesses and who claim allyship to really step up and make things happen, and we need to look for ways that we can bypass those people when they won't do what's right.

Build communities and networks. Gas your friends up. Give your own awards. Know your worth and don't give discounts.

You've got this. X

# Contributors

**Aja Barber** is a writer and personal stylist in London whose work focuses on intersectionality and the fashion industry. Aja's writing can be found in the *Guardian* and *Eco Age*.

**Candice Brathwaite** is a *Sunday Times* Bestselling Author, TV presenter and contributing editor at *Grazia* Magazine.

**Daniellé Scott-Haughton** works as a scripted comedy and drama Development Executive at Balloon Entertainment, where she works with underrepresented, emerging voices.

**Destiny Ekaragha** is a BAFTA award-winning director who was named BAFTA breakthrough Brit in 2014. Her award-winning feature comedy *Gone Too Far!* premiered at London Film Festival. Destiny directed *Danny and the Human Zoo*, written by the acclaimed comedian Lenny Henry, primetime UK television *Silent Witness*, international drama including *Riviera* and most recently the second half of the BAFTA-winning season 2 of *The End of the F\*\*\*ing World* for Netflix.

**June Angelides**, MBE is a banker turned entrepreneur turned investor, best known for starting coding school, Mums in Tech. Named by the *Financial Times* as the 6th Most Influential Tech Leader and by Computer Weekly as one of the most Influential Women in Tech, June recently received an Honorary Fellowship at the Institute of Engineering and Technology and was awarded an MBE for services to women in technology.

**June Sarpong**, OBE, is one of the most recognisable British television presenters and broadcasters and a prominent activist, having co-founded the WIE Network (Women: Inspiration and Enterprise) and the Decide Act Now summit. In 2019, she was appointed the first-ever Director of Creative Diversity at the BBC.

**Lekia Lée** is a former broadcast journalist who has worked both in Nigeria and the UK. In 2010, inspired by her then 5-year-old daughter, she founded Project Embrace to end hair discrimination, increase afro hair representation and encourage her daughter and girls like her to embrace their afro-textured hair.

**Liv Little** is an award-winning journalist, cultural consultant, creative director, author and curator. She's also the founder of gal-dem, a media company committed to spotlighting the creative talents of women and non-binary people of colour. Liv's career spans audio, journalism and TV and film. Liv has been voted a Future Leader, LGBTQI+ broadcaster of the year, a rising star at WOW and included in the inaugural BBC's *100 Women* series.

**Lopè Ariyo** is a former chef, food writer, cookbook author, recipe developer and software engineer. In the food world, her focus is on elevating foods and cuisines that are often both misrepresented and underrepresented in the UK.

**Munroe Bergdorf** is a writer, model, activist and Doctor of Letters, and has become recognised globally for her activism. In August 2020, not only did *British Vogue* name her in the Top 25 Most Influential Women in the Country (alongside Rihanna and the Queen), but *Teen Vogue* featured her on the cover of their coveted September issue. Munroe has most recently been announced as the winner of *Attitude*'s Hero Award 2020, presented by Edward Enninful.

**Nana Bempah** is an executive producer working in film and advertising, and founder of Pocc – a creative community, support network and organisation seeking to accelerate equality for ethnically diverse people in the creative industries. In addition to rapidly becoming the leading community to connect Black, brown and ethnically diverse creatives for help, support, opportunities and collaboration within the industry, Pocc brings about transformation through campaigns using non-traditional ideas, behaviours and activism.

**Naomi Ackie** is an award-winning actress and writer from East London. She has starred in *Star Wars: The Rise of Skywalker*, *Lady Macbeth* and *The End of the F***ing World*.

**Naomi and Natalie Evans** are anti-racist activists and educators based in the UK. They run successful Instagram platform @everydayracism_ as well as being highly sought out professional speakers and soon to be authors.

**Natalie Lee** runs a blog called *Style Me Sunday*. She is a big advocate of in encouraging women to feel comfortable in their skin and likes to stick a middle finger up to society's standards and norms. A mother of two girls, she is a fierce supporter of women and a huge lover of beauty and fashion. Natalie talks about many things, from alopecia to ageing to wanting to see more diverse images in the media. She has a podcast, *The Everything Project*, and runs events such as 'The Warrior Woman Project' in association with Dove and Feeling Myself.

**Vanessa Sanyauke** is an award-winning and globally recognised diversity, inclusion and innovation professional. She is also the Founder and CEO of Girls Talk London, a global community for Millennial women.

# Endnotes

## Introduction

1. Intersectionality is a term originated by Kimberlé Crenshaw
2. Jeff Desjardins, 'Meet Generation Z: The Newest Member to the Workforce', *Visual Capitalist*, February 2019, https://www.visualcapitalist.com/meet-generation-z-the-newest-member-to-the-workforce/
3. Vivian Hunt, Dennis Layton and Sara Prince, 'Diversity Matters', McKinsey & Company, February 2015, https://www.mckinsey.com/business-functions/organization/our-insights/~/media/2497d4ae4b534ee89d929cc6e3aea485.ashx
4. Sylvia Ann Hewlett and Tai Green, 'Black Women Ready to Lead', Center for Talent Innovation, 2015 https://www.talentinnovation.org/_private/assets/BlackWomenReadyToLead_ExecSumm-CTI.pdf
5. 'Women in the Workplace 2020', McKinsey & Company and LeanIn.Org, September 2020, https://www.mckinsey.com/featured-insights/diversity-and-inclusion/women-in-the-workplace

## Chapter 1

1. Kristen Bialik and Richard Fry, 'Millennial Life: How Young Adulthood Today Compares with Prior Generations', Pew Research Centre, Washington D.C., February 2019, https://www.pewsocialtrends.org/essay/millennial-life-how-young-adulthood-today-compares-with-prior-generations/
2. Richard Fry, 'Millennials Aren't Job-hopping Any Faster than Generation Z Did', April 2017, https://www.pewresearch.org/fact-tank/2017/04/19/millennials-arent-job-hopping-any-faster-than-generation-x-did/
3. Being Black in Corporate America: An Intersectional Exploration', Coqual, 2019, https://www.talentinnovation.org/_private/assets/BeingBlack-KeyFindings-CTI.pdf
4. 'Young, Underemployed and Optimistic: Coming of Age, Slowly, in a Tough Economy', Pew Research Centre, Washington D.C., February 2012, https://www.pewsocialtrends.org/2012/02/09/young-underemployed-and-optimistic/
5. ibid.
6. ibid.

## Chapter 2

1. Jennifer L. Berdahl and Celia Moore, 'Workplace Harassment: Double Jeopardy for Modern Women', *Journal of Applied Psychology*, 2006, https://pdfs.semanticscholar.org/c5cd/8934b5d10b331560b24bcc3d7dc3c4a4818d.pdf

Hannah Green, 'Disparity in Discrimination: A Study on the Experience of Minority Women in the Workplace', 2017, https://www.csustan.edu/sites/default/files/groups/University%20Honors%20Program/Journals/hannah_green.pdf

2. 'Being Black in Corporate America: An Intersectional Exploration', Coqual, 2019, https://www.talentinnovation.org/_private/assets/BeingBlack-KeyFindings-CTI.pdf

3. Claudia Goldin, 'Female Labor Force Participation: The Origin of Black and White Differences, 1870 and 1880', *Journal of Economic History*, 1977, https://dash.harvard.edu/handle/1/2643657

4. Nina Banks, 'Black Women's Labor Market History Reveals Deep-Seated Race and Gender Discrimination', February 2019, https://www.epi.org/blog/black-womens-labor-market-history-reveals-deep-seated-race-and-gender-discrimination/

5. 'The Status of Black Women in the United States', Institute for Women's Policy Research, June 2017

6. 'Zero Hours Contracts and Impact on Black Workers', UNISON, January 2014, https://www.unison.org.uk/motions/2020/conference-type/zero-hours-contracts-and-impact-on-Black-workers-i/

7. Georgina Bowyer and Morag Henderson, 'Race Inequality in the Workforce: Exploring Connections Between Work, Ethnicity and Mental Health', 2020, https://www.obv.org.uk/sites/default/files/images/Race-Inequality-in-the-Workforce-Final.pdf

8. David Cooper, 'Workers of Color Are Far More Likely To Be Paid Poverty-Level Wages Than White Workers', Economic Policy Institute, June 2018, https://www.epi.org/blog/workers-of-color-are-far-more-likely-to-be-paid-poverty-level-wages-than-white-workers/

9. ibid.

10. ibid.

11. 'The Status of Black Women in the United States', Institute for Women's Policy Research, June 2017

12. https://www.ethnicity-facts-figures.service.gov.uk/work-pay-and-benefits/pay-and-income/household-income/latest

13. Sarah Jane Glynn, 'Breadwinning Mothers Continue To Be the U.S. Norm', Center for American Progress, May 2019, https://www.americanprogress.org/issues/women/reports/2019/05/10/469739/breadwinning-motherscontinue-u-s-norm/ as quoted: https://www.nationalpartnership.org/our-work/resources/economic-justice/fair-pay/african-american-women-wage-gap.pdf

14. https://data.census.gov/cedsci/table?q=S0201&tid=ACSSPP1Y2018.S0201 and https://www.nationalpartnership.org/our-work/resources/economic-justice/fair-pay/african-american-women-wage-gap.pdf

15. 'The Status of Black Women in the United States', Institute for Women's Policy Research, June 2017

16. 'Black Women Aren't Paid Fairly and That Hits Harder in an Economic Crisis', Lean In, https://leanin.org/data-about-the-gender-pay-gap-for-black-women

17. 'Women in the Workplace 2020', McKinsey & Company and LeanIn.Org, September 2020, https://www.mckinsey.com/featured-insights/diversity-and-inclusion/women-in-the-workplace

18. 'Being Black in Corporate America: An Intersectional Exploration', Coqual, 2019, cited in https://fortune.com/2020/02/24/black-history-month-workplace-racism/

19. Sabrina Barr, 'One in Three Adults Have Experienced or Witnessed Racism at Work, Study Finds', *The Independent*, October 2019, https://www.independent.co.uk/life-style/racism-work-discrimination-gender-lgbt-sexuality-ageism-glassdoor-a9167256.html 'Diversity and Inclusion Study 2019', Glassdoor, https://www.glassdoor.com/about-us/app/uploads/sites/2/2019/10/Glassdoor-Diversity-Survey-Supplement-1.pdf

20. Olivia Petter, 'One in Four Ethnic Minority Workers Report Experiencing Bullying and Harassment Despite Zero-Tolerance Policies', *The Independent,* October 2019, https://www.independent.co.uk/life-style/bullying-harassment-work-racism-equality-zero-tolerance-policy-a9128951.html

21. 'The McGregor-Smith Review: Race in the Workplace', https://assets.publishing.service.gov.uk/government/uploads/system/uploads/attachment_data/file/594336/race-in-workplace-mcgregor-smith-review.pdf

22. ibid.

23. 'The 2018 State of Women-Owned Business Report', Empower Women, 2018, https://www.empowerwomen.org/en/resources/documents/2019/01/the-2018-state-of-women-owned-business-report?lang=en

24. 'Facts About Women in Business', Prowess, https://www.prowess.org.uk/facts

## Chapter 3

1. Katy Waldman, 'A Sociologist Examines the "White Fragility" that Prevents White Americans From Confronting Racism', *New Yorker*, July 2018, https://www.newyorker.com/books/page-turner/a-sociologist-examines-the-white-fragility-that-prevents-white-americans-from-confronting-racism

2. William Petersen, 'Success Story, Japanese-American Style', January 1966, *New York Times Magazine*, https://www.nytimes.com/1966/01/09/archives/success-story-japaneseamerican-style-success-story-japaneseamerican.html

3. Lockhart, P.R, 'After more than 200 attempts, the Senate has finally passed anti-lynching legislation', *Vox*, December 2018 https://www.vox.com/identities/2018/12/21/18151805/senate-lynching-legislation-hate-crimes-booker-harris-scott

4. www.congress.gov/bill/116th-congress/house-bill/35/text)

5. 'Saving Lives, Improving Mothers' Care', MBRRACE UK Maternal Report, November 2018

6. P. Goff, M. Jackson, B. Di Leone, M. Culotta and N. DiTomasso, 'The Essence of Innocence: Consequences of Dehumanizing Black Children', *Journal of Personality and Social Psychology*, 2014, https://www.apa.org/pubs/journals/releases/psp-a0035663.pdf

7. 'Statistics on Race and the Criminal Justice System 2016', Ministry of Justice, November 2017, https://assets.publishing.service.gov.uk/government/uploads/system/uploads/attachment_data/file/669094/statistics_on_race_and_the_criminal_justice_system_2016_v2.pdf

8. Samuel Osborne, 'Black Women Become Most Educated Group in US', *The Independent*, June 2016, https://www.independent.co.uk/news/world/americas/black-women-become-most-educated-group-us-a7063361.html

9. 'Degrees Conferred by Race and Sex', National Center for Education Statistics https://nces.ed.gov/fastfacts/display.asp?id=72

10. Joan C. Williams and Marina Multhaup, 'For Women and Minorities to Get Ahead, Managers Must Assign Work Fairly', *Harvard Business Review*, March 2018, https://hbr.org/2018/03/for-women-and-minorities-to-get-ahead-managers-must-assign-work-fairly

11. Linda Babcock, Maria P. Recalde and Lise Vesterlund, 'Why Women Volunteer for Tasks That Don't Lead to Promotion', *Harvard Business Review*, July 2018, https://hbr.org/2018/07/why-women-volunteer-for-tasks-that-dont-lead-to-promotions

12. 'Sticking women with the office housework', *Washington Post*, April 2014, https://www.washingtonpost.com/news/on-leadership/wp/2014/04/16/sticking-women-with-the-office-housework/

**Chapter 4**

1. Alasdair Rae, 'Residential Mortgage Lending by Postcode Shows Gaps Across Britain', *The Guardian*, 20 March 2015, https://www.theguardian.com/uk-news/2015/mar/20/residential-mortgage-lending-by-postcode-shows-lending-gaps-across-the-country

2. Amani M. Allen et al., 'Racial Discrimination, the Superwoman Schema, and Allostatic Load', *Annals of the New York Academy of Sciences*, 2019, as covered in 'How the "Strong Black Woman" Identity Both Helps and Hurts', *Greater Good Magazine*, December 2019, https://greatergood.berkeley.edu/article/item/how_the_strong_Black_woman_identity_both_helps_and_hurts

3. Roxanne A. Donovan and Lindsey M. West, 'Stress and Mental Health: Moderating Role of the Strong Black Woman Stereotype', *Journal of Black Psychology*, November 2014, https://www.researchgate.net/publication/280770795_Stress_and_Mental_Health_Moderating_Role_of_the_Strong_Black_Woman_Stereotype

4. Daniel Mayer, 'Introducing Gen Z: "Millennials on Steroids"', Calabrio https://www.calabrio.com/wfo/workforce-management/introducing-gen-z-millennials-on-steroids/

5. Richard Partington, 'Number of Zero-Hours Contracts in UK Rose by 100,000 in 2017 – ONS', *The Guardian*, April 2018, https://www.theguardian.com/uk-news/2018/apr/23/number-of-zero-hours-contracts-in-uk-rose-by-100000-in-2017-ons

6. Jenny Roper, 'BAME Workers More Likely To Be in Insecure Work', *HR Magazine*, June 2017, https://www.hrmagazine.co.uk/article-details/bame-workers-more-likely-to-be-in-insecure-work

7. 'Millennials in the workplace update: what they want, what they're changing & more', YPulse, April 2016 https://www.ypulse.com/article/2016/04/25/millennials-in-the-workplace-update-what-they-want-what-theyre-changing-mor/

8. 'ICD-11 for Mortality and Morbidity Statistics', WHO, September 2020, https://icd.who.int/browse11/l-m/en#/http://id.who.int/icd/entity/129180281

9. Ryan Pendell, 'Millennials Are Burning Out', Gallup, July 2018, https://www.gallup.com/workplace/237377/millennials-burning.aspx

10. Josh Cohen, 'Minds Turned to Ash', *The Economist*, June 2016, https://www.economist.com/1843/2016/06/29/minds-turned-to-ash

11. 'Time Off and Vacation Usage', US Travel Association, https://www.ustravel.org/toolkit/time-and-vacation-usage

12. 'The Problem of the American Work Martyr', Project: Time Off as featured in *The Atlantic*, https://www.theatlantic.com/sponsored/project-time-off/the-problem-of-the-american-work-martyr/1257/

13. ibid.

14. Martha C. White, 'It's the Millennials' Fault You Can't Take a Vacation', *Money*, August 2016, https://money.com/millennial-workers-vacation-shame/

15. Bartolucci, G.B., Capozza, D., De Carlo, N.A., et al. 'The Mediating Role of Psychophysic Strain in the Relationship Between Workaholism, Job Performance, and Sickness Absence: A Longitudinal Study,' *Journal of Occupational and Environmental Medicine*, 2013

16. John Pencavel, 'The Productivity of Working Hours', *Stanford University and the Institute for the Study of Labour*, 2013

17. Shawn Acor and Michelle Gielan, 'The Data-Driven Case for Vacation', *Harvard Business Review*, July 2016 https://hbr.org/2016/07/the-data-driven-case-for-vacation

18. Hillary Hoffower and Allana Akhtar, 'Lonely, Burned Out and Depressed: The State of Millennials' Mental Health in 2020', *Business Insider*, October 2020, https://www.businessinsider.com/millennials-mental-health-burnout-lonely-depressed-money-stress?r=US&IR=T

19. 'The Economic Consequences of Millennial Health', Blue Cross Blue Shield, November 2019, https://www.bcbs.com/sites/default/files/file-attachments/health-of-america-report/HOA-Moodys-Millennial-10-30.pdf

20. 'Two Million Commercially Insured Americans Diagnosed with Major Depression Are Not Seeking Any Treatment', Blue Cross Blue Shield, March 2019, https://www.bcbs.com/the-health-of-america/articles/two-million-commercially-insured-americans-diagnosed-major-depression-not-seeking-treatment

21. Hillary Hoffower, 'Depression Is On the Rise Among Millennials But 20% of Them Aren't Seeking Treatment – and It's Likely Because They Can't Afford It', *Business Insider*, June 2019, https://www.businessinsider.com/depression-increasing-among-millennials-gen-z-healthcare-burnout-2019-6?r=US&IR=T

22. Olugbenga Ajilore, 'On the Persistence of the Black-White Employment Gap', Center for American Progress, February 2020, https://www.americanprogress.org/issues/economy/reports/2020/02/24/480743/persistence-Black-white-unemployment-gap/

23. 'Underemployment', https://datacenter.kidscount.org/data/tables/107-children-in-single-parent-families-by-race

24. Nancy Beauregard, et al. 'Gendered Pathways to Burnout: Results from the SALVEO Study'. *Annals of Work Exposures and Health*, April 2018

25. Neil Schoenherr, 'Suicide Attempts Among Black Adolescents On the Rise', *The Source* (Washington University in St. Louis), October 2019, https://source.wustl.edu/2019/10/suicide-attempts-among-black-adolescents-on-the-rise/

26. Inger E. Burnett-Zeigler, 'Young Black People Are Killing Themselves', *New York Times*, December 2019, https://www.nytimes.com/2019/12/16/opinion/young-black-people-suicide.html?action=click&module=Opinion&pgtype=Homepage

27. James H. Price and Jagdish Khubchandani, 'The Changing Characteristics of African-American Adolescent Suicides, 2001–2017', *Journal of Community Health*, May 2019, https://link.springer.com/article/10.1007/s10900-019-00678-x

28. 'Report: Day-to-Day Experiences of Emotional Tax Among Women and Men of Color in the Workplace', Catalyst, February 2018, https://www.catalyst.org/research/day-to-day-experiences-of-emotional-tax-among-women-and-men-of-color-in-the-workplace/

29. Anni Ferguson, 'The Lowest of the Stack: Why Black Women Are Struggling With Mental Health', *The Guardian*, February 2016, https://www.theguardian.com/lifeandstyle/2016/feb/08/black-women-mental-health-high-rates-depression-anxiety

30. 'The Impact of Racism on Mental Health', Synergi, March 2018, https://synergicollaborativecentre.co.uk/wp-content/uploads/2017/11/The-impact-of-racism-on-mental-health-briefing-paper-1.pdf

31. David R. Williams, 'Stress and Mental Health of Populations of Color: Increasing Our Understanding of Race-Related Stressors', *Journal of Health and Social Behavior*, December 2018, https://www.ncbi.nlm.nih.gov/pubmed/30484715

32. 'Race at Work 2015', Business in the Community, November 2015, https://www.bitc.org.uk/report/race-at-work-2015/

33. 'The McGregor-Smith Review: Race in the Workplace' https://assets.publishing.service.gov.uk/government/uploads/system/uploads/attachment_data/file/594336/race-in-workplace-mcgregor-smith-review.pdf

34. Inger E. Burnett-Zeigler, 'The Strong and Stressed Black Woman', *New York Times*, April 2018, https://www.nytimes.com/2018/04/25/opinion/strong-stressed-black-woman.html

35. 'Race Disparity Audit', Cabinet Office, October 2017, https://assets.publishing.service.gov.uk/government/uploads/system/uploads/attachment_data/file/686071/Revised_RDA_report_March_2018.pdf

36. Jayne Cooper et al., 'Ethnic Differences in Self-harm, Rates, Characteristics and Service Provisions', *The British Journal of Psychiatry*, 2010, https://www.cambridge.org/core/services/aop-cambridge-core/content/view/CDBA53F0AC230909E892C263781A0A51/S0007125000015762a.pdf/ethnic_differences_in_selfharm_rates_characteristics_and_service_provision_threecity_cohort_study.pdf

37. 'Race Disparity Audit', Cabinet Office October 2017, https://assets.publishing.service.gov.uk/government/uploads/system/uploads/attachment_data/file/686071/Revised_RDA_report_March_2018.pdf

38. ibid.

39. 'Mental Health and Wellbeing in England', NHS Digital, 2014, https://files.digital.nhs.uk/pdf/q/3/mental_health_and_wellbeing_in_england_full_report.pdf

40. Inger E. Burnett-Zeigler, 'The Strong and Stressed Black Woman', *New York Times*, April 2018, https://www.nytimes.com/2018/04/25/opinion/strong-stressed-black-woman.html

41. 'Black, Asian and Minority Ethnic (BAME) Communities', Mental Health Foundation, June 2019, https://www.mentalhealth.org.uk/a-to-z/b/black-asian-and-minority-ethnic-bame-communities

42. 'Health Disparities and Stress', American Psychological Association, 2012, https://www.apa.org/topics/health-disparities/fact-sheet-stress

43. Arline T. Geronimus et al., 'Do US Black Women Experience Stress-Related Accelerated Biological Aging?', *Human Nature*, March 2010, https://www.ncbi.nlm.nih.gov/pmc/articles/PMC2861506/

44. Shirley A. Thomas and A. Antonio González-Prendes, 'Powerlessness, Anger, and Stress in African American Women: Implications for Physical and Emotional Health', *Health Care for Women International*, December 2008

45. Jalana Harris, 'Adherence to the Strong Black Woman Archetype and Sexual Agency: An Intersectional Exploration of Sexual Assertiveness, Towards Deconstructing Black Women's Sexual Health', *Health Care for Women International*, May 2009

## Chapter 5

1. Peter Dreier, 'Rosa Parks: Angry Not Tired', Dissent, Winter 2006, https://core.ac.uk/download/pdf/73342562.pdf

2. Audre Lorde, 'The Uses of Anger: Women Responding to Racism', June 1981, https://www.blackpast.org/african-american-history/speeches-african-american-history/1981-audre-lorde-uses-anger-women-responding-racism/

3. Shirley A. Thomas and A. Antonio González-Prendes, 'Powerlessness and Anger in African American Women: The Intersection of Race and Gender', *International Journal of Humanities and Social Science*, June 2011

4. Melissa V. Harris-Perry, *Sister Citizen: Shame, Stereotypes, and Black Women in America*, Yale University Press, 2011

5. Victoria D. Gillon, 'The Killing of an "Angry Black Woman": Sandra Bland and the Politics of Respectability', 2016, https://pdfs.semanticscholar.org/6fab/b9401bcaaed44b676305f941d32dfdb40e66.pdf

6. Christine Grandy, 'How "The Black and White Minstrel Show" spent 20 Years on the BBC', January 2019, https://www.thebritishacademy.ac.uk/blog/how-black-and-white-minstrel-show-20-years-bbc/

7. Lindsay Kimble, 'Michelle Obama Confesses Caricature of Angry Black Woman "Knocked Me Back"', *People*, May 2015, https://people.com/celebrity/michelle-obama-commencement-speech-at-tuskegee-university-2015/

8. Fusion Comedy, 'How Microaggressions Are Like Mosquito Bites', https://www.youtube.com/watch?v=hDd3bzA7450

9. Gurjit Degun, 'D&AD to Review Speaker Fees Policy', *Campaign*, May 2019, https://www.campaignlive.co.uk/article/d-ad-review-speaker-fees-policy/1584779

10. A. Antonio González-Prendes, 'Powerlessness and Anger in African American Women: The Intersection of Race and Gender', *International Journal of Humanities and Social Science*, June 2011, http://www.ijhssnet.com/journals/Vol._1_No._7_%5BSpecial_Issue_June_2011%5D/1.pdf

11. 'Women of Colour in the Workplace', National Committee on Pay Equity, https://www.pay-equity.org/info-race.html

12. Sarah Jane Glynn, 'Breadwinning Mothers Continue To Be the U.S. Norm', Center for American Progress May 2019, https://www.americanprogress.org/issues/women/reports/2019/05/10/469739/breadwinning-motherscontinue-u-s-norm/

13. Kimberlé Williams Crenshaw, 'Black Girls Matter: Pushed Out, Overpoliced and Underprotected', Center for Intersectionality and Social Policy Studies and African American Policy Forum http://static1.squarespace.com/static/53f20d90e4b0b80451158d8c/t/54dcc1ece4b001c03e323448/1423753708557/AAPF_BlackGirlsMatterReport.pdf

14. Victoria L. Brescoll and Eric Luis Uhlmann, 'Professional Women Suffer Negative Consequences for Displays of Emotion in the Workplace, While Professional Men are Accorded Benefits for Similar Behaviors', *Psychological Science*, March 2008, https://gap.hks.harvard.edu/can-angry-woman-get-ahead-status-conferral-gender-and-expression-emotion-workplace

15. Bridget Goosby, Elizabeth Straley and Jacob E. Cheadle, 'Discrimination, Sleep, and Stress Reactivity: Pathways to African American-White Cardiometabolic Risk Inequities', *Population Research and Policy Review*, October 2017, https://www.researchgate.net/publication/317004359_Discrimination_Sleep_and_Stress_Reactivity_Pathways_to_African_American-white_Cardiometabolic_Risk_Inequities

16. Matthew Gavidia, 'High Levels of Chronic Stress, High Blood Pressure Linked in African Americans', *American Journal of Managed Care*, October 2019, https://www.ajmc.com/view/high-levels-of-chronic-stress-high-blood-pressure-linked-in-african-americans

17. Traci Pedersen, 'Your Brain First Notices Race & Gender Before All Else', *PsychCentral*, August 2018, https://psychcentral.com/news/2013/10/12/your-brain-first-notices-race-gender-before-all-else/60650.html

## Chapter 6

1. Dan Cassino and Yasemin Bresen-Cassino, 'Race, Threat and Workplace Sexual Harassment: The Dynamics of Harassment in the United States, 1997–2016', *Gender, Work and Organization*, June 2019 https://onlinelibrary.wiley.com/doi/10.1111/gwao.12394 as cited in Opheli Garcia Lawler, 'Black Women Are More Likely to Get Sexually Harassed at Work Than White Women, Study Says', *Mic*, June 2019, https://www.mic.com/p/Black-women-are-more-likely-to-get-sexually-harassed-at-work-than-white-women-study-says-18147714

2. Joel R. Andersen, Elise Holland, Courtney Heldreth et al., 'Revisiting the Jezebel Stereotype: The Impact of Target Race on Sexual Objectification', *Psychology of Women Quarterly*, August 2018, https://journals.sagepub.com/doi/10.1177/0361684318791543# citing K. Sue Jewell, *From Mammy to Miss America and Beyond*, Routledge, 1993

3. Le Grand v. Darnall, 27 U.S. 664, 1829, https://casetext.com/case/le-grand-v-darnall

4. Cathy Scarborough, 'Conceptualizing Black Women's Employment Experiences', *Yale Law Journal*, May 1989, citing Jacob D. Wheeler, 'A Practical Treatise on the Law of Slavery', 1837

5. Carolyn M. West and Kalimah Johnson, 'Sexual Violence in the Lives of African American Women', National Online Resource Center on Violence Against Women, May 2013, https://vawnet.org/sites/default/files/materials/files/2016-09/AR_SVAAWomenRevised.pdf

6. Jalana Harris, 'Adherence to the Strong Black Woman Archetype and Sexual Agency: An Intersectional Exploration of Sexual Assertiveness, Towards Deconstructing Black Women's Sexual Health', May 2018, https://www.academia.edu/37409894/Adherence_to_the_Strong_Black_Woman_Archetype_and_Sexual_Agency_An_Intersectional_Exploration_of_Sexual_Assertiveness_towards_deconstructing_Black_Womens_Sexual_Health_A_Dissertation_Presented

7. David Pilgrim, 'The Jezebel Sterotype', July 2002 https://www.ferris.edu/HTMLS/news/jimcrow/jezebel/index.htm

8. Carolyn M. West and Kalimah Johnson, 'Sexual Violence in the Lives of African American Women', National Online Resource Center on Violence Against Women, May 2013, https://vawnet.org/sites/default/files/materials/files/2016-09/AR_SVAAWomenRevised.pdf citing D. M. Sommerville, *Rape and Race in the Nineteenth-Century South*, University of North Carolina Press, 2004

9. Joel R. Andersen, Elise Holland, Courtney Heldreth et al., 'Revisiting the Jezebel Stereotype: The Impact of Target Race on Sexual Objectification', *Psychology of Women Quarterly*, August 2018, https://journals.sagepub.com/doi/10.1177/0361684318791543# citing Tim Butcher, 'Freak Show African Going Home, *Telegraph*, April 2002, http://www.telegraph.co.uk/news/worldnews/africaandindianocean/southafrica/1392207/Freak-show-African-going-home.html

10. 'Coming Home', *The Guardian,* February 2002, https://www.theguardian.com/education/2002/feb/21/internationaleducationnews.highereducation

11. ibid.

12. Joel R. Andersen, Elise Holland, Courtney Heldreth et al., 'Revisiting the Jezebel Stereotype: The Impact of Target Race on Sexual Objectification', *Psychology of Women Quarterly*, August 2018, https://journals.sagepub.com/doi/10.1177/0361684318791543#

13. ibid. citing S. Plous and D. Neptune, 'Racial and Gender Biases in Magazine Advertising', *Psychology of Women Quarterly*, 1997, https://psycnet.apa.org/record/1997-38412-009

14. Angela Neal-Barnett, 'To Be Female, Anxious and Black', Anxiety and Depression Association of America April 2018, https://adaa.org/learn-from-us/from-the-experts/blog-posts/consumer/be-female-anxious-and-black

15. Joel R. Andersen, Elise Holland, Courtney Heldreth et al., 'Revisiting the Jezebel Stereotype: The Impact of Target Race on Sexual Objectification', *Psychology of Women Quarterly*, August 2018, https://journals.sagepub.com/doi/10.1177/0361684318791543# citing Roxanne Donovan, 'To Blame or not to Blame: Influences of Target Race and Observer Sex on Rape Blame Attribution', *Journal of Interpersonal Violence* June 2007

Linda Foley, Christine Evancic, Karnik Karnik et al., 'Date Rape: Effects of Race of Assilant and Victim and Gender of Subjects on Perceptions,' *Journal of Black Psychology*, February 1995

Jennifer Katz, Christine Merrilees, Jill C. Hoxmeier, et al., 'White Female Bystanders' Responses to a Black Woman at Risk for Incapacitated Sexual Assault', *Psychology of Women Quarterly*, February 2017

16. Josina Calliste, 'R. Kelly's Abuse Raises Questions About the Sexual Exploitation of Black British Girls, Too', *gal-dem*, January 2014, https://gal-dem.com/r-kellys-abuse-raises-questions-the-sexual-exploitation-of-black-british-girls-too/

17. Joel R. Andersen, Elise Holland, Courtney Heldreth et al., 'Revisiting the Jezebel Stereotype: The Impact of Target Race on Sexual Objectification', *Psychology of Women Quarterly*, August 2018, https://journals.sagepub.com/doi/10.1177/0361684318791543#

18. 'Sexual Harassment of LGBT People in the Workplace', Trades Union Congress, April 2019, https://www.tuc.org.uk/sites/default/files/LGBT_Sexual_Harassment_Report_0.pdf

19. 'Sex Stereotypes of African Americans Have Long History', NPR, May 2007, https://www.npr.org/templates/story/story.php?storyId=10057104

20. 'Nearly Two in Three Young Women Have Experienced Sexual Harassment at Work, TUC Survey Reveals', Trades Union Congress, August 2016, https://www.tuc.org.uk/news/nearly-two-three-young-women-have-experienced-sexual-harassment-work-tuc-survey-reveals

21. Maya Oppenheim, 'Black Women More Likely to Experience Sexual Harassment in the Workplace, Study Finds', *The Independent*, July 2019, https://www.independent.co.uk/news/world/americas/black-women-sexual-harassment-abuse-work-study-a8997296.html citing Dan Cassino and Yasemin Bresen-Cassino, 'Race, Threat and Workplace Sexual Harassment: The Dynamics of Harassment in the United States, 1997–2016', *Gender, Work and Organization*, June 2019, https://onlinelibrary.wiley.com/doi/10.1111/gwao.12394

22. Hannah Green, 'Disparity in Discrimination: A Study on the Experience of Minority Women in the Workplace', 2017, https://www.csustan.edu/sites/default/files/groups/University%20Honors%20Program/Journals/hannah_green.pdf

23. Amanda Rossie, Jasmine Tucker and Kayla Patrick, 'Out of the Shadows: An Analysis of Sexual Harassment Charges Filed by Working Women', The National Women's Law Center, August 2018, https://nwlc-ciw49tixgw5lbab.stackpathdns.com/wp-content/uploads/2018/08/SexualHarassmentReport.pdf

24. Maya Oppenheim, 'Black Women More Likely to Experience Sexual Harassment in the Workplace, Study Finds', *Independent*, July 2019, https://www.independent.co.uk/news/world/americas/black-women-sexual-harassment-abuse-work-study-a8997296.html

25. Hannah Green, 'Disparity in Discrimination: A Study on the Experience of Minority Women in the Workplace,' citing T. K. Hernandez, 'Sexual Harassment and Racial Disparity: The Mutual Construction of Gender and Race', *Journal of Gender, Race, and Justice*, 2000, https://ir.lawnet.fordham.edu/cgi/viewcontent.cgi?article=1011&context=faculty_scholarship

26. Errin Haines Whack, 'Why Few Women of Color in Wave of Accusers? "Stakes Higher"', *AP News*, November 2017, https://apnews.com/article/34a278ca43e24c5587c911ead5fac67c

27. Memo on 'Key Findings From a Survey of Women Fast Food Workers', Hart Research Associates, October 2016, https://hartresearch.com/wp-content/uploads/2016/10/Fast-Food-Worker-Survey-Memo-10-5-16.pdf

28. Maya Oppenheim, 'Black Women More Likely to Experience Sexual Harassment in the Workplace, Study Finds', *The Independent*, July 2019, https://www.independent.co.uk/news/world/americas/black-women-sexual-harassment-abuse-work-study-a8997296.html

29. ibid.

30. Jennifer L. Berdahl and Celia Moore, 'Workplace Harassment: Double Jeopardy for Modern Women', *Journal of Applied Psychology*, 2006, https://pdfs.semanticscholar.org/c5cd/8934b5d10b331560b24bcc3d7dc3c4a4818d.pdf

31. Rebecca Fishbein, 'Salma Hayek Says Weinstein Went After Women of Color Because "We Are the Easiest" to Discredit', *Jezebel*, May 2018, https://jezebel.com/salma-hayek-says-weinstein-went-after-women-of-color-be-1826000383

32. Stuart Oldham, 'Salma Hayek Says Harvey Weinstein Only Responded to Her and Lupita Nyong'o's Harassment Claims Because Women of Colour Are Easy to Discredit', *Variety*, May 2018, https://variety.com/2018/film/news/salma-hayek-says-harvey-weinstein-only-responded-to-her-and-lupita-nyongos-harassment-claims-because-women-of-color-are-easier-to-discredit-1202808828/

33. Isha Aran, 'Harvey Weinstein is Saving His Nastiest Smear Attempts for Women of Color', *Splinter*, December 2017, https://splinternews.com/harvey-weinstein-is-saving-his-nastiest-smear-attempts-1821293136

34. 'Sexual Harassment in the Workplace', House of Commons Women and Equalities Committee, July 2018, https://publications.parliament.uk/pa/cm201719/cmselect/cmwomeq/725/725.pdf

35. Data.Parliament.UK

    1) The Equality and Human Rights Commission: http://data.parliament.uk/writtenevidence/committeeevidence.svc/evidencedocument/women-and-equalities-committee/sexual-harassment-in-the-workplace/written/80811.html

    2) The Everyday Sexism Project: http://data.parliament.uk/writtenevidence/committeeevidence.svc/evidencedocument/women-and-equalities-committee/sexual-harassment-in-the-workplace/written/80681.html

    3) NGO Safe Space: http://data.parliament.uk/writtenevidence/committeeevidence.svc/evidencedocument/women-and-equalities-committee/sexual-harassment-in-the-workplace/written/80292.html

    4) Close the Gap: http://data.parliament.uk/writtenevidence/committeeevidence.svc/evidencedocument/women-and-equalities-committee/sexual-harassment-in-the-workplace/written/80301.html

36. 'Sexual Harassment in the Workplace', House of Commons Women and Equalities Committee, July 2018, https://publications.parliament.uk/pa/cm201719/cmselect/cmwomeq/725/725.pdf

37. Dr Rachel Fenton, Oral Evidence for 'Sexual Harassment in the Workplace', House of Commons Women and Equalities Committee, May 2018, http://data.parliament.uk/writtenevidence/committeeevidence.svc/evidencedocument/women-and-equalities-committee/sexual-harassment-in-the-workplace/oral/83116.html

38. 'Sexual Harassment in the Workplace', House of Commons Women and Equalities Committee, July 2018, https://publications.parliament.uk/pa/cm201719/cmselect/cmwomeq/725/725.pdf

39. Oral Evidence for 'Sexual Harassment in the Workplace', House of Commons Women and Equalities Committee, May 2018, http://data.parliament.uk/writtenevidence/committeeevidence.svc/evidencedocument/women-and-equalities-committee/sexual-harassment-in-the-workplace/oral/83116.html

40. 'ACAS Publishes New Guidance on Non-Disclosure Agreements', ACAS, February 2020, https://www.acas.org.uk/acas-publishes-new-guidance-on-non-disclosure-agreements-ndas

41. Written Submission to the House of Commons Women and Equalities Committee, March 2018, http://data.parliament.uk/writtenevidence/committeeevidence.svc/evidencedocument/women-and-equalities-committee/sexual-harassment-in-the-workplace/written/80083.html

42. 'Sexual Harassment in the Workplace', House of Commons Women and Equalities Committee, July 2018, https://publications.parliament.uk/pa/cm201719/cmselect/cmwomeq/725/725.pdf

43. Sandra L. Fielden, Marilyn J. Davidson, Helen Woolnough and Carianne Hunt, 'A Model of Racialized Sexual Harassment of Women in the UK Workplace', *Sex Roles*, November 2009, https://www.academia.edu/30307158/A_Model_of_Racialized_Sexual_Harassment_of_Women_in_the_UK_Workplace

44. ibid.

45. ibid.

46. ibid.

47. ibid.

48. ibid.

49. Oral Evidence for 'Sexual Harassment in the Workplace', House of Commons Women and Equalities Committee, May 2018, http://data.parliament.uk/writtenevidence/committeeevidence.svc/evidencedocument/women-and-equalities-committee/sexual-harassment-in-the-workplace/oral/83116.html

50. 'Sexual Harassment in the Workplace', House of Commons Women and Equalities Committee, July 2018, https://publications.parliament.uk/pa/cm201719/cmselect/cmwomeq/725/725.pdf

## Chapter 7

1. 'Race at Work 2015', Business in the Community, 2015, https://www.bitc.org.uk/report/race-at-work-2015/ as quoted in 'The McGregor-Smith Review: Race in the Workplace', https://assets.publishing.service.gov.uk/government/uploads/system/uploads/attachment_data/file/594336/race-in-workplace-mcgregor-smith-review.pdf

2. 'Addressing Barriers to BAME Employee Career Progression to the Top', CIPD, December 2017, https://www.cipd.co.uk/Images/addressing-the-barriers-to-BAME-employee-career-progression-to-the-top_tcm18-33336.pdf

3. Keisha Edwards Tassie and Sonja M. Brown Givens, 'The Double Outsiders' Challenges to Professional Success', https://www.academia.edu/2767826/The_Double_Outsiders_Challeneges_to_Professional_Success?email_work_card=title citing 'Report: Advancing African-American Women in the Workplace: What Managers Need to Know', Catalyst, February 2004

4. Kimberley Giles, 'When You Mistakenly Hire People Just Like You', *Forbes*, May 2018, https://www.forbes.com/sites/forbescoachescouncil/2018/05/01/why-you-mistakenly-hire-people-just-like-you/#3eb9ba503827

5. ibid.

6. 'Women in the Workplace 2020', McKinsey & Company and LeanIn.Org, September 2020, https://www.mckinsey.com/featured-insights/diversity-and-inclusion/women-in-the-workplace

7. Keisha Edwards Tassie and Sonja M. Brown Givens, 'The Double Outsiders'

Challenges to Professional Success', https://www.academia.edu/2767826/The_Double_Outsiders_Challeneges_to_Professional_Success?email_work_card=title

8. 'Race at Work 2015', Business in the Community, 2015, https://www.bitc.org.uk/report/race-at-work-2015/ as quoted in 'The McGregor-Smith Review: Race in the Workplace', https://assets.publishing.service.gov.uk/government/uploads/system/uploads/attachment_data/file/594336/race-in-workplace-mcgregor-smith-review.pdf

9. Veena Vasista, '"Snowy Peaks": Ethnic Diversity at the Top', Runnymede Trust November 2010, https://www.runnymedetrust.org/uploads/publications/pdfs/SnowyPeaks-2010.pdf citing H. Hooker, N. Jagger and S. Baldwin, 'Recruitment of Under-Represented Groups into the Senior Civil Service', Department for Work and Pensions, May 2008

10. Veena Vasista, '"Snowy Peaks": Ethnic Diversity at the Top', Runnymede Trust, November 2010, https://www.runnymedetrust.org/uploads/publications/pdfs/SnowyPeaks-2010.pdf citing 'Different Women, Different Places', The Diversity Practice, 2017

11. Veena Vasista, '"Snowy Peaks": Ethnic Diversity at the Top', Runnymede Trust November 2010, https://www.runnymedetrust.org/uploads/publications/pdfs/SnowyPeaks-2010.pdf citing 'Taking Talent to the Top', Runnymede Trust

12. 'Entry to, and Progression in, Work', Joseph Rowntree Foundation, July 2015, https://www.jrf.org.uk/report/entry-and-progression-work as quoted in 'The McGregor-Smith Review: Race in the Workplace', https://assets.publishing.service.gov.uk/government/uploads/system/uploads/attachment_data/file/594336/race-in-workplace-mcgregor-smith-review.pdf

13. Sylvia Ann Hewlett and Tai Green, 'Black Women Ready to Lead', 2015, Center for Talent Innovation, 2015, https://www.talentinnovation.org/_private/assets/BlackWomenReadyToLead_ExecSumm-CTI.pdf

14. 'Report: Advancing African-American Women in the Workplace: What Managers Need to Know', Catalyst, February 2004 as cited in Keisha Edwards Tassie and Sonja M. Brown Givens, 'The Double Outsiders' Challenges to Professional Success', https://www.academia.edu/2767826/The_Double_Outsiders_Challeneges_to_Professional_Success?email_work_card=title

15. John Crowley, 'You Can't Stop Employees Discussing Their Pay', People, May 2018, https://www.peoplehr.com/blog/2018/05/09/you-cant-stop-employees-discussing-their-pay/

16. 'Can You Tell Coworkers Your Salary?', Chron, July 2020, https://work.chron.com/can-tell-coworkers-salary-7204.html

17. Mary Leisenring, 'Women Still Have to Work Three Months Longer to Equal What Men Earned in a Year', United States Census Bureau, March 2020, https://www.census.gov/library/stories/2020/03/equal-pay-day-is-march-31-earliest-since-1996.html#:~:text=Women%20Still%20Have%20to%20Work,Men%20Earned%20in%20a%20Year&text=For%20the%20first%20time%20and,gender%20pay%20gap%20is%20narrowing.

18. Anthony Breach and Yaojun Li, 'Gender Pay Gap by Ethnicity in Britain – Briefing', Fawcett Society, March 2017, https://www.fawcettsociety.org.uk/Handlers/Download.ashx?IDMF=f31d6adc-9e0e-4bfe-a3df-3e85605ee4a9

19. Kayla Fontenot, Jessica Semega and Melissa Kogar, 'Income and Poverty in the United States: 2017', United States Census Bureau, September 2018, https://www.census.gov/library/publications/2018/demo/p60-263.html

20. 'The Wage Gap: The Who, How, Why, and What to Do', National Women's Law Center, October 2018, https://nwlc-ciw49tixgw5lbab.stackpathdns.com/wp-content/uploads/2018/10/The-Wage-Gap-Who-How-Why-and-What-to-Do-2018.pdf

21. ibid.

22. Jasmine Tucker, 'Women and the Lifetime Wage Gap: How Many Woman Years Does It Take to Equal 40 Man Years?', National Women's Law Center, March 2019, https://nwlc-ciw49tixgw5lbab.stackpathdns.com/wp-content/uploads/2019/03/Women-and-the-Lifetime-Wage-Gap-v1.pdf

23. Anthony Breach and Yaojun Li, 'Gender Pay Gap by Ethnicity in Britain – Briefing', Fawcett Society, March 2017, https://www.fawcettsociety.org.uk/Handlers/Download.ashx?IDMF=f31d6adc-9e0e-4bfe-a3df-3e85605ee4a9

24. 'Black Women Aren't Paid Fairly and That Hits Harder in an Economic Crisis', Lean In, https://leanin.org/data-about-the-gender-pay-gap-for-black-women

25. 'The 2018 State of Women-Owned Businesses Report', American Express, 2018 https://www.empowerwomen.org/en/resources/documents/2019/01/the-2018-state-of-women-owned-business-report?lang=en

26. 'Facts About Women in Business', Prowess, https://www.prowess.org.uk/facts

27. 'Availability of Credit to Small Businesses', US Federal Reserve, September 2017 https://www.federalreserve.gov/publications/2017-september-availability-of-credit-to-small-businesses.htm

28. Kerry Hannon, 'Black Women Entrepreneurs: The Good and Not So Good News', *Forbes*, September 2018

29. Nina Zipkin, 'Out of $85 Billion in VC Funding Last Year, Only 2.2 Percent Went to Female Founders. And Every Year Women of Color Get Less Than 1 Percent of Total Funding', *Entrepreneur*, December 2018, https://www.entrepreneur.com/article/324743

30. 'ProjectDiane Report 2018: The State of Black and Latinx Women Founders', digitalundivided, 2018, https://www.projectdiane.com/, as quoted in 'Report: The Number of Black Women-Led Startups Has More Than Doubled Since 2016', The Case Foundation, June 2018', https://casefoundation.org/press_release/report-the-number-of-black-women-led-startups-has-more-than-doubled-since-2016-according-to-digitalundivideds-latest-research-projectdiane-2018/

31. 'The 2018 State of Women-Owned Businesses Report', Empower Women, American Express, 2018 https://www.empowerwomen.org/en/resources/documents/2019/01/the-2018-state-of-women-owned-business-report?lang=en

32. Kerry Hannon, 'Black Women Entrepreneurs: The Good and Not So Good News', *Forbes*, September 2018

33. Nina Zipkin, 'Out of $85 Billion in VC Funding Last Year, Only 2.2 Percent Went to Female Founders. And Every Year Women of Color Get Less Than 1 Percent of Total Funding', *Entrepreneur*, December 2018, https://www.entrepreneur.com/article/324743

34. Paul A. Gompers and Sophie Q. Wang, 'Diversity in Innovation', Harvard Business School Working Paper, January 2017, https://www.hbs.edu/faculty/Pages/item.aspx?num=52168

35. Paul Gompers and Silpa Kovvali, 'The Other Diversity Dividend', *Harvard Business Review*, July–August 2018, https://hbr.org/2018/07/the-other-diversity-dividend

36. Paul A. Gompers and Sophie Q. Wang, 'And the Children Shall Lead: Gender Diversity and Performance in Venture Capital', Harvard Business School Working Paper, 2017 https://www.hbs.edu/ris/Publication%20Files/17-103_5768ca0e-9b35-4145-ab02-4a081b71466e.pdf

37. Paul Gompers and Silpa Kovvali, 'The Other Diversity Dividend', *Harvard Business Review*, July–August 2018, https://hbr.org/2018/07/the-other-diversity-dividend

38. Lauren Cohen, Andrea Frazzini and Christopher Malloy, 'The Small World of Investing: Board Connections and Mutual Fund Returns', *Journal of Political Economy*, October 2008, https://www.jstor.org/stable/10.1086/592415?seq=1

39. Paul A. Gompers et al., 'The Cost of Friendship', *Journal of Financial Economics*, March 2016, http://dx.doi.org/10.1016/j.jfineco.2016.01.013

40. Paul Gompers and Silpa Kovvali, 'The Other Diversity Dividend', *Harvard Business Review*, July–August 2018, https://hbr.org/2018/07/the-other-diversity-dividend

41. Keisha Edwards Tassie and Sonja M. Brown Givens, 'The Double Outsiders' Challenges to Professional Success', https://www.academia.edu/2767826/The_Double_Outsiders_Challeneges_to_Professional_Success?email_work_card=title citing 'Report: Advancing African-American Women in the Workplace: What Managers Need to Know', Catalyst, February 2004

## Chapter 8

1. 'Women in the Workplace 2019', McKinsey & Company and LeanIn.Org, 2019, https://wiw-report.s3.amazonaws.com/Women_in_the_Workplace_2019.pdf

2. Dominic-Madori Davis, 'There Are Only Four Black Fortune 500 CEOs. Here They Are', *Business Insider*, February 2020, https://www.businessinsider.in/thelife/news/there-are-only-four-black-fortune-500-ceos-here-they-are-/articleshow/74407852.cms

3. Caroline Bologna, 'Why the Phrase "Pull Yourself Up By Your Bootstraps" is Nonsense', *HuffPost US*, August 2018, https://www.huffingtonpost.co.uk/entry/pull-yourself-up-by-your-bootstraps-nonsense_n_5b1ed024e4b0bbb7a0e037d4?ri18n=true

4. 'Women in the Workplace 2018', LeanIn.Org, 2018, https://leanin.org/women-in-the-workplace-report-2018

5. 'What Being an "Only" at Work is Like', from 'Women in the Workplace 2018', McKinsey & Company and LeanIn.Org, 2018, https://leanin.org/women-in-the-workplace-report-2018/what-being-an-only-at-work-is-like

6. David Rock, Heidi Grant and Jacqui Grey, 'Diverse Teams Feel Less Comfortable – and That's Why They Perform Better', *Harvard Business Review*, September 2016, https://hbr.org/2016/09/diverse-teams-feel-less-comfortable-and-thats-why-they-perform-better

7. Cedric Herring, 'Does Diversity Pay?: Race, Gender, and the Business Case for Diversity', *American Sociological Review*, April 2009, https://journals.sagepub.com/doi/abs/10.1177/000312240907400203

8. David Rock, Heidi Grant and Jacqui Grey, 'Diverse Teams Feel Less Comfortable – and That's Why They Perform Better', *Harvard Business Review*, September 2016, https://hbr.org/2016/09/diverse-teams-feel-less-comfortable-and-thats-why-they-perform-better

9. Ella Jessel and Pamela Buxton, 'Drop in BAME Architects Across UK's Top Practices, New Data Reveals', *Architects' Journal*, June 2019, https://www.architectsjournal.co.uk/news/drop-in-bame-architects-across-uks-top-practices-new-data-reveals/10043128.article

10. Simon Gwynn, 'BAME Representation Drops at UK Agencies, IPA Census Reveals', *Campaign*, April 2020, https://www.campaignlive.co.uk/article/bame-representation-drops-uk-agencies-ipa-census-reveals/1681653

11. Katy Waldman, 'A Sociologist Examines the "White Fragility" that Prevents White Americans From Confronting Racism', *New Yorker*, July 2018, https://www.newyorker.com/books/page-turner/a-sociologist-examines-the-white-fragility-that-prevents-white-americans-from-confronting-racism

12. Jeff Desjardins, 'Meet Generation Z: The Newest Member to the Workforce', *Visual Capitalist*, February 2019, https://www.visualcapitalist.com/meet-generation-z-the-newest-member-to-the-workforce/

13. Gavin Jackson, 'Young people's earnings affected by gender and ethnicity', *Financial Times*, October 2018, https://www.ft.com/content/aaa900ea-d6b9-11e8-a854-33d6f82e62f8

## Chapter 9

1. Jesse D. McKinnon and Claudette E. Bennett, 'We the People: Blacks in the United States', US Census 2000 Special Reports, August 2005 https://www.census.gov/prod/2005pubs/censr-25.pdf

2. 'Black Britons: The Next Generation', *Economist*, January 2016, https://www.economist.com/britain/2016/01/28/the-next-generation

3. Jeff Desjardins, 'Meet Generation Z: The Newest Member to the Workforce', *Visual Capitalist*, February 2019, https://www.visualcapitalist.com/meet-generation-z-the-newest-member-to-the-workforce/

4. ibid.

5. Steve Crabtree, 'Worldwide, 13% of Employees Are Engaged at Work', Gallup, October 2013, https://news.gallup.com/poll/165269/worldwide-employees-engaged-work.aspx

6. Vivian Hunt, Dennis Layton and Sara Prince, 'Diversity Matters Report', McKinsey & Company, February 2015, https://www.mckinsey.com/business-functions/organization/our-insights/~/media/2497d4ae4b534ee89d929cc6e3aea485.ashx

7. 'Hacking Diversity with Inclusive Decision Making', Cloverpop, September 2017, https://www.cloverpop.com/hubfs/Whitepapers/Cloverpop_Hacking_Diversity_Inclusive_Decision_Making_White_Paper.pdf

8. Vivian Hunt, Dennis Layton and Sara Prince, 'Diversity Matters', McKinsey & Company, February 2015, https://www.mckinsey.com/business-functions/organization/our-insights/~/media/2497d4ae4b534ee89d929cc6e3aea485.ashx

9. 'Women in the Workplace 2017', McKinsey & Company and LeanIn.Org, 2017, https://wiw-report.s3.amazonaws.com/Women_in_the_Workplace_2017.pdf

10. Sylvia Ann Hewlett and Tai Green, 'Black Women Ready to Lead', Center for Talent Innovation, 2015, https://www.talentinnovation.org/_private/assets/BlackWomenReadyToLead_ExecSumm-CTI.pdf

11. 'The McGregor-Smith Review: Race in the Workplace', https://assets. publishing.service.gov.uk/government/uploads/system/uploads/attachment_data/ file/594336/race-in-workplace-mcgregor-smith-review.pdf

12. ibid.

13. Sabrina Barr, 'One in Three Adults Have Experienced or Witnessed Racism at Work, Study Finds', *The Independent*, October 2019, https://www.independent.co.uk/ life-style/racism-work-discrimination-gender-lgbt-sexuality-ageism- glassdoor-a9167256.html

14. Olivia Petter, 'One in Four Ethnic Minority Workers Report Experiencing Bullying and Harassment Despite Zero-Tolerance Policies', *The Independent,* October 2019, https://www.independent.co.uk/life-style/bullying-harassment-work-racism-equality- zero-tolerance-policy-a9128951.html

'The Race at Work Charter Report', Business in the Community', October 2019 https://www.bitc.org.uk/report/the-race-at-work-charter-one-year-on-2019/

## Chapter 10

1. Elizabeth Judge, 'Women on Board: Help or Hindrance?', *The Times*, November 2003, https://www.thetimes.co.uk/article/women-on-board-help-or-hindrance-2c6fnqf 6fng?wgu=270525_54264_15797847457767_ a1d37d5f3a&wgexpiry=1587560745&utm_source=planit&utm_ medium=affiliate&utm_content=22278

2. Michelle K. Ryan and S. Alexander Haslam, 'The Glass Cliff: Exploring the Dynamics Surrounding the Appointment of Women to Precarious Leadership Positions', *The Academy of Management Review*, April 2007, https://www.jstor.org/ stable/20159315

3. '2018 CEO Success Study: Succeeding the Long-Serving Legend in the Corner Office', Strategy&, 2018, https://www.strategyand.pwc.com/gx/en/insights/ceo-success.html

4. Jena McGregor, 'Here's why women CEOs are more likely to get sacked from their jobs', *Washington Post*, May 2014 https://www.washingtonpost.com/news/ on-leadership/wp/2014/05/02/heres-why-women-ceos-are-more-likely-to-get-sacked- from-their-jobs/

5. Alison Cook and Christy Glass, 'Above the Glass Ceiling: When are Women and Racial/Ethnic Minorities Promoted to CEO?', *Strategic Management Journal*, June 2013, https://onlinelibrary.wiley.com/doi/abs/10.1002/smj.2161

6. Michelle K. Ryan and S. Alexander Haslam, 'The Road to the Glass Cliff: Differences in the Perceived Suitability of Men and Women for Leadership Positions in Succeeding and Failing Organizations', *Leadership Quarterly*, October 2008, https://ore.exeter.ac.uk/repository/handle/10871/8362?show=full

7. Michelle K. Ryan, S. Alexander Haslam, Mette D. Hersby et al., 'Think Crisis-Think Female: The Glass Cliff and Contextual Variation in the Think Manager-Think Male Stereotype', *Journal of Applied Psychology*, May 2011, https://pubmed.ncbi.nlm.nih. gov/21171729-think-crisis-think-female-the-glass-cliff-and-contextual-variation-in-the- think-manager-think-male-stereotype/

8. Emily Stewart, 'Why Struggling Companies Promote Women: The Glass Cliff, Explained', *Vox*, October 2018, https://www.vox.com/2018/10/31/17960156/what-is- the-glass-cliff-women-ceos

9. 'Women in the Workplace 2019', McKinsey & Company and LeanIn.Org, 2019, https://wiw-report.s3.amazonaws.com/Women_in_the_Workplace_2019.pdf

10. Michael L. McDonald, Gareth D. Keeves and James D. Westphal, 'One Step Forward, One Step Back: White Male Top Manager Organizational Identification and Helping Behavior toward Other Executives Following the Appointment of a Female or Racial Minority CEO', *Academy of Management Journal*, April 2018, http://ns.umich.edu/Releases/2018/Feb18/One-step-forward-two-steps-back-study-20180213.pdf

11. ibid.

## Chapter 11

1. 'The McGregor-Smith Review: Race in the Workplace', https://assets.publishing.service.gov.uk/government/uploads/system/uploads/attachment_data/file/594336/race-in-workplace-mcgregor-smith-review.pdf

2. Coles, S. M., & Pasek, J. (2020), 'Intersectional Invisibility Revisited: How Group Prototypes Lead to the Erasure and Exclusion of Black Women', in *Translational Issues in Psychological Science* 6(4), 314–324.

3. Valerie Purdie-Vaughns, 'Why So Few Black Women are Senior Managers in 2015', *Fortune*, April 2015, https://fortune.com/2015/04/22/black-women-leadership-study/

4. Berdahl, J. L., & Moore, C. (2006). 'Workplace harassment: Double jeopardy for minority women' in *Journal of Applied Psychology*, 91(2), 426–436

5. 'The McGregor-Smith Review: Race in the Workplace', https://assets.publishing.service.gov.uk/government/uploads/system/uploads/attachment_data/file/594336/race-in-workplace-mcgregor-smith-review.pdf

6. Sheryl Sandberg and Adam Grant, 'Speaking While Female', *New York Times*, January 2015, https://www.nytimes.com/2015/01/11/opinion/sunday/speaking-while-female.html?_r=0

7. Victoria L. Brescoll, 'Who Takes the Floor and Why: Gender, Power, and Volubility in Organizations', *Administrative Science Quarterly*, February 2012, https://journals.sagepub.com/doi/abs/10.1177/0001839212439994

8. Emily Crockett, 'The Amazing Tool that Women in the White House Used to Fight Gender Bias', *Vox*, September 2016, https://www.vox.com/2016/9/14/12914370/white-house-obama-women-gender-bias-amplification

9. Bill Carmody, 'Six Steps to Overcoming Impostor Syndrome', *Forbes*, July 2018 https://www.forbes.com/sites/forbesagencycouncil/2018/07/27/six-steps-to-overcoming-imposter-syndrome/?sh=2cc7682c3152

10. Carl Richards, 'Learning to Deal With the Impostor Syndrome', *New York Times*, October 2015, https://www.nytimes.com/2015/10/26/your-money/learning-to-deal-with-the-impostor-syndrome.html

# Acknowledgements

**W**hat an experience the process of writing *Millennial Black* and putting it out into the world has been. Aside from sample chapters, this book was written entirely during 2020, a year of both lockdowns and civil rights uprisings. One of the hardest years in many of our lives.

I want to thank my agent, Hattie Grunewald, for believing in *Millennial Black*, and in me, right away. You're amazing and I'm glad I know you. Let's make more things together very soon.

I also want to thank the wonderful Rachel Kenny who commissioned this book – it quite literally wouldn't have happened without you.

Thanks to the team from HQ, particularly Kate Fox, Nira Begum and Jo Kite, who I've worked with to make both *Millennial Black* and *Anti-Racist Ally* a reality. Thanks for being there on the journey from a pink and black Google slides presentation (book proposals can be much simpler than that, who knew!) to a real life book. Two books, even! It's been wild! Working together during a pandemic means that we've never physically met, I think we've managed our long-distance editorial relationship well, from Zooms to Google Docs and sliding into Instagram DM.

Thank you also for letting me pause on this manuscript, with only one week left before delivery, when we saw there was a need to refocus our efforts and attentions on another project. Your flexibility and faith allowed us to write, and bring out, *Anti-Racist Ally* in record time. You not only trusted a debut author in backing *Millennial Black*, you trusted me to do what was needed – and to bring what should have been my second book out before my first.

To all of the amazing Black women who agreed to be featured in the book, in excerpts and quotes, and who shared your favourite things about being who you are with me, thank you. I love you. I am in awe of you. You inspire and teach me, truly.

I want to thank my Lady Gang, every day, for everything we achieve together, and everything we help one another to achieve. You astound me. Whilst I can't mention everyone I want to give special shout-outs to those who have played a huge part in helping make 2020 bearable, and so, have made this book possible. Thank you Anna Woolf, Joe Buckingham, Rory O'Neill, Rebecca Patts Davies, Laura May Coope, Kate Cliffen, Hugh Smith, Cameron Sheers, and Jake and Tesh.

I'm also glad that, in some ways, 2020 hasn't been all bad, and has actually meant that new, online friendships have flourished in unexpected and amazing ways, adding new members to the Lady Gang from near and far. Thank you for being there for this, Naomi and Natalie from @EverydayRacism_, Erika @TheQueenOfConfidence, Pippa Vosper, Erica @TheRestJustFallsAway, Sulaiman Khan, Lisette Henry, and Carly Findlay OAM – your long-distance support and encouragement has meant the world to me, and I've been blown away by your achievements too. You are all so different to me, and to each other, and I learn so much from you all.

Though they will never see it, I also want to thank Ann Friedman and Aminatou Sow, the hosts of *Call Your Girlfriend*. I truly believe that listening to your podcast every week for the last goodness knows how many years has fundamentally changed who I am and how I think and express myself, all for the better.

Wouldn't it be funny if I were just like, 'And now, to wrap things up, here are all of the people who have wronged me, alphabetically . . .' but no, that's not how we'll close this out. Instead I'll close out like this.

Thank you, always, to Lawrence Brand – my partner in all things. You make everything possible. It's not that I couldn't do it without you, it's that I simply wouldn't want to. You are amazing. You inspire me, and push me to be better in all ways, personal and professional. There's no one else I would have spent a year in a one-room flat with – open-plan living seems fun until you're sitting in the shower you tried to renovate yourself, to do calls. Let's keep making all of the things and having all of the fun.

# Appendix

## We Wear the Mask

### Paul Laurence Dunbar

We wear the mask that grins and lies,
It hides our cheeks and shades our eyes,—
This debt we pay to human guile;
With torn and bleeding hearts we smile,
And mouth with myriad subtleties.

Why should the world be over-wise,
In counting all our tears and sighs?
Nay, let them only see us, while
    We wear the mask.

We smile, but, O great Christ, our cries
To thee from tortured souls arise.
We sing, but oh the clay is vile
Beneath our feet, and long the mile;
But let the world dream otherwise,
    We wear the mask!

# Thank yous and Quotes Sources

Angelou, Maya, *George Stroumboulopoulos Tonight* interview, 2013

Gay, Roxanne, *Bad Feminist*, 2014

Lorde, Audre, 'Learning From the 60s' presentation, 1982

Lorde, Audre, The Transformation of Silence into Language and Action',
   1977

Lorde, Audre, *I am Your Sister: Black Women Organizing Across
   Sexualities*, 1985

Lorde, Audre, *Sister Outsiders: Essays and Speeches*,1984

Morrison, Toni, Ohio Arts Council annual meeting, 1981

Morrison, Toni, *O* magazine interview, 2009

Morrison, Toni, 'The Work You Do, The Person You Are', *The New
   Yorker*, 2017

Waheed, Nayyirah, *Salt*, 2019

ONE PLACE. MANY STORIES

Bold, innovative and
empowering publishing.

FOLLOW US ON:

@HQStories